Young Wives' Tales

NEW ADVENTURES IN LOVE AND PARTNERSHIP

Edite

Jill Corral and Lisa Miya-Jervis

Foreword by bell hooks

Seal Press

Cover design by Christine Sienkiewicz
Text design by Christina Henry de Tessan
Cover photograph by Stephen Webster/Photonica

Library of Congress Cataloging-in-Publication Data

Young wives' tales: new adventures in love and partnership / edited by Jill Corral and Lisa Miya-Jervis.
    p. cm.
    ISBN 1-58005-050-6 (pbk.)
    1. Wives—United States. 2. Young women—United States. 3. Marriage—United States. 4. Generation X—United States. I. Corral, Jill. II. Miya-Jervis, Lisa.

HQ759 .Y66 2001
306.872'0973—dc21   2001020638

Printed in the United States of America
First printing, June 2001

10   9   8   7   6   5   4   3   2   1

Distributed to the trade by Publishers Group West
In Canada: Publishers Group West Canada, Toronto, Ontario
In Australia: Banyan Tree Book Distributors, Kent Town, South Australia
In the United Kingdom, Europe and South Africa: Hi Marketing, London
In Asia and the Middle East: Michelle Morrow Curreri, Beverly, MA

For Peter, my hero.
—J.C.

For Christopher, without whom it's all just theory.
—L. M-J.

Acknowledgments

Almost any book, and an anthology in particular, benefits from the generous advice and support of many people who assist in their individual ways. We are grateful to all those who helped make this project a reality.

Endless thanks to everyone at Seal Press, especially Jennie Goode, our fabulous editor, for her indefatigable professionalism, sharp and insightful eye and steady stream of good karma.

Thanks to bell hooks, for her honest and inspiring writings on love (and everything else) and for generously giving of her time to contribute to this project.

Thanks to Ophira Edut, for allowing our paths to cross.

Huge thank yous also to Andi Zeisler, Ben Shaykin, Dana McDole, Pia Guerrero, Leigh Cotnoir, Celia White, Rachel Payne, Robin Finkelstein and the Jervis and Corral clans for their kindness, love and constant support.

And of course to our wonderful contributors (all those who submitted and all those whose work appears here), for words they have written and those they have yet to write, and for their patience with us and our editorial whims.

Table of Contents

Foreword

Finding Freedom and Knowing Love

"If women and men want to know love, we have to yearn for feminism. For without feminist thinking and practice we lack the foundation to create loving bonds." These are my favorite lines in the chapter on love from my recent book, *Feminism is for Everybody*. All women hope to have happiness, all women want to exercise power in their lives, but all women do not yearn for feminism. And yet feminism defined simply as a movement to end sexism—sexist exploitation and oppression—has helped many women come to power, whether they exercise that power by choosing among a variety of sexual preferences; by choosing to get married or remain single; parenting or not; pursuing education and a career; or combining a number of these options.

The journey to power and the journey to feminism, though arduous and difficult, are ultimately easier to chart than the journey to happiness. Yet together feminism and power make us better able to pursue happiness. The feminist movement I joined more than thirty years ago—as a young, unhappy, powerless, southern black teenage girl from a fundamentalist Christian background who still longed to remain close to God and to know love—ridiculed religion and mocked love (the partnership I longed for, the motherhood I admired and respected). I challenged that narrow notion of feminism then, and I challenge it today. It was often wrongheaded, yet its founding principle—the belief that sexism must end if women and men, boys and girls, are to know constructive power, happiness and love—remains essentially true.

As a militant feminist teen I believed with my whole heart that, more than anything, feminist freedom held the promise of choice in a world where challenging patriarchal notions of love and committed partnership would be a constant, in-your-face struggle. It is easier to stand before a public world and demand justice (equal pay for equal work, reproductive freedom and more) than it is to stand in the space of our private longings for love and connection and call for a change in how we make love, how we create partnerships. In that intimate space our deepest fears about abandonment and loss surface. And our longing to hold onto familiar ways of bonding can be just as tempting as our longing to let go and dare to create new ways to mate and make lasting committed bonds.

At that time I desperately wanted a feminist dialogue about love and partnership, complete with a how-to guide telling us all how to be self-loving and how to love others. I wanted a feminist discourse on love and committed partnership that would link feminist discourse with spiritual practice. I wanted a feminist discourse that would join a passion for justice with the will to love. Now, more than thirty years later, I am constantly writing about love and the connection between our capacity to love and our efforts to create meaningful political revolutions that aim to transform all our lives. That intense yearning to know love and to create partnerships rooted in a vision of feminist justice and mutuality is the revolutionary heartbeat of all the essays in *Young Wives' Tales*.

In *Feminist Theory: From Margin to Center*, first published more than ten years ago, I insisted that we needed a movement that would affirm the variety of choices for women and men staying at home, entering the workforce, getting married or not (issues raised now in many right-wing books bashing feminism, albeit from a different perspective). No one has been a sharper critic of feminism than myself, but then and now my desire was not to bash feminism but to make it a better, stronger politic that would include a realistic understanding of the interconnections of race, sex and class: a politic that would transform the lives of girls and boys, men and women, so that we would all have more power and a greater chance for happiness.

Nowadays antifeminist critics suggest that it is feminist politics that have intensified women's unhappiness. This is not so. Most women and men in our society have no understanding of visionary feminism. The feminism they know most intimately is brought to them by patriarchal mass media, by opportunistic thinkers who have never been engaged in feminist activism or the creation of feminist thought, who set themselves up as the movement's harshest critics. (No wonder, then, that the feminism they write about is flat, stereotypical and merely echoes every negative statement made about the movement since its inception.) But the purpose of feminist politics was never to make us happy. Rather, by enhancing our civil rights and providing us freedom, it grants us greater access to all the ways to be fully self-actualized and empowered, and as a consequence be more able to embrace psychological well-being, joy and happiness. Then and now visionary feminism offers us the means to seek our happiness: a vision of mutuality in partnership that affirms and enhances our capacity to know love. There can be no love without justice. When we do the work of ending domination, we are doing the work of love.

Young Wives' Tales is filled with stories of this work. Militantly mapping new directions and relentlessly soul searching, the women in this anthology eagerly share their struggle to create revolutionary bonds of love. Their spirited voices are not only feminist and proud—they are not ashamed to speak with raw honesty about how hard it is to build partnerships, to be practicing feminism when the patriarchal culture of marriage and committed relationships has changed so little. These young women offer daring new visions of peer partnership, ones that are sometimes rooted in conventional thinking about marriage and coupling, but mostly combine the radical new with the radical old. It's an enticing and seductive mix. These courageous young voices resonate with everything I have told the world about my struggles both in the past and in the present to make loving partnerships—bonds that nurture and sustain.

Women and men of all ages are eagerly searching for new ways to think about relationships, for concrete ways to express and build caring connections that are not rooted in domination. *Young Wives' Tales* opens up the space, offering new possibilities. Uniting feminism and love, feminism and partnership, these essays take us into the feminist future. Speaking to our hearts about how hard it is, about the pleasure and pain of it all, the fun, the risk and the recklessness, they dare to remind us that we can embrace feminism and we can open our hearts to love, that we can connect and commit. They tell us that our yearning can be fulfilled—that we can find freedom and we can know love.

bell hooks

Introduction

Young Wives' Tales, like the offspring of so many eager couples, was conceived in a car—and what began as a simple ride to the subway station became a years-long exploration of love and its modern manifestations. At twenty-six, Jill had been living across the San Francisco Bay from her mate of eight years, an arrangement chosen by two solitary types who enjoyed having rooms of their own. Lisa—newly married after a few months of dating preceded by years of emphatic singlehood—was adjusting to the rhythm of daily life with a partner and acclimating to the identity whiplash she experienced when folks spied the ring on her finger. Naturally, the conversation turned to life lived as part of a couple: balancing needs and desires with those of a partner; the way the word "married" still conjures up outmoded and inadequate images in too many people's minds. We recognized in each other's words an urgency for a public, feminist reconfiguring of those images, for validation that committed relationships take a multitude of forms and for recognition of the constant struggle to construct a relationship that truly embodies our principles of respect and mutuality.

In this conversation (most of which took place sitting in the car outside the station, since we arrived at our destination long before we were ready to stop talking), we discovered how hungry we were to hear how our peers—others who were raised in the heyday of feminism's second wave—were negotiating these issues and solving these conflicts. Love, partnership and marriage present a unique challenge to twenty- and thirtysomething women. Many young feminists want the love, support and companionship that come with long-term commitment, but we don't necessarily want the rigid gender roles, strict monogamy or "settling down" that have traditionally defined it. Feminism's messages of self-reliance and critique of heterosexuality—its imperatives and its institutions—have transformed the way we see relationships: We wrestle with marriage's sordid social and economic history, including the exclusion of many of us based on sexual orientation and the treatment of women as property. We no longer see singlehood as some limbo to be rushed through headlong on the search for a mate. We no longer see those mates as necessarily male. We seek out romantic commitments for the personal and emotional satisfaction they can bring—not to avoid "spinsterhood." We have the opportunity to forge relationships informed by our feminist principles right from the start (a very different situation from those in our parents' generation, who if they came to feminism did so when the rules and habits of a partnership were already established). We come armed with the knowledge that it's all too easy to lose oneself in a relationship, and we are determined not to.

But for all these options, we're still caught in a cultural tug of war: In spite of feminism's profound effects, the notion that marriage is a woman's ultimate goal still carries an alarming amount of currency. Everyone, from toy companies to sitcom writers, seems to think that the XX chromosome is inextricably linked to fantasizing and planning "the most important day of our lives" from gown to cake, before ever having laid eyes on the eventual groom (and, of course, they assume it will be a groom). From ubiquitous how-to-find-the-perfect-man advice in women's magazines to clueless questions from well-meaning relatives ("How come a nice girl like you hasn't found a husband yet?"), we are assumed to be searching for a man to make an honest woman of us. Our insistence that we are already honest—honestly struggling to find the right balance of interdependence, honestly and extralegally married to another woman, honestly enriched by our partnerships but not defined by them, honestly happy to be as we are—too often goes unheeded.

So we engage in constant struggles to bring public perceptions of couplehood in line with the private workings of our partnerships. Even if our pop cultural and social institutions will not recognize it, the desire to love and be loved in return crosses generational and political and gender lines: There are as many ways to be a strong, loving couple as there are couples. Realistic views of love mean we are willing to compromise with our partners for the sake of the relationship, but not to compromise ourselves, our values or our goals in order to have a relationship at all.

The time is ripe for an exploration of the new meanings of romantic partnership. The rigid structure of the past—marriage, mortgage, children, in that order—has been dislodged. Religion, family and restrictive social expectations used to serve as compasses to guide us, but now we must be guided by our own minds, hearts and beliefs. We are left with the burden of choices, with the burden of freedom. We are compelled to forge new visions of what relationships can be, tossing aside the parts that don't work for us and making up new rules—personal and individual rules—to take their place.

And what do these partnerships look like? As we enter into them, we are both looking back and looking ahead, determined yet unsure, ambivalent and hopeful. One set of expectations is gone—that of the dutiful helpmeet who runs the household and puts her own desires second—but it's up to us to find new ones. We're finding our way in the dark; we crave advice that rings true for us, that is relevant to our political and generational landscape. We wonder how much to take from tradition and how much to discard. We wonder how much—and how—we can reinvent marital traditions. The bridal imperative of "something borrowed, something new" has taken on new meaning.

In our discussions with each other and with friends, co-workers and countless acquaintances, we've come across a tremendous and insistent curiosity about the state of committed relationships among women our age. We want to know how others are doing it, why they're doing it, how they make it work and stay sane amid the blizzard of mixed messages and desires for love, careers, homes, money, freedom and dreams. So we set out to collect and share these stories of bliss, invention, introspection and trial alike, lending an ear to true tales of the first generation to be blazing this path.

Some, like Bhargavi C. Mandava, find themselves reclaiming traditional rites, as she does ancient Vedic vows in "A Suitable Union." Others choose to make rites conform to their dictates. In "The Crossing of Arms," Denise Brennan Watson reconciles her Catholic upbringing with her and her husband's pagan spirituality to create a ceremony that celebrates family heritage while honoring the couple's political ideals.

Of course, more than just ceremonies have been reconstructed. Kitsey Canaan creates her own name, and her daughter's, in "Naming Daisy Canaan." Georgette Chen balances love and career through a long-distance relationship odyssey in "The Two-Body Problem." Ellen Anne Lindsey finds that her ideal partnership numbers more than expected in "Table for Three, Please." And Faith Haaz-Landsman, in "One Queer Family," puts a very modern twist on boy meets girl.

Alternative arrangements notwithstanding, we acknowledge there is much to learn from women who have preceded us. The dignity and inner reserve of older wives strengthen Carrie Jones in "Off the Map," as she finds solace and self-reliance where she least expected it. Kate Epstein's "A Marriage of My Own" traces her attempts to create an egalitarian partnership as she reflects on her mother's marital legacy.

For others, the legacy begins now; it is only recently that queer women have openly experienced gay unions and commitment ceremonies on a large and public scale. Jane Eaton Hamilton takes a humorous look at the "Twenty-One Questions" one asks when planning a wedding between two women, Diane Anderson-Minshall and her partner do "The Lesbian Baby Dance" and Leigh Cotnoir ("One Size Does Not Fit All") examines the pressures of being a married lesbian in a world where successful long-term couplings carry the weight of an entire community's hopes and political goals.

And with legalization of same-sex marriage persistently in the headlines yet still out of reach, can a politically-minded straight girl marry with a light heart? In "Why I Don't," Rachel Fudge recounts the joys and hurdles of partnered, heterosexual and unmarried living; Jennifer Maher, in "My Best Friend's Not Coming to My Wedding," does walk down the aisle, but must confront her misgivings on the way.

While most of us refuse to "honor and obey," we still say a heartfelt "I do!" to steamy sex with our partners. In "Sex and the Shacked-Up Girl," Stacy Bierlein plans for eighty years of sizzle, while Lori L. Tharps goes "In Search of the Elusive Orgasm" when she learns that love is definitely *not* all you need.

Of course, embracing feminist sensibilities does not mean that cultural and family pressures are left behind. Juhu Thukral and her partner choose peace of mind over idealism in "Reluctant Bride and Groom." "So Yoro Ka Djan (Home Is Far Away)" is native southerner Lauren Smith's attempt at making a mutual homeland in the Midwest with her Burkinabé husband.

Sometimes relationships that don't last are as illuminating as those that do. In "Raw Material," Sonya Huber ponders her habit of serial engagement and how she learned that a "good enough" man isn't good enough; "Teenage Army Bride" Bee Lavender recounts the evolution (and dissolution) of her first marriage as she and her husband reached adulthood. In "Answering Homer," Katie Hubert finds that idealism and a gender-reversed mythology are not enough to keep a couple together.

Many of the contributors to *Young Wives' Tales* have found themselves asking, like the Talking Heads, "How did I get here?" We grew up and surprised ourselves by crossing the country to be with a lover—or by staying close while living a thousand miles away. We married wives of our own—or determined we never wanted to become one. We discovered we wanted to raise children—or resolutely stopped the family at two. We actually found partners with whom we could be fully ourselves. Whether or not we ever dreamed of wedding cakes or matching toothbrushes, we're now discovering how to create meaningful and fulfilling partnerships in which we and our companions thrive.

So we're hitched. Devoted. In love. Shacked up. Happy. Working on it. Committed. Free-wheeling. Bonded. Swept off our feet. Independent. Interdependent. Straight. Gay. Other. Domesticated. Untamed. Traditional. Rebellious. Coupled.

But no matter what lives we find ourselves living, we're altogether aware of having chosen them—and that has made all the difference.

Jill Corral and Lisa Miya-Jervis

Young Wives' Tales

A Bride's Anxiety

Karen Eng

If I were a bride-to-be by the book, I'd probably be reveling smugly in the long-awaited arrival of my prince, poring over china patterns and plucking my bridesmaids from a bevy of eager maidens. Come to think of it, I'd probably be younger. But I'm not. I'm thirty-two, always-been-and-always-expected-to-be single, polygamous in theory, serially monogamous in practice and guarded.

Then, a few months ago, Iain and I got formally engaged. At the tail end of a long, tearful fight one afternoon, he lowered the bottom third of his body to the living room floor and told me he looked forward to fighting with me like this for a lifetime. I hugged his head and wept even more because I hold him in the highest esteem, and I never expected to be so lucky.

We had naturally and quietly come to this decision together long before that moment. But once it became official, the invasion of privacy by others—even the threat of it—threw me right out of whack. At least a month went by before I told even my closest friends, and then I mostly just let word leak out.

Why was I so filled with dread?

My trepidation partly revolves around the accoutrements, the public display, the time and energy, the dubious limbo state of being engaged. I'm feeling overly defensive. I'm preparing to react to strange women squealing over me, men asking where the ring is, bitter friends' grudging acknowledgment, people asking whether I've set the date, what I'm going to wear and what flavor the cake will be, and whether they'll be invited.

Partly it's just that I just want things to go on as usual, until we can sneak off to city hall and then have a feast with family and friends. I wear no big rock, rarely refer to Iain as "my fiancé," try to avoid small talk involving wedding plans. But, as time goes on, I also realize the wedding anxiety is only one end of the telescope. At the other, marriage is a hugely magnified, abstract thing beyond our little relationship, loaded with assumptions too vast and varied to form a cohesive picture.

When we were seven or eight years old my best friend and I played lots of pretend. We were angels looking down at winter clouds reflected in the big rain puddles on the blacktop, thinking about diving down through those aerial windows to visit humans on Earth. We'd be miners searching for fool's gold in her backyard, or gardeners pulling marigold seeds out of their calyces and planting them.

Frequently we'd play Writer or Artist, switching off between creating works of art and playing The Dog—a loyal pet who'd fetch blank paper and crayons. It was a *kind* of marriage fantasy, I guess. Pretty foresightful, too. As adults we both make our living in magazines—although until now, neither of us has come within spitting distance of the magistrate.

So as far as picturing any kind of husband, imagination apparently restricted me to animal life. I knew I couldn't marry someone like my dad, a real patriarch who—faith rooted both in Confucian duty and science—oversaw my every move. Consequently, I hate being told what to do; inevitably, the first serious boyfriend I brought home turned out to be just as controlling. I was nineteen, he was twenty-five, and he "let" me do whatever I wanted.

To my mother's credit, she saw this and warned me, perhaps having learned from experience. "You're too independent for him," she said. I disagreed with her, thinking she was just trying to exert control. But she was right about him—and me.

"You don't need a husband," she said. "You need a wife."

This being Orange County in the 1980s, wifely partners for sheltered young ladies were in short supply, so once I came to my senses and left him at twenty, I bumped along more or less on my own—never even living with a man—until I was thirty. Until then I read lots of Anaïs Nin and Colette and decided I could be alone happily, with (just to keep things interesting) lovers dropping in to agitate me in my solitary bliss well beyond menopause, like another of my favorite celebrity libertines, Jeanne Moreau. I learned to do everything for myself: cook and clean, work and pay the bills, garden and guard my privacy, take company in cats—looking forward to the day I would finally be one of those dirty old women who avail themselves of their friends' pubescent sons.

At twenty-two I moved to Berkeley—virtually a resort for solitary women—where I acquired two close older female friends who'd each raised a son on her own. At twenty-seven I bought into a cooperative: an apartment with room for one in a small, like-minded community. Like my friends, I could and would do it all myself. Husbands, like those my sister and high-school friends were acquiring, receded even further, like pleasant but innocuous features in a landscape.

Funny—faced with marriage now, I realize there's an upside to having prepared for indefinite solitude: I'd trained myself not to get what I wanted, but I *am* well-equipped to recognize what I want when I see it. (The downside, of course, is that I'm also more intolerant, more stubborn, more quick-tempered and less inclined to compromise.) Iain is self-contained, patient and humble. He possesses a yielding nature tempered by integrity and a sharp mind. He's contemplative, so he knows himself and doesn't take out what he doesn't know on me. He is compassionate and patient but not at all spineless, making him, at age twenty-four, more mature than I am. ("What would Iain do?" I sometimes ask myself in hairy situations.) He likes me in all my goofy glory, too, so I don't have to worry about keeping up appearances.

I don't think we're incredibly unconventional. We each try to support the other's ambitions while maintaining a respectful distance. He wants to be the one to stay home with our (eventual) baby, even though he's worried my maternal instincts will kick in and I won't let him. "Fat chance," I say. I'm accustomed to using up all my energy on work, and I'm hoping that his youthful stamina and natural patience will prevail when I'm too tired to drag my middle-aged ass out of bed to deal with the kid in the middle of the night. Right now, as I type, he's at the laundromat doing our laundry because I want to finish this. He hauls the baskets out, kisses me good-bye and steps into the evening, saying, "Don't be discouraged. You can do it." All this, and he makes coffee in the morning and does the dishes at night.

Now, I'm set in my ways. So all of Iain's good qualities didn't make me automatically decide marriage was the way to go. My sister, three years younger but married at twenty-three, pushed me over *that* ledge. As the first hapless human to intrude on my private world, she knows better than anyone my ferocious need for a place of my own. (She knows, for instance, I will wake up ready to kill if roused unexpectedly in the morning—unless the rouser is armed with a cup of hot, black coffee.) Not long after my relationship with Iain began, she and I had a little talk. I told her I liked having him with me more than anyone—more than I liked being alone.

She said: "Marry him." It wasn't a suggestion. It was a directive. (She probably thought it was my last chance.)

"I can see how I could," I said, tentatively. "But . . . I've never really wanted to get married before."

"That's the *point*," she said. "You're not supposed to want to marry just anybody."

She was right, as always. To my amazement, the idea of agreeing to be with Iain as indefinitely as possible has settled into me comfortably. It excites me to think about all the perks and possibilities marriage affords. We can plan ahead, pool our efforts to pursue our dreams, wake up together and share guilty pleasures. So when it comes to the actual act, why do I still feel like running away?

I do know what I want from our wedding. We've decided we constitute a family, so we want formal acceptance as such. I like the idea of being able to choose my relatives. I like having Iain's family as my extended family; they felt like mine from the beginning. Getting the world to recognize our relatedness seems to demand some ceremony, even if it's not state sanctioned. The idea of building family onto family and starting a franchise of our own sounds (I have to admit) nice. This makes it easier to let go of that old idea of my solitary self.

High-mindedness aside, now I've got practicalities to deal with, and a lot of my animosity comes from the nitty-gritty. I'm looking forward to friends meeting each other for the first time, the food and the dance, but more often, I feel put upon. Not that I begrudge anyone a party: It's just not something I've ever craved doing, and I don't want to do it now. I'd rather stay in bed with a book.

Worse, while I respect marriage in general, I generally abhor weddings. I especially object to the uniformity of typical weddings. They tend to involve the following, which doubles as a list of things I loathe or find embarrassing: smelly bridal magazines; dresses that look like three-tier wedding cakes; three-tier wedding cakes; big cartoony diamond rings; raised parquet dance floors; DJs playing "We Are Family" by the Pointer Sisters; engagement parties; the whole business with the garter; bridesmaids; engraved invitations with ten million bits of paper falling out of each envelope; handwringing mothers-in-law; public vows (especially self-written ones—they make me blush); caterers; tuxes; video cameras in the face when one is trying to eat a drippy hors d'oeuvre; "So when are *you* getting married?"; insipid conversations with ridiculous strangers sporting large hair; small dresses and too much perfume; and showers leading to the gratuitous giving of utterly useless gifts.

As Iain and I don't have religious considerations but do want more than anything to bring our families together, we're looking to cultural heritage for guidance. We're both children of immigrant parents (mine are from China and Hong Kong, his mother is from Aberdeen, Scotland), and we're very attached to our families. To take care of legalities, we'll get papers signed by a close mutual friend who's an ordained Universal Life Minister.* Then in Los Angeles, where most of my family lives, Iain will come to my mother's house to bargain with my cousins and siblings for my hand and take me back to his waiting family. Both families later will celebrate with a big Chinese banquet.

Back in the Bay Area, we'll exchange rings and party to live Scottish music, ensure a blessed and demon-free future with a traditional Chinese

---

* *An all-inclusive religious organization founded in 1962 that will ordain anyone in a matter of moments over the web, legally sanctioned by the state to perform wedding duties. For more information, see www.ulm.org.*

lion dance and eat Peruvian food cooked by Iain's Peruvian stepfather as well as a bite of his mother's national dish, haggis. No bouquet fling, no vows (except between us), no garter striptease, no bridesmaid politics.

We're trying to accommodate and honor everyone to our satisfaction, but this has caused its own problems. A traditional white wedding is, by all accounts, stressful enough. But one traditional Chinese plus one multitraditional wedding creates twice the decisions and more than twice the details. And because we've written out the "You are now husband and wife" moment entirely and each event has its own guest list, more than one person has, at some point, been convinced that the party they haven't been asked to *must* be the one where the *real* wedding is happening. The same friends who scoff at marriage are the ones concerned about getting invited to the one where the governmental wand gets waved over our heads. It's like pregnant women getting their bellies touched by total strangers: People lose all sense of self-restraint.

"This is why people elope," say the cynics. I don't have the heart for that, and in my ongoing struggle to be tolerant I am developing perspective. I'm coming to know, for instance, that weddings are a way for people to participate in a way they understand. They're scripted moments for an overwhelmingly emotional situation that makes people feel defenseless. (A friend of mine wrote, in response to a distress call, "Of course you're overwhelmed—people stampede individuals who seek a lifetime of exclusivity.") Maybe weddings are a palliative for the part of us that finds such unions painful and unnatural or feels that weddings mainly represent loss. Thus the tears.

Probably I'm being too unforgiving. But I have at least begun to realize that the default white-wedding template exists precisely because we live among many different cultures and we need a place to start, a common ritual. Mothers get to wring their hands, friends get to attend to friends, the family's small children get to bear rings and flowers, and so on. If we had a more homogeneous population with common spiritual and cultural values, weddings might be closer to the heart and easier. Iain and I could go from decision to engagement to wedding without my having to do anything but show up, with no new ideas to cause conflict.

Announcing my intention to marry has pushed me up against people's expectations of weddings, of wedlock, what it all means—whether I like it or not. I can't pretend to understand what marriage symbolizes to people in the culture at large. I don't understand where the script comes from; I simply don't relate. Marriage is so complex, it can't mean any single thing to any single individual, much less to an entire culture, especially one as wildly complex as ours. You could argue that it all boils down to values. Considering the barrage of opinions I've been enduring, though, nothing seems farther apart in people's minds than marriage values and weddings. The oddest of all the pessimistic or thoughtless attitudes volleyed at me in the course of being engaged is this: Marriage is so scary because it's so *permanent*. At this I snort, and inwardly I wish it were true. In fact, I'm certain only that nothing goes on forever, that my desire for Iain takes the form of wanting to be with him from moment to moment into a future I can't see. Marriage is only as permanent as I am, and what am I? A resilient bag of blood. Life is fragile and brief—from where I stand it's nowhere near a long enough time with the person I want closest by me.

A Marriage of My Own

Kate Epstein

"For we think back through our mothers if we are women," said Virginia Woolf of the woman writer in *A Room of One's Own*. Marriages are, like writing books, a collaboration. A spouse, like a writer, may have influences and models. As a young wife, I think back to my mother.

April 2, 1967. My mother's wedding. The bride wears a short white dress. Her cropped hair is longer on top, accentuating a slim neck. The slender groom is in a suit. His thick-rimmed glasses define his face, picking up the darkness of his hair and clothes. The photographs show a string of people standing with their arms around one another's shoulders, the varying heights requiring bent knees and torsos. There are none of the clean lines and carefully positioned uprightness of most wedding photographs.

"It was a stupid wedding," my mother said to me once. She'd wanted to have it in the apartment she had secretly been sharing with my father for a year. Her mother insisted on a hotel function room. It was a major concession; to socialist-leaning young people of the sixties, it was important to minimize the bourgeois.

∞

August 3, 1997. I wear a wedding gown of silk organza, simple and unadorned. A band of silk makes a V at my waist and ends in two roses at the small of my back. A white veil hangs down my back. Tiny flowers in my headpiece pick up the pink. The skirt stands out in a slender bell over my petticoat. When I move the fabric falls softly, like snowflakes. The train sweeps the floor gently.

Ethan wears a dark suit and red tie. His mass of long, curly hair is tidy. After the ceremony he has on two rings, each a set with my two, one for the engagement and one for the wedding. It was his idea.

"If I just buy you a ring, it's like me making you mine," he explained. We had our engagement rings custom-made, mine a more delicate version of his, with matching pieces of jade peeking out through the gold like a deep green eye. People ask about his—they're not used to seeing engagement rings on men. He loves to explain it.

I would have been content to wait for the wedding for a ring. My father never gave my mother an engagement ring—they both thought engagement rings too old-fashioned and "middle-class"—so I didn't think it was necessary. My mother's nascent feminism, which I believe lurked in her leftist leanings, made adherence to traditional wedding rituals unthinkable.

Thirty years later, I still see the vestiges of male dominance in wedding traditions, but I also believe that traditions have beauty and power that I'm entitled to tap into: Two rings are better than none; the white dress signifies new life, not virginity; sexual commitment enriches our pleasure in each other, without possession or domination. Instead of Mr. and Mrs. Handelman, we stayed Kate Epstein and Ethan Handelman: the Epstein-Handelmans (or the Handelman-Epsteins, if you ask *him*). We broke two glasses under two heels at the ceremony's conclusion, claiming our cultural tradition but discarding the asymmetry. The veil framed my face but didn't shield it. In a world changed by feminism, we took what we wanted from tradition and left the rest.

This is how my parents got engaged: They lived together for a year in secret, on the opposite coast from their parents. My father decided to move to Nebraska for school. My mother, in the midst of her junior year at UC Berkeley, said that without any kind of commitment she felt free to see other people. She made a date with a man from one of her classes.

My father asked her to marry him.

She broke her date.

"Now she's feeling scared," Mom explained. Maria on *Sesame Street* was singing to her reflection as she got ready for her wedding.

Mom, my brother and I had gathered in front of the television to watch Maria and Luis's wedding. We were years too old for *Sesame Street*, no longer viewers, but we'd heard about the event from a friend.

"Getting married is really a leap in the dark," Mom said. "I'm glad we did it when we were young, because God knows if we'd have had the courage later."

Her marriage was starting to show cracks. My parents had fought fairly regularly for as long as I could remember, but that was normal, for them. I didn't think *divorce*. I was a child of the divorce generation. I knew such children. I played with them. They seemed to be set slightly apart from the rest of us, as if they bore a mark.

I started to see the cracks when I was about eleven. But only once before I entered junior high did I suspect that I might soon bear the mark. I confronted my parents as they sat across from each other at the dining table. "You guys fight *all the time*." "All the time" seemed stark in my mouth. It was the closest I could come to saying "divorce."

Things seemed to get better soon after I said it, as if I had warned them of a precipice they were standing near, and they had decided to come back.

It was a reprieve.

This is how I got engaged: The July after my college graduation, I stayed up all night with my roommate the night before her wedding. The ice cream we ate bubbled painfully in my stomach until dawn, a sign of my developing intolerance for lactose. I was getting too old to eat ice cream.

The sky outside was beginning to gray when I realized why Cathy's wedding was making me so anxious I couldn't sleep. I wanted to get married.

I wasn't sure I was old enough to be married. I wasn't sure if Cathy was, either, and she knew it. She was changing her name, and I was afraid she would lose a lot more than that. Would her marriage, to a man in the Army, get in the way of her career? Could she become her own person if she married when she was barely grown up? My mother's shadow loomed over me. But Cathy and I had choices. Career and independence held their charms: We didn't need men to give us status.

I had vowed not to marry young—which was a moderate position. When my parents broke up during my teens, I'd announced that I would never marry at all, so disgusted was I by the raw pain created in all of us by the divorce. I always thought my parents would have worked out better if they hadn't been so young, so fresh and unformed, when they married. Or that they might not have married at all had they waited until they were older and wiser. Wasn't that what Mom had said as she watched Maria and Luis on *Sesame Street*?

But I've always looked to my friends to see what I'm old enough to do. I started wanting to date when one friend went out; I started wearing a bra after noticing a strap on another friend's back; I began shaving my armpits and legs when others turned up hairless one spring. Cathy's wedding was like a push: She stood on the other side of the gap, holding her hand out, as I watched the sun rise on the morning she'd be a bride. My heart was poised for a leap, and it was dragging my mind along.

I've never been religious, but I've always acknowledged the validity of faith, belief without proof. There is no guarantee that a marriage will last, or that it will turn out to be the best choice. I suppose that everyone, in part, marries for the same reason my father did: to avoid being alone. Ethan and I loved each other and were happy together. Marriages made by older people break up too, I reasoned. No matter how old you are when you marry, you'll change. A few more years wouldn't make a big difference. Independence doesn't require loneliness. The remaining gap between doubt and certainty was pretty small, and I could feel my heart stretching to bridge it.

The next time I got Ethan alone, driving home from Cathy's wedding, I explained to him how I'd felt in the early morning.

"If we get married . . . " I said, late in the conversation.

"I think we've decided about *if*, just not *when*," Ethan said calmly, glancing away from the road.

"Oh." I guessed we had decided *if*. It took four months for us to muster up the courage to decide *when*. But in November we were officially engaged, buying rings and choosing halls and talking to rabbis. We would celebrate our leap of faith.

In the early seventies, soon after my mother joined a feminist consciousness-raising group, my father reported a strange event. "I have the impression I peed in the oven last night," he said one morning.

My mother turned the oven on. It was not a dream.

"No matter how much I cleaned that oven, I couldn't get the smell out. We had to move away," Mom reports.

He said he was confused, and it was an accident. She said the oven and the toilet were not in the same room and that opening an oven door requires the opposite motion from raising a toilet seat. She said he was responding to her joining the women's movement.

Perhaps it is because I am a mama's girl, attuned to the quiet anger that festered and then erupted in my mother—but never seemed to change my father—that I believe her. Or maybe it's because neither of them ever mentions him scrubbing the oven.

When we were dating, I once asked Ethan if he was a feminist.

He said he wasn't sure.

"Well," I said, "what's a feminist?"

He said, "If feminism means supporting the equality of women, I'm definitely a feminist."

I adored him for the whole conversation. I even liked his initial hesitation. If he were just saying what he thought I wanted to hear, he wouldn't have paused.

I feel I've come rather far from finding urine in the kitchen. And anyway, our oven is self-cleaning.

When I was eleven my parents discussed sharing household duties because my mother was considering getting a job. They were sitting apart from the rest of us but within earshot, near my grandparents' backyard swimming pool. The memory is very green, with the grass around the pool.

Their main goal was to decide whether she should get a job at all.

Mom had been working at home as a novelist, freelance copyeditor, mother and housekeeper since my birth. After some discussion of an equitable division of housework, she said to Dad, "I think the thing that appeals to me the most about taking the job is that you'd do the grocery shopping."

"Lin, if that's all it is, I'll do the grocery shopping either way," he promised.

She didn't take the job, and neither of them remembered the conversation. A couple of months later I mentioned it to her, but she waved me away. Nothing changed until she got a job.

"I would expect you to do more if you worked from home," Ethan said. He says this because full-time, paycheck-earning work hasn't been all I expected it to be, and I've been considering stopping. I've even fantasized about living in a much cleaner home, which seems possible if I were freelancing and had more time for housework. Mostly I fantasize about how great it would be to have more time for writing.

"Of course, I'd miss cooking," he mused.

"We'll work it out," I reassured.

Several weeks later, I came back with a different tune.

"I don't see why I should do all the housework if I work at home." We've never tied his sometimes-fluctuating graduate-student income to housework. I'd just read Alix Kates Shulman's essay "A Marriage Disagreement, or Marriage by Other Means" in the *Feminist Memoir Project,* which describes the agreement she wrote for the equal distribution of childcare and housework with her husband.

Before reading that essay, I'd been modeling our duties after my parents', unconsciously. Maybe I'd also thought of staying home as a guilty pleasure that I should pay for with extra housework. Or I just liked the idea of the grout being clean.

"I don't assume you'll do everything." Ethan doesn't always remember our conversations. Much to his irritation, I remember everything. I repeated his earlier remarks.

The first principle of Shulman's marital agreement was that paid work was not to be ascribed the most inherent value. "The ability to earn more money is a privilege which must not be compounded by enabling the larger earner to buy out of his/her [household and childcare] duties."

I'm not in complete agreement with her here. It's true that earning more money is a privilege traditionally and unfairly awarded to men. But being able to choose *not* to earn a living wage is also a privilege. Right now, I'm granting that privilege to Ethan while he's in graduate school. Someday he may give it to me. But we've been living by Shulman's idea in that he hasn't taken on all the housework in exchange. So why should I?

Ethan made excuses. Hadn't I always said that breaks were an important part of writing? Why wouldn't I put in some laundry on a break? Was I sure I would work forty hours a week as a freelance writer, that I would even want to? Indeed, I might find I get as much writing done in thirty hours a week as I do in forty. It's a quirky job. But there was something of the knee-jerk going on, also: Men's work is more important than women's; caring for a home is a female activity.

Deciding who does the dishes can set the tone of a marriage. I have conflicting feelings about staying at home: I dream of it and yearn for it, but the potential consequences frighten me. We've agreed to take it as it comes, revising our division of labor until it seems right, if and when I decide to work at home. We'll remain vigilant. Because deciding who makes the money can set the tone of a marriage, too.

"I didn't even think divorce was an option until I got a job," my mother told me last week. I had asked her if she still thinks my father's financial support was her gilded cage. She says yes.

I think that period was when I learned divorce was an option, as well—not quite consciously, and not because of Mom's job, but because of the tension that rang constantly. Once again, they were fighting *all the time*. This time I couldn't even confront them. Our family was like a house of cards, everything delicately leaning on itself. I knew that a tiny breeze, the word "divorce" in my thoughts, the question asked, would bring it down.

The breeze came from a door that Mom's paycheck opened. In nineteen years of marriage she hadn't known the door was there. Within two years of collecting a paycheck, she walked through it—away from her marriage.

I remember my father saying proudly to me, "I'm the breadwinner."

"Doesn't Mommy make money, too?" She freelanced for several book publishers.

"I'm the *primary* breadwinner."

I'd always planned to exhibit some of my father's arrogance about my moneymaking capacities. At eight I found my calling in the form of weekly school compositions. I wanted to be a writer. But I would have another job for income, as my writer-parents always advised. They thought I'd succeed, just not right away, and not necessarily so spectacularly as to make a living. By the time I was a teenager, my mother was emphasizing financial independence.

I agreed with her completely: "I never want to confuse financial dependence with love," I was known to explain. "Nothing's pure if you do it for money," Mom said. It was all so obvious. Sting had sung, "If you love someone, set them free." No one, I was sure, could be free without her own money. Marital happiness must come from knowing that love, not money, kept you together. This credo would supply the support for the house of cards, the foundation holding it up. The first card could lean on something more substantial than another card.

Unfortunately, I've found that this credo can make *professional* happiness difficult. Ethan's professional happiness involves a certain level of financial dependence right now. He could barely live on the money he earns as a graduate student. Similarly, I would be happier professionally if I could be a full-time writer. And when it's my turn, that's what I want to do.

Will it be so dangerous? At times I still think so, especially since we're also planning on children. I can imagine my future, a kerchief around my head, tending to household, children and husband, a slave to their needs, all my brain cells suffocating, atrophying. This woman is a familiar figure—I think she's in an episode of the *Brady Bunch*. Her image brands my decisions: "unfeminist."

But life is more complicated than TV. And feminism is more complicated than a simple rejection of everything the tube shows. Women need access to equal paychecks, but that doesn't mean that each woman must exercise that freedom. I am truest to feminism when I understand my own priorities—writing and raising children—and make decisions accordingly. Sometimes I wish these weren't my priorities, since both mean I'll be overworked and underpaid, but I've come to accept that they are. And I've chosen a partner eager to share them with me. When it comes time to decide about childcare, it won't be the choice between me or a professional—it'll be about how we split the time we take from the work he loves and the work I love, and how we balance that with our feelings about (and budget for) professional care.

The support under my house of cards isn't financial dependence—it's love. I have a tendency to reach inside that house and nudge the foundation. "Do you really love me? Is this what we want? Is this working? Are we communicating?" "Divorce," I intone, reacting to those two years I was silent before my parents' divorce. "Yeah, well, divorce me," I say, and then take it back. It's my way of dealing with the fact that Mom and I have similar priorities. She was a full-time writer for a while. She was married to my father for a while. Neither one made her look like the woman with the kerchief, most of the time. Both stopped working for her, and she quit both.

It's too bad it took Mom so long to realize her marriage was unhappy. The door that swung open when she got a job had been there all along. I hope that having seen her go through it ensures that I'll always remember. Hope seems to be the key.

December 24, 1992. My mother's second wedding. The bride wears blue, the groom wears a black suit. The Unitarian minister's study is intimate. I wear red. I am given the floor at one point in the ceremony.

I ramble. Though I had the opportunity to prepare, I didn't. I say nice things about my stepfather, a welcome addition to my parent collection. I talk about how my mother is always saying, "T!"—her nickname for him—"Look!" when she sees something worth looking at. As if seeing were for sharing. What better endorsement for moving through life together than that you want to see the same things?

Then I tell them both, "You've made me maybe-kinda-sorta believe in marriage again."

It is true. I like who they are together. My stepfather exhibits his unwavering devotion to my mother after decades, he says, of unrelieved flirting. And my mother has become a much kinder, more open person. The years since the wedding have ticked by without their love ever flagging, their constant and easy companionship always evident. When I call—long-distance—they get on separate extensions and periodically lapse into just talking to each other; it's annoying.

But it's inspiring, too. My mother embraced hope, and that influenced my marriage more than anything else she's ever done. In the five years between their ceremony and ours, my mother and stepfather got me to believe in marriage. If Mom could believe again, I could too. "Maybe-kinda-sorta" dropped out of the sentence.

Naming Daisy Canaan

Kitsey Canaan

I was lying in the big hospital Jacuzzi waiting for the placenta to come out while the nurses took my firstborn across the room to clean her up under the warm lights. My husband leaned against the side of the tub and said to me, "I think she should have your last name because you worked so hard." I *had* worked hard: Labor had been hell beyond belief, far beyond anything I'd prepared for.

"Okay," I said without a second's hesitation. That's how we settled an eight-month debate.

I knew within twenty-four hours of meeting Doug Ryan that I would marry him, and in our first love-drunk weeks together I felt a sappy, wistful connection to his Irish surname. I'm three-quarters Irish and I look Irish, but I inherited Ellman, my father's vaguely Jewish name. Even in that romantic cloud, however, I knew I could never take my husband's name, whether or not I preferred it to my own. I just couldn't do it. Mrs. Ryan? No way. It simply was not possible.

When Doug and I first talked about having kids, we agreed that hyphenated names were not for us. As a poet, I care about the musical quality of words. I didn't want to saddle our offspring with two names that sounded as monotonous linked together as ours would. Doug's reasoning was less aesthetic, more logical. What happens when two people with hyphenated names have children? Do their children have four last names?

Our first, whimsical solution was to rename ourselves, choosing a family name that we would both assume. One tipsy evening we came up with Cucumber-Lovely, but the next morning we realized that hadn't solved the hyphenation problem.

Years later, when I was pregnant and we had to face the issue more seriously, we talked it through again. It quickly became clear that we each wanted the baby to have our own last name. How to resolve this? Not, we decided, on any political basis. We would stick strictly to aesthetics. Whichever name, his or mine, sounded better with the child's first name would be the one. So far we agreed. The problem arose when we couldn't agree which sounded better.

I was surprised to find how much the issue mattered to me. Earlier in my life I don't think I'd have cared that much. I'd never liked my last name. Ellman was dull, even ugly. And it was my father's name. I had no affection or respect for him, and sharing his name irked me.

In the mid-seventies, when I was thirteen, my oldest sister came home from Smith College and brought feminism with her. Among the other aspects of consciousness-raising in which she engaged me, she mentioned she had considered changing to our mother's maiden name because her family's culture was really the one we were raised in; my father had virtually no contact with his family of origin. More to the point, she hated the "man" suffix. To compensate, her college friends called her Sheila Ellwoman.

At the time I thought changing one's name a rather frivolous, even pretentious thing to do. Still, I felt strongly that names were important. I cared passionately about my own first name. I was christened Catherine, but my family had never called me that. I grew up as Kitsey, and having an unusual name was an important part of my identity. It was annoying, though, to have to fill out forms as Catherine and then explain later what I preferred to be called.

I decided to change my name when, at thirty-four, I went through a deep, suicidal depression. As I emerged from that state, it became clear to me that I needed a new name to symbolize my rebirth. I didn't know what the last name would be, but I knew I would jettison Catherine, make Kitsey my legal first name and find a new surname to go with it. It took about a week to choose one. I knew I wanted a name to begin with a C, a hard C. It had to complement Kitsey musically. I went to the dictionary and read carefully through the Cs, making a list of possibilities. It took no time at all to select Canaan. Though I'd long before rejected Christianity, the name's resonance felt right to me: the promised land, the land of the living to which I had thought I would never return.

Having chosen that name made it precious. A year later, pregnant, I wanted my child to have that name, too. I wanted to found a line of Canaans. It was a surprise, because I used to ridicule this "passing on a name" sentiment when it was voiced by a man. It reeked of the patriarch's ownership of children. But my chosen name did not have value because it represented a family line or tradition from the past. It was an affirmation of the future, a rejoicing that I would *have* a future; that I could renounce suicide and come back to life, love and joy; that I could even give birth to new life. I wanted to pass on this affirmation. And, frankly, I didn't want to be the only Canaan. I wanted to share the name with those closest to me. (When I chose my name I invited Doug to assume it as well, but he declined. Now I call him an honorary Canaan.)

The summer before our daughter was born, Doug and I would take slow walks in the woods, trying out different names (Daisy, Chloe, Lucy, Avery, Rory) and playing with their variations (Chloe Ryan, Lucy Canaan). It seemed silly, though, to choose the baby's name before we met it, so we made a short list and decided to see who she or he turned out to be.

I gave Doug a lot of credit for considering my surname as an option for our daughter, something most men I know would not be comfortable with. But I also knew about his family's relationship to the name Ryan. The first time I ate dinner with his parents and sister, Doug's dad joked about having "the luck of the Irish." Underneath their amusement at people's assumption that they were Irish—with their olive complexions, they look anything but—there was something else, some deep ambivalence. Over the years I began to understand. Doug's father, Terry

Ryan, carries the name of two slaveholders. Terry's mother, Julia Terry, was the biracial descendant of the slave-owning Terrys of Lynchburg, Virginia. Terry's father was Reginald Ryan, whose last name came from the master of the Georgia plantation where *his* father, Billy Ryan, had been born, although Billy's father was not Master Ryan but the white overseer, a man named Schears, and his mother was a slave. So Doug's dad was the child of two biracial parents.

Doug's grandmother was dark-skinned, but his grandfather could pass for white. So could Doug's father, and that's what his parents insisted he do. They lived in a white neighborhood in Cleveland, but still some people knew they were of mixed race. When Terry was drafted in World War II, however, his passing became complete. With the Army still segregated, he was placed in a white unit and lived as a white man ever after. And paid a high price. Even after the civil rights movement and the social changes of the seventies and eighties, Terry's psychological relationship to the world was one of passing, of being in some sense a liar, an interloper. His wife is white, their children look white, but the whole family lives with the sense of not quite being part of white America.

When it came to choosing his child's surname, Doug's inherited ambivalence surfaced. "I never really felt like it was *my* name," he said during one of our walks. "It was always more of a family joke," and by that I knew he meant not something funny, but a sore spot. Later, he elaborated. "I feel like my name's 'Doug Ryan,' but not that I'm 'a Ryan,'" he said. "The fact that I have that name just means that names are totally arbitrary anyway." Before I renamed myself, I would have agreed with him. Now I felt differently.

As I entered my ninth month, we still had not decided whose name our child would carry. Two weeks before my due date my contractions began, fifteen minutes apart for a *week* until finally, when I was utterly drained and exhausted, I began the eight hours of intense hard labor that brought our daughter into the world. During that week I was not thinking about names. I was praying that either I would not have another contraction or that they would just get going and be done with.

Labor was a thousand times worse than I ever imagined. I was delirious from the pain. Somewhere in the middle of the long night, I demanded of my doctor why no one had ever told me how much it would hurt. He smiled a comforting smile, rubbed my back and said, "Because you wouldn't have believed it." He was right—I had been warned and hadn't believed. Doug hadn't believed either. He was in tears as often as I was.

I had never related the ordeal of labor to the right to name our child before Doug came to the side of the Jacuzzi and made his offer. But it instantly seemed right. Not because I'd "won" our debate and gotten my own way. Giving Daisy (it was immediately obvious to us that she was Daisy) my name was only partly my reward for having gone through so much pain. It was much more. It was a sign that I had grown her in my body, that her flesh, blood and bone were created from mine, that I had made her. It was a sign that through the initiation of labor I had taken on new responsibility, entered a new role, a new relationship. If Doug had, at that moment, insisted on naming her Daisy Ryan, I would have rebelled. I had earned her name for her.

Now, nearly four years later, Doug jokes that people will think Daisy is his stepdaughter. This doesn't seem to bother him, especially as Daisy looks so much like him. I tell him he can still be an honorary Canaan. And I tell Daisy that we are the "Canaan women." I always feel great pride saying that to her. (Lately, though, she's begun to correct me: "No, you're a woman. I'm the Canaan girl.")

The week before Christmas, Doug and Daisy took a bus to New York City to visit his sister and let me catch up on work for a few days before I followed them down in our car. It was Daisy's first time on a bus, and, Doug reported, she watched out the window utterly fascinated. Their route took them through North Canaan, Massachusetts. Daisy can't read yet, but she recognizes her name. After Doug pointed out the first sign, she saw her name everywhere. "That's Canaan, just like me!" she exclaimed gleefully each time she spotted it. She was so happy, Doug told me later. Hearing the story, I felt a rush of warmth and satisfaction. I'd given my daughter yet one more thing I'd never had as a child: not just a love of life, not just a secure and happy family, but pride in her own name.

Twenty-One Questions

Jane Eaton Hamilton

One: The question that engenders all the rest.
Two homosexual women shiver in February at Long Beach, on the west coast of Vancouver Island, beachcombing during low tide, wearing anoraks, fleeces, heavy boots. They are not whispery, vaporous, gauzy. The waves crash behind them, wild and combustible. There is an unholy wind, which has driven heterosexuals indoors to moon at each other over oysters Rockefeller. In the case of our women, the wind does not whip hair, because our women have short hair. Very short, in fact, with razor trims above their ears. Gelled tufts atop. Already we are in the realm of queer. Shyly, one woman asks the other woman if she thinks they should maybe get married. Maybe. It sounds like a castoff comment, like nothing special. Except that it is Valentine's Day.

"Married?" says the second woman, her voice sucked away by the wind. She does not understand this as a proposal; her lover is hardly on bended knee.

"I want to be with you all my life," says the first woman.

The second woman just frowns. "I want to be with you, too," she says. "But, jiminy crickets, do you have to call it marriage?"

"But marriage is what I want," says the first woman. "I think."

She sighs. She is the first to admit it. For lesbians, the words are clumsy, the institution clumsier. "I think it's what I want. I want to marry you."

The women are drawn to each other like moths to light bulbs, like fingers to sea anemones. They are gooily in love.

"Oh, heck." The second woman laughs, joy surging through her. Though they are on uneasy footing there among the rocks, she lifts the first woman, swings her and shouts, "Yes, yes, yes!"

Two: Marriage? But what is marriage between women?
What are the women intending to say to each other by marrying? What are they saying to their community? Neither of them really knows. They just have an inchoate longing toward a deep, secure future. They sit over dinner discussing it, falling silent, mooning.

"But marriage! Isn't marriage—" The second woman thinks to herself that it's goofy. Just downright goofy. To mimic heterosexuals? Isn't it just embracing rituals that haven't even brought heterosexuals much joy? Isn't it selling out lezzie culture? Anyhow, don't marriages fall apart at a heady clip? What's the failure rate—50 percent? That's something to ape?

The women talk about marriage versus commitment ceremonies, but here they agree: They are already as committed as they would be following such a ceremony. Marriage must hold more meaning, or hets wouldn't bother. Why do they, though? What's the draw? "Divorce?" asks the second woman. "Maybe people head into marriage more seriously because it's hard to get back out."

"Or maybe they just love each other more," says the first woman, "and they have to find a way to express it."

The second woman says, "I love you more."

"Honeybunch," says the first woman, taking her lover's hand. "I love you more, too."

Marriage, then. The women settle, hesitantly, on marriage.

But now what? Where do they go from here? Back to Vancouver, for starters, because they both have work in the morning. And, also, they want to look at rings, those walkabout symbols that tell everyone else what has transpired. But what kind of rings? Should there be one, or two? If they try to toe the heterosexual line, they will have to choose a diamond (a girl's best friend) for at least one of them. But neither of our women is femme. Neither of them is butch. They cling to the amorphous muddle at the middle where diamonds and dresses—well, ugh. All right, then. Two simple silver bands as engagement rings, and each of them can choose her own accompanying wedding band.

"My fiancée," breathes the first bride that night in bed as she strokes her lover's face.

"My fiancée," whispers the second bride back and giggles.

They cannot get used to the ludicrous sound of the word on their tongues. "Are we really engaged?" asks the first bride.

Are they? That's a question about queer marriage: Is there even any such thing? If you think there's an easy answer, you're mistaken. In heterosexual marriage, traditions are a given, and they add a significance that's understood by a wider community. Nothing is that simple with queer marriage. Arguments start up.

Three: For instance, what is the best month for a wedding?
"June," says the first bride without hesitation.

"I hate June," says the second bride. "It always rains in Vancouver in June."

"August, then," says the first bride.

"Uh, no," says the second bride after an obvious hesitation.

"Why not?"

"I just can't, okay?"

"Tell me. I want to know why not."

"It doesn't matter, really," says the second bride.

"It does matter. To me it matters."

"Carol and I held our commitment ceremony in August."
Silence.

"Honey?" says the second bride. "Does that bother you? What's wrong? That shouldn't bother you. It wasn't a wedding, at least."

"Nothing," says the first bride, turning away her face.

"Nothing?"

"Nothing, all right? I said nothing. Didn't you hear me? I'm glad you had your ceremony in August, therefore wrecking the month for me for all time."

"Snookums?"

"Leave me alone."

"Honeybunch? Let's just do it in July."

Four: What should the brides wear?
"White wedding gowns?" jokes the second bride.

The first bride hoots and says, "That'd work for you, because technically, you're a virgin. But me! I've had sex so often I'd have to wear—well, all right, let's say it: black."

The second bride is absurdly hurt. "Are you ridiculing me? You are. You are ridiculing me. I shouldn't be put down just because I don't like penetration. Just because I haven't had the sleazy kind of past you have. Just because I've never slept with a man."

The same question again: What should the women wear?

They could both wear gowns. They could both wear tuxedos. One could wear a gown and one could wear a tuxedo. They could flip for it. But neither of them has worn a dress in ten years. They could just wear everyday clothes, but would that signal to their guests how much all this means? How would that say wedding?

And also, what should the maids of honor wear? Should they even be called maids of honor? Would coupled lesbians be matrons of honor, or only if they'd been through a commitment ceremony?

"Why can't we just call them 'best women?'" asks the second bride.

"Fine by me," says the first bride, grinning devilishly. "As long as we get to dress them in ruffled pink gowns."

Five: What is a queer wedding for?
It's not licensed. There's no marriage certificate, after all. The government doesn't suddenly open up with spousal pension benefits. There are still no joint tax returns. There's no financial incentive—no community property laws. It is merely a cleaving. Unto each other. Of two brides. Do the brides care about sickness and health?

"What if I had an accident and became a paraplegic?" says the first bride. "Would you stay with me then?"

"Of course I would, snookums," says fiancée two.

"The law wouldn't make you."

"The law wouldn't make me if we were straight, either."

"They'd make you pay alimony," says the first bride. "So what if I were a quadriplegic? Then?"

"Well, yeah, I think so."

"You think so?" The first bride gives the second bride a little kick.

"I know so. Okay? I know so."

"No, you don't. You'd leave me. I can tell you'd leave me. The stress would get to be too great and you'd run off with what's-her-name. Your ex. The French one. Fifi."

"Well, what would you do if I were the one who had the accident?"

"I'd run off with Fifi."

Six: Do our brides care about richer or poorer?

"Share money?" says the first bride. "But I earn three times as much as you do! You expect me just to fork it over?"

"Fork it over?" says the second bride.

"I'm sorry. But still, how is that fair?"

"That's what heterosexuals do. It deepens the commitment, don't you think? One for all and all for one."

"Can't we be a little progressive here? We're not heterosexual, or hadn't you noticed? My money is mine. Your money is yours."

"Fine," says the second bride through gritted teeth.

"You're mad. Are you mad? You're always mad, lately."

"I'm not mad. Why would I be mad? Just because my wife will have to take her tropical vacations without me because I can't afford to go? Honestly, I'm not mad. Good golly, no. Don't be absurd."

"I'm just against you getting too dependent on me," says the first bride.

"Screw you," says the second bride. "And screw the bank account you rode in on."

Seven: What about the vow "until death us do part"?

"Death, whoa," says the second bride. "'Til death us do part. That's a really long time."

There. It is finally out. This is what they are talking about when they talk about marriage. Forsaking—all others. Forsaking the ones with giddy laughs. The ones who snake around the dance floor at the club. The ones with snapping eyes. The ones who are short and just slightly overweight. The exes, with whom it is possible to tumble accidentally into bed. The tall chunky ones. The lithe ones. The ones who wear dresses and high heels. The ones who wear black jackets. The one who pitches in the all-girl softball league, with whom the second bride has been flirting recently.

"What?" says the first bride. "Did you just say what I think you just said? How could you be so cruel? I thought you loved me, but let me tell you, lately I'm questioning the depth of your commitment. I didn't twist your arm here. You said yes. You said you wanted to do this."

There is a long pause, then: "Occasionally, once in a while," admits the second bride, "maybe I have a doubt or two. Don't you?"

"I don't. No way. I don't."

"You're always mad lately. You're mad every time I come home from softball."

"So? So? I mean, geez Louise. You're gone a lot. Are you going to be gone this much after we're married? I mean, yeah. I wish you'd hang out with me instead of going to play ball. Why does it have to be all day every Sunday?"

"I thought you liked that I play ball. I thought maintaining our independence was so important to you."

"I'm a softball widow, that's all."

"How could you possibly be a widow? We aren't even married yet. And besides, why should I stay home, when all you do all day long on Sunday is clean?"

"Someone has to wash the floors. We don't have time all week. But oh no: You think I should do all the grunt work, don't you? You do, don't you?"

"The grunt work? I take out the garbage. I fix the washing machine. That's the real grunt work."

Eight: Where should the ceremony be performed?

And what kind of ceremony? How many guests should the brides invite?

"Listen," says the second bride, "I know we talked about a church wedding. But I have to tell you, I've been having real qualms. It feels wrong when I'm an atheist. It goes against everything I believe in. I know it would seem more formal, but—"

"You're not an atheist," says the first bride. "You're agnostic. You're keeping an open mind. At least, that's what you told me. There's a big difference between atheism and agnosticism."

"Well, you believe in reincarnation. You've been dabbling in Wicca."

"Outdoors, then. We can get married at Jericho Beach with just our nearest and dearest present. No fuss. Less expense. We can limit the guest list to—"

"Ten," says the second bride.

"Ten? I have six married brothers and thirteen nieces and nephews. Fifty, maybe, though a hundred would be more realistic."

"My mother won't come."

"She'd let you get married and not attend?" says the first bride.

"You know she thinks it's not a real marriage. You know she just thinks I need to meet the right young fellow."

"Aren't I your nice young fellow?"

"Oh, you are, little snooglebums. My honeybunch bruiser. I love you so, so much."

"I love you too, popsicle. Pumpkin. Puddingdrop."

Nine: Here's a basic question. Are there really two brides?
Or are there a bride and groom? Or two grooms? Let's face it, neither of these women is particularly feminine. They divide the labor around the house according to preference. The first bride cooks because the second bride stinks at it. The second bride takes the garbage out when the first bride doesn't get to it. The second bride does all the mending. The first bride does the laundry and changes the spark plugs in the car. Neither wears dresses, ever. Who knows why? They're dykes. They don't like them.

"I don't mind being called a bride," says the first bride.

"Ugh," says the second. "It sounds like you're a Barbie doll."

The first bride says, "Well, you be the groom. Do you want to be the groom?"

"I don't think of myself as a man. I'm a woman. But I'm not a dippy woman."

"You're saying brides are dippy?"

"It's a dippy word. It comes from when women were considered their husband's property. What about 'marrying partner'?"

"Oh, that's just great. Very simple, easy on the tongue: 'Aunt Sylvia, I'd like you to meet my "marrying partner,"' yup. Very nice ring to it. Very nice indeed." The first bride thinks a minute. "Nope, I think I'd rather be your property."

Ten: Will they register a china pattern?

"I don't like those plates. Too many roses. Look at these. Brown. Plain. I like these ones more," says the second bride.

"Do you think anybody's going to buy us china anyhow?"

"Of course they'll buy us china. Heterosexuals aren't totally stupid. They'll know we have to eat."

"We don't eat," says the first bride. "Lesbians just have sex. Everybody knows that. All day every day."

"Yum," says the second bride and squeezes her fiancée's hand.

The first bride says, "I still like that pattern best."

"I don't even see why we have to register."

"People want to know what to get us. Anyhow, isn't that half the point of marriage? The presents? Don't you have a dowry?"

The second bride laughs. "One left-handed baseball glove, one pair of slightly worn cleats, a huge Visa bill, an '82 Honda. Lucky you."

The first bride squeezes her hand. "I *am* lucky. I'm really lucky."

The second bride smiles. "Do you think people will get us good presents? I mean, we're queer. It isn't actually legal. Won't they just expect us to break up eventually? They might not want to spend much. They might just hedge their bets."

Eleven: Who will officiate? And what will the brides say to each other?

There is also the question, and it is a big one, of whether the second bride's Uncle Thomas should be invited. Last Thanksgiving, Uncle Thomas was heard hooting when the brides (at that point girlfriends, now life as opposed to marrying partners) kissed.

"What are you doing there?" asks the second bride.

"I'm addressing the invitations. Someone has to get to it."

"But you're using a Bic."

"So?" says the first bride.

"I just thought we decided on calligraphy. I know we talked about this, and we said calligraphy would be more elegant."

"Did we? I'm so tired." The first bride swipes a hand over her face. "Honey, you smell like sweat. Did you win? Sometimes I wish we'd just—"

"What?"

"Elope."

The second bride holds her shoulders. "There's a lesbian minister at the United Church who could officiate."

"Is there? How do you know that?"

The second bride shrugs. "She married Mary and Sue."

"Mary and Sue got married? When?"

"Before your time. Back when you lived in Montreal."

"That's—fifteen years ago. Sixteen. They're still together."

"Of course they're still together, silly. They're married."

Twelve: What about flowers?

"I'm not carrying flowers," says the second bride adamantly. "No way I'm going down the aisle carrying a bouquet like some simpering straight girl."

"You're walking down the aisle?"

"Well, I don't know. I never really thought about it. Aren't you?"

"I never thought about it either. Maybe I'll wait at the altar."

"There isn't an altar. It's outside. There isn't an aisle, either."

"Well, at the seagull poop then. Whatever, we still need bouquets," says the first bride. "We can't get married and not have any flowers."

"Why can't we?"

"I love flowers. They're very hopeful. I always saw myself carrying stephanotis."

"You did? You're not kidding? You know what? You're a closet femme. I'll bet you played with Barbie dolls."

"I had two Barbie dolls. They were queer. They got married and had babies together. They harvested one Barbie's eggs, fertilized them in a petri dish and implanted them in the other Barbie. They had three daughters. Barbie, Barbie and Barbie. They lived happily ever after."

Thirteen: Who will pay for the wedding?
The brides themselves, proportionate to their earnings—or split expenses down the middle?

"I talked to my father today," says the first bride. "He's going to pay for everything."

"Your father is going to pay for you to marry a woman?"

"Yes, he is," insists the first bride. "Even the honeymoon."

"We're going on a honeymoon?"

"Now we are."

"I've always dreamed of going mountain climbing," says the second bride.

The first bride replies, "You know where I've always dreamed of honeymooning?"

"You've dreamed of honeymooning?"

"Niagara Falls."

Fourteen: There is still the question of who will stand up with them.
"Who do you want to be your maid of honor?" asks the first bride.

"I thought we were calling them best women."

"Best women, then. Are you still thinking about asking Dorothy? Because she was really snotty to me at the party on Sunday."

"But Dorothy's my best friend," says the second bride.

"I'm just saying."

"What are you saying?"

"I'm saying: If we're a team now, shouldn't we be making joint decisions?"

"About who I want to stand up for me?!"

"If we're a team. Are we a team?"

"We're a team, but I still want Dorothy," says the second bride. "You're asking Claire."

"What's wrong with Claire? Suddenly there's something wrong with Claire? Claire happens to be one of the best people I know."

"Well, so is Dorothy, if you'd give her half a chance. And she's the most important person in the world to me."

"I thought I was."

Fifteen: Is queer marriage even safe?
The second bride's mother is convinced it might not be. She tries to convince the women to reconsider having an outdoor ceremony. They have to apply for a permit—what if word gets out? Bystanders could take exception. The press could show up. Wackos could bring guns.

"Because of two people pledging their undying love?" says the second bride.

"Don't pretend you don't know what I mean," says her mother. "You know very well what I mean."

"We have the right to do this in front of everyone. We won't hide."

"People might not like it, is all I'm saying."

"That's their problem, then."

"Unless they pump bullets into you. Then it's yours."

"I plan to say I love this woman. I plan to say it right out loud. This is our marriage, Mom." The second bride reaches for the first bride's hand.

"I don't like it," says her mother. "It's not what I wanted for you."

Sixteen: There is always, always, the question about shaving.
"Are you planning to shave your armpits?" asks the second bride.

"Are you out of your mind? Why would I do that? I thought I might shave my mustache, is all. Or maybe wax it."

"I thought I'd shave my armpits. Along with my legs. I mean, if you're going to slide a garter down my leg—"

"I could go for that."

"Mmm," says the second bride. "Me too. Now that I think about it. Me too. But wouldn't we have to take our pants off first?"

Seventeen: And the question about names.
"Are you going to take my last name?" asks the first bride.

"Are you going to take mine?" asks the second.

"We could hyphenate."

"Let's just keep our own names," says the second bride.

"You don't want my name? But you could become Mrs. Squat."

"Well, you could become Mrs. Idono."

"Mrs. and Mrs. Idono Squat!"

Eighteen: Should the brides hire a professional photographer?
Or just someone they know?

Oops. It seems the first bride neglected to tell the second that once, in a life far away (Kelowna—a day's drive to the interior) and long ago (two years earlier), she and the photographer happened to be lovers.

"It was not a serious affair," says the first bride. "Merely a fling."

But the second bride is not mollified. She feels defiled. "When were you going to tell me? When I was grinning into the lens? Everyone at the wedding would have known but me!"

"So?"

"So! How many women have there been? Honestly, now. Is it more than ten? More than twenty? More than fifty?"

Nineteen: There are too many questions and too few answers.
To reach the simplest of answers proves exhausting.

The second bride throws herself across the bed and says she wants to call the whole thing off. "I can't do this," she wails. "It's not even legal."

"It's legal in my heart," says the first bride.

"I don't want to get married unless I can really get married. Otherwise, what's the point?"

"I thought *I* was the point."

"I can cleave without a wedding," says the second bride, sniffling.

"Don't cry," says the first bride. "If it means that much to you, we don't have to go through with it."

"You don't want to go through with it? Is that what you're saying? You don't want to be my wife?"

"I want to be your husband."

"Very funny."

"I'm sorry. I do want to marry you. That's not what I was saying."

"You do want to? I want to, too. I do. I really do."

"C'mere. Give me a hug."

Twenty: Finally, it's time—July 14.
If there are questions now, other than on the lips of the guests milling about near the duck ponds at Jericho Beach, it's too late to ask. It's

sunny; the ocean is as flat as a mirror. Gulls wheel across the sky calling raucously. The mountains in the distance look like blue reclining nudes. Tables of food are set up.

But look—the second bride's mother wasn't wrong. There are protesters, fortunately held back by police.

The second bride wears a tux, and the first bride wears a very off-white gown. This is because the second bride is pretending to be butch (she is packing), and the other, femme (she is also packing, but only for the honeymoon trip to Niagara Falls). The first bride's mother sits on a white folding chair in the front row dabbing her eyes with a tissue. The first bride's father nods his head sagely.

The second bride's mother is there, but out of sight behind some bushes, peeking in, also weeping.

The brides promise a justice of the peace that they will love, honor and cherish each other forever. A small emerald is placed on the ring finger of the first bride. A labyris is slid onto the ring finger of the second bride.

Protesters hold up placards saying, "God hates fags." Saying, "Die, Sodomites." They try to drown out the ceremony with their shouts.

When the women kiss, the guests clap and cheer.

So do the protesters, only their cheers are jeers.

At the reception, the brides sign a registry (which isn't really anything more than a form printed out on the second bride's computer) on the dotted line, but not quite on the dotted line. Being queer, they sign a little outside the line, and it is requested that they use crayons. The usual color is of course lavender, a vibrant, solidaritous lavender, but they are free to choose whichever color most pleases them. There are no thought police here! Except suddenly there's horrid Uncle Thomas—where did he come from?—holding apples against his chest, dancing around the floor air-kissing men.

Twenty-one:
They have ordered up the honeymoon suite at a Niagara Falls hotel, but when they register the clerk says, "I have Mr. and Mrs. Idono Squat registered. There must be some mistake, ladies. That suite is reserved for honeymooners."

"Us!" say the brides, exultant.

The clerk's lips thin. "Oh, I don't think so. Perhaps—we have a room on the first floor that surely would be perfect."

"We paid for the honeymoon suite," insists the first bride. "We reserved it."

"I'll have to talk to my manager."

Finally, after tears and threats of legal action, the matter is sorted out. The brides are shown, holding hands, into the honeymoon suite, where a vase of red roses waits beside a bottle of chilled champagne and two champagne flutes. The bed is red and heart shaped. There is a red whirlpool bath.

"Holy toots," says the first bride and throws down her backpack.

"Jesus Christ," says the second bride and flops down on the bed on her back.

"Could you believe that jerk? I couldn't believe that jerk. Like lesbians aren't allowed to fall in love. Like there's something unsavory about us."

"Never mind him." The second bride rolls on her side. "Are you unsavory? I'm feeling a little unsavory. In fact, never mind unsavory. I'm feeling a little perverted. A little—married."

"Are we really married?" says the first bride, grinning, clambering onto the bed.

And that, of course, is the last question: Are they?

Why I Don't

Rachel Fudge

For more than seven years now, Hugh and I have made a home together. We've created the perfect recipes for Vietnamese rice noodles and black bean burritos, learned to accept the other's bizarre food tastes (he says Marmite, I say peanut butter), juggled the demands of paid work and housework and come to terms with the fact that we'd rather stay in than go out. We're still figuring out how to keep houseplants alive and, most important, what to call each other.

All the existing terms are woefully inadequate. "Boyfriend" and "girlfriend," aside from sounding very junior high, are applied to such a broad range of relationships that they're practically meaningless. When I was fourteen I had a "boyfriend": We pretty much ignored each other when we were with our friends because we were too insecure to actually be seen together in public, that being the nature of early teen "dating." Seeing as how Hugh and I aren't embarrassed to be seen together, and we show our affection in ways that don't involve sarcastic putdowns, stealing the other's notebook or sending messages through our friends, I really think we ought to find a different word.

Besides, when you tell people you're living with your boyfriend, they're genetically programmed to inquire whether any wedding bells are in the future. To your negative reply, they're further compelled to respond with one of the more irksome stock phrases: "Ah, so you're just having fun, then." (I suspect that this is a nominally more discreet way of saying, "Oh, so you're just in it for the sex," but I have yet to confirm it.) Um, yes, we *do* have fun, lots of it—but we also have to pay bills, take the garbage out and do our laundry. This line of questioning sometimes takes the equally annoying approach: "Is it [your relationship, that is] serious?" While intellectually I understand that the asker is often just trying to get a hold on the nature of our relationship by using commonly understood (if awkward and imprecise) language, my first impulse is always to kick my interrogator in the shin and run away.

Implicit in the boyfriend/girlfriend appellation is the increasingly archaic and, to Hugh and to me, completely foreign concept of "dating." Whole volumes could be written about shifts in dating patterns, heterosexual courtship and gender relations in the twentieth century. But seeing as how I've been on only one actual date—which at the time I refused to acknowledge as such, since I resented the fact that the friend who'd asked me out was mucking up the friendship by trying to make it into something else—I'm not the one to tackle that topic.

So, clearly, "boyfriend" is right out. "Lover," "significant other" and our own tongue-in-cheek invention, "special peer," just don't cut it either. And while the Census Bureau's brand-new, oh-so-PC designation "unmarried partner" is a giant step up from having to check the "single" box, I don't like defining my relationship by what it *isn't*.

Then there's the always understood, if slightly dishonest, "fiancé." This one didn't occur to me until a few years ago, when I set up an IRA and made Hugh my beneficiary. Under "relationship" I had written "domestic partner," but the account manager erased it in favor of "fiancé"—it was easier that way, he explained. In theory, I guess it works—after all, Hugh and I are engaged in a long-term relationship—but in practice "fiancé" falls flat. Not only does it sound slightly ridiculous in a Jane Austen sort of way, but it describes a temporary post-dating, pre-marriage state characterized by endless discussions about florists, swing bands and bickering relatives. And don't even get me started on the whole diamond-ring-'n'-bended-knee quagmire.

"Partner" is now the *mot du jour,* but despite its increasing use, its multiple interpretations—business partner? sex partner? domestic partner?—still confound. Sometimes that lack of specificity—and gender neutrality—is welcome, especially when it's really no one's business. (To the smarmy young Canadian customs agent who asked what the nature of our relationship was, Hugh and I replied, "Partners." "Partners in what? Crime?" he asked with a smirk. Instead of blurting out, "Yes, partners in crime, you moron, and you're our first victim," we scowled and mumbled, *"Domestic* partners.")

So what are we? None of the existing terms accurately describes the way we feel about each other, the way we share our lives. While Hugh and I are perfectly content *not* to apply labels, there are times when some sort of explanation, however vague, is required. I get the feeling that everyone, from parents to insurers to Census workers, would heave a sigh of relief if we'd just get married and make clear the terms of our relationship.

Labels aside (for now), if Hugh and I opted for marriage, we would be reaffirming our relationship in the eyes of our family and friends, who would toast our union and shower us with gifts, and legitimizing it to the government, which would take some blood and some money and bestow us with a bounty of rights and responsibilities. We'd gain access to those really romantic things like health insurance, power of attorney and tax credits, along with an astonishing array of kitchen gadgets. By bidding farewell to the allegedly immature, carefree days of simply living together, we'd be taking the first step down the road to legal legitimacy and social maturity.

Legal protection and Le Creuset crockpots notwithstanding, there's more to this marriage business than meets the eye. What, exactly, does all this talk of legitimacy and maturity have to do with me, with Hugh, with *us?* Given that neither Hugh nor I feel a need to "take the next step" or to "make it honest," is my concern with the semantics of marriage nothing more than a straw man (straw bride?) I've concocted out of my general discomfort with institutions and gender roles? What is it about marriage that has even me, a nonbeliever, all tied up in knots and stumbling to clarify my opposition?

Well, for starters, I'm not crazy about the prospect of an actual wedding, never having been one for pomp and circumstance. Although I've been thoroughly moved by my friends' weddings and commitment ceremonies, I'm extremely reluctant to be the guest of honor. I've always found graduations, birthdays, awards ceremonies and the like embarrassing and a little demeaning, rife as they are with expectations and caricatures—the triumphant graduate, the delighted birthday girl—that don't usually jibe with my more conflicted feelings about these so-called big events, not to mention my general discomfort in large groups. A wedding would be all that and more—just thinking about it makes me queasy.

Instead, Hugh and I have built our relationship on everyday domestic habits, not on grand gestures: the early evening cheese, crackers and cocktails hour; the daily junk-mail exploration and commentary; the weekly perusal of event listings in our local alterna-paper, with the knowledge that most likely we will not drag ourselves out of the house to attend any of them. I'm not just being contrary when I say Hugh and I experience the relationship in a different language altogether, one rooted not in mythologized traditions and ceremonial/symbolic accoutrements but in the ongoing process of questioning what seems taken for granted. In fact, Hugh and I were drawn together by the thrilling realization that we could be wallflowers together. By banding together, we could feel a little less out of place—or, rather, we could create our *own* place, one in which what is "natural" is what feels right to us, not what is "normal" to the outside world.

This is all well and good (wonderful, in fact), but I also realize that we live in an imperfect world, where my commitment to Hugh is policed not just by me and him but by a large bureaucracy that doesn't have time to consider the nuances and verbal contracts of each and every relationship. Because we can't live on love alone—at least, we can't acquire health insurance, bank loans and discounts on renter's insurance with it—some sort of formal legal agreement eventually will be necessary. (We've already done a pretty good job of convincing the people who really matter—our families and close friends.) This is a conscious choice, based on pragmatics rather than ideology, to live within the system rather than to opt out of it entirely. The reality is that there are certain legal, financial and social benefits and protections that I want in on, like the right to access affordable health insurance and the right to be at Hugh's side should he require major medical care.

But rather than settling for the single shot of marriage and its avalanche of benefits and obligations, I prefer to find a backdoor route through measures like living wills, legal guardianship and domestic partnership (knowing all the while, of course, that certain rights will remain off-limits). Hard as it is to resist the appeal of the wedding-gift registry, we'll register instead as domestic partners—in the city of San Francisco, because California's state-level registry is open only to same-sex couples and mixed-sex couples sixty-five or older. We'll hire a lawyer to make certain our durable powers of attorney and living wills are in good shape. If we're lucky enough to become homeowners, we'll apply jointly for mortgages and both names will appear on all the paperwork. Put together, all these smaller measures might well spell out something very close to "marriage"—just as our emotional commitment to each other looks very much like marriage—but it will be on our terms, by our making. Romantics might shudder at the seemingly cold-hearted technicality of this, but it's no different from the legalistic nature of the standard marriage contract.

People have suggested that if I'm willing to go to such complicated lengths to achieve legal legitimacy, I should just grit my teeth and tie the knot. Sure (their argument goes), marriage is a problematic institution with a dubious history, but you don't have to chuck out the bride with the bathwater—why make life more difficult when a suitably mutable option exists? And think of all the fun you could have in reinterpreting all those old wedding chestnuts with feminist flair: You could skip down the aisle solo—or with your whole freakin' family; your best friend could get a minister-for-a-day license and officiate; you could substitute Huggy Bear's riot-grrl anthems for Wagner's processional. Use the textual and visual elements of the ceremony itself to make explicit the deconstructed and reconstituted aspects of your wedding vows. You could subvert marriage from within, help redefine our common conceptions of marriage by applying the structure to unconventional or nontraditional relationships (such as same-sex or nonmonogamous marriages).

Indeed, that's exactly what plenty of my peers are doing: cooking up new recipes for weddings and labeling them transgressive and unconventional. Call it alternative, and they will come to the altar. After all, we girls have been dreaming about this day since we were tots, right? All we needed was a way to walk down the aisle without compromising our feminist/radical/outsider status.

When it comes to deconstructing meaning and reclaiming formerly negative or derogatory terms, I'm usually more than game (Exhibit A: my college yearbook entry, where "nasty bitch" is listed as one of my activities). On the wedding question, however, I'm just the grrl who can't say yes. Fun though it might be to throw an anti-wedding, these symbolic gestures refigure only the wedding ceremony, not the marriage itself. All the hard work of an egalitarian partnership still lies ahead, in the cozy bedroom and the dirty bathroom, at grandma's house and the office holiday party. The larger cultural meanings and expectations attached to marriage still apply, and people who didn't attend your pro-feminist, nonhierarchical wedding won't be clued in to the true nature of your partnership. And if I'm going to have to explain to everyone I meet what my marriage means and signifies, I might as well explain why marriage isn't for me.

These days—post sexual, feminist and queer revolutions—it's hard to pinpoint the essence of a marriage. Some would say that any long-term monogamous relationship is no different from a marriage. I'm not so sure I disagree; after all, the same themes of fidelity and lifelong commitment resonate. Strip away the myths and symbols and two basic elements of marriage emerge: the legal contract, which is often also expressed as a religious vow, and the personal contract, which is an emotional commitment to the idea of fidelity and life partnership. The legal contract sets up a relationship of mutual interest between a wife and a husband; individual states—and religions, too—regulate the specific rights and obligations of that contract with hundreds of laws.

Those basic terms—a union of man and woman—are integral to both the legal status and the cultural function of the marriage contract, yet they are often taken for granted by most straight couples. These terms are coldly biological and entirely separate from notions of romance, partnership, commitment or emotion. I don't subscribe to the "opposites attract," Mars/Venus theory of gender relations, and removing the "man and wife" language from the wedding ceremony doesn't affect the underlying requirement. The personal vow holds greater possibilities for adaptation—but no matter how heartfelt, the personal contract is not legally binding.

Individual marriages, of course, adopt widely varying legal and personal contracts, and with the growing popularity of the prenuptial agreement, the contractual nature of marriage has become more apparent. Many people, however, still embark upon a marriage without a clear understanding of the contract (which is at once simple and incredibly vague), so bowled over are they by the spiritual and personal components. I'm not knocking those—indeed, I find that personal vow, the verbal contract, the most appealing part of the whole production. But if you sign that dotted line, shouldn't you know what you're agreeing to? More to the point: If I'm going to be a party to the contract, I want to be its creator. Just as most couples freely edit or altogether discard the standard wedding vows (to have and to hold, to honor and obey, man and wife), so too could they rewrite the paper contracts—but not if they marry. That is, while a couple can enact additional contracts (such as prenuptials) to modify or clarify the terms of the marriage contract, they *can't* escape the highly specified terms as laid out by the states.

What it comes down to is this: I'm not invested in making marriage into something that works for me, because I already have a relationship that works. These days, Hugh and I are not inclined toward reform. Polite refusal is more our style. Don't get me wrong—some things can, and should, be changed, and those things are well worth fighting for. But when it comes to marriage, maybe we should take a cue from *Ladies' Home Journal* and ask that decades-old question with a twist: Is marriage worth saving?

Even if we can't resolve the question of marriage's future, I think it's high time we exploded that cultural myth of all girls dreaming of their wedding day. While that may have held a grain of truth in the past, when girls were taught that their highest achievement was to be a good wife and mother, it's a pretty specious claim today. I can't deny that I did in fact indulge in other girlish dreams of femininity (becoming a ballerina, wearing ungodly shades of pink), but I gave little thought to being a bride. It wasn't until I graduated from femininity to feminism that I became interested in marriage—not as a girlish fantasy but as a hotbed of gender stereotypes to be analyzed, critiqued and, I assumed, discarded.

I was easily seduced by the language of radical feminism circa 1969: the brilliant manifestos, the cleverly cutting wordplays and, above all, the sense of absolute righteousness. The revolutionary lingo thrilled me, as it did many other collegiate born-again radical feminists in the supposedly post-feminist early 1990s. I eagerly embraced the all-or-nothing certainty of seventies feminism, including the automatic denunciation of marriage as a tool of the patriarchy. I had no inkling then that in a scant few years marriage would be wielded as a revolutionary tool for same-sex couples—and even by a handful of straight couples who travel in such rigorously nonconformist circles that an obvious embrace of tradition seems transgressive.

Times (and I) have changed, to be sure, and my stance on marriage is no longer based on a knee-jerk reaction. Times haven't changed enough, though, that I can afford to throw away those old manifestos. Despite the efforts of feminist deconstructionists and same-sex-marriage advocates, marriage remains rooted in gender difference, one that is expressed both structurally and semantically.

I learned this lesson when I was young, though its full implications didn't become clear until I was older. I grew up in a liberal community where labels of any kind were suspect and we children were raised to see people, not their titles. To be sure, this egalitarian conditioning created some awkward moments with more conservative elders, but my parents also did their best to practice what they preached. For more than thirty years, my mother has gently but steadfastly refused to be called "Mrs. Fudge." It's not that she objects to sharing my father's last name, but that, as she has said countless times, "'Mrs. Fudge' is a title, 'Emily' is my name." Instead of opening up the notion of marriage for me, though, my mother's reasoning—that being a wife doesn't necessarily make you an adjunct of your husband—has made me more determined than ever to find a new set of meanings that don't resort to legally codified biological distinctions. For the truth is, the *Free to Be . . . You and Me* promises of my upbringing have yet to be fulfilled, and despite my mother's positive example, prescriptive images of wifehood and motherhood still flourish. Just this year a friend of a friend of mine was heard to ask my mother, in a surprised tone, "You work?" It just goes to show that in spite of the best efforts of all the gender-role critics (from Marlo Thomas to Mom and Dad), those old stereotypes hold firm.

Like my mother, I do not want to become a Mrs. So-and-So. I don't want to become a "bride," let alone a "wife." I don't want to have a "husband." I don't want any part of those roles, no matter how earnest the subversive intentions. Words do have the power to define our behaviors and others' expectations, and the real danger is when the meaning of symbols contained in the wedding extend into married life in the form of titles and entitlement. It's not that I think marriage automatically would turn Hugh into a boorish Archie Bunker and me into a shrill Donna Reed. What concerns me more are the myriad small ways that "husband" and "wife" are acted out and, even more significant, how those roles are viewed by others. When we received the creatively misaddressed mail solicitation that trumpeted, "Mrs. Hugh Hynes, you are the woman featured in *Essence* magazine!" it cracked us up—a twentysomething white guy is the *Essence* woman? It didn't occur to me until much later, after the hilarity had subsided, that *Essence*'s marketers were targeting *me*. The magazine's retro assumption that the *Essence* woman is content to be "Mrs. Man" rankled, and it's one made by many people other than direct-mail marketers.

Those little things tend to stick in my craw and make me ever more stubborn in my resistance: the automatic assignation of dominant status to the husband in such diverse undertakings as filing taxes, making household decisions with telemarketers and signing mortgages. By refusing the labels inherent in marriage, Hugh and I can keep these roles, and expectations, at arm's length. And even though I've argued fervently that these symbols and rituals don't speak to me, I'm not immune to their pull—they still have a stranglehold on social mores and public expectations. As irksome as it is to keep explaining my stance vis-à-vis marriage, it's still better than slipping into a conventional, easily understood (and misunderstood) role. Marriage might seem the easy way out, but a little discomfort is often a very good thing. In some small way, my and Hugh's relationship can challenge expectations and perceptions in a way that marriage does not, no matter how radical the married individuals.

It isn't just the labels I dislike, but the assumptions about maturity. Lately, many a relative has politely asked my parents if Hugh and I are "making any plans to settle down" (i.e., planning a wedding). Meanwhile, our dirty little secret is that Hugh and I *have* settled down and opted for domestic bliss; we *have* gotten "serious," to use that hated word. But because we've done it gradually, at a pace so natural to us as to go nearly unnoticed, we've escaped a certain kind of detection and social approbation.

Ironically, my own relationship looks a lot more like a marriage than like any of the other nontraditional family structures out there. So why is it so important to me that our partnership not become a marriage? What it really boils down to is this: Marriage feels wrong. My life with Hugh feels very, very right. Marriage is irrelevant to the daily hubbub of our relationship; the same joys and tribulations attend as to a state-sanctioned union—without the feeling I'm being sold a bill of goods. Marriage is like lipstick or high heels or party dresses: so incredibly foreign and so clearly the trappings of someone else's idea of womanhood. And while drag is fun and potentially subversive, it can't be the basis of my relationship.

What we are is Rachel and Hugh, Hugh and Rachel: two individuals creating a family together. Hence the joint bank account and all the aforementioned nonmarital agreements. As long as it's just the two of us, of course, the repercussions of resisting formal recognition of our relationship are fairly minor, and we can follow our natural inclination to derive legitimacy and security not from institutions but from our families and ourselves. If, down the road a ways, offspring should arrive, we'll enact whatever new measures seem necessary—and that means I won't rule out the possibility that someday we may find ourselves slinking off to city hall (or Las Vegas) to utter those fated words. If we do, though, it will be a legal deal, not a social/emotional milestone: As far as we're concerned, the true commitments were made long ago.

Seven years along, Hugh and I continue to struggle with the terminology. We sometimes even pass as a married couple if it's in our best interest and doesn't harm anyone. This don't-ask-don't-tell policy came in handy when we traveled in rural Scotland last summer. Our initial concerns over awkward encounters with kindly yet puritanical bed-and-breakfast owners proved unfounded: Most proprietors simply assumed we were married, or didn't really want to know if we weren't. While at first I felt like a hypocrite for assuming the married-couple privilege, I realized that, once again, it was all about those pesky labels. That is, what the Scots saw—a nice, responsible, young (married) couple—and who we are—a nice, responsible, young (unmarried) couple—were not that far off.

In other contexts, such as among well-meaning but confused family friends, passing isn't an option, nor is it particularly desirable. At times like these, adequate words are even harder to come by. On one such occasion a few years ago, a family friend asked my mother what she should call Hugh. "Hugh," my mother replied. "No," the friend said, "that's not what I mean." "I know what you mean," my mom said, "but 'Hugh' will do just fine." I couldn't have said it better myself.

One Queer Family:

The Ultimate Mixed Marriage

Faith Haaz-Landsman

Recently, I picked up an issue of *Out* magazine that profiled a "nontraditional" couple. It was about a straight woman and a gay man in love. The article described the evolution of their partnership and their friends' and former friends' reactions. The magazine made them seem like the most interesting thing that had happened to the modern gay relationship since monogamy. I can beat that nontraditional marriage blindfolded, with one hand tied to the bedpost.

Michael and I had been friends for more than seven years when we were married in Las Vegas on February 6, 2000, by Pat, the Clark County commissioner. We since have gone on to live as husband and wife, with a twist.

Michael is a nice Jewish gay man raised in a New York suburb. He is tall and handsome, known for his stylishness. He is clever and efficient in speech and action. Michael was diagnosed with HIV in 1990 and was approaching the point on his doctor's timetable for imminent illness and demise when we met.

I am a nice Jewish lesbian born and raised in Southern California. From the age of sixteen, I figured I would meet the woman of my dreams, fall deeply in love and spend the rest of my days nestled under threadbare flannel sheets with her. Throughout the eighties and early nineties I was a classic lesbian feminist. I tried for the long-term monogamous relationship, complete with the stereotypical second-date U-Haul. But my lovers in college, whether they were cute dreadlocked freshmen, husky sorority girls or bisexual starfuckers, were primarily baby dykes clamoring to spend the night with the charismatic girl quoted daily in the campus newspaper. These were not really commitment thangs. I rigidly adhered to the dogma: I wore tie-dye and "raged against the machine" à la Seattle grunge aesthetic; I abstained from the use of razors; I listened to Holly Near records (one of the only decisions I regret in life); and I became director of the school's Women's Center. I went through a very brief butch phase, but have since found my inner Barbie. Unfortunately, due to my non-traditional-lesbo appearance and my affinity for gay men, a few dykes have questioned my allegiance to the gender. In fact, two Birkenstock-wearing, softball-playing, Andrea Dworkin–reading dykes once actually called me a "male-coddling fembot." Very creative turn of phrase. These assumptions are probably due not only to the high heels and general lack of "lesbian aura," as one date put it, but also to the man to whom I am married.

In May 1992, after emphasizing my political involvement and over-emphasizing my work experience to the pale-faced director of human resources, I landed a job at an agency that provided services to people with HIV. And so, inside a powder-gray building with scant architectural appeal, I began a career, friendships and eventually a family I could not have imagined.

The place teemed with gay men and straight women, a few lesbians and—deep in the heart of facilities management—one lone heterosexual male. As the human resources assistant in a rapidly expanding agency, my access to new employees immediately ingratiated me to the vultures, who wanted to know the names of the cute ones and whether they put a lover or their mother as the beneficiary on their life insurance forms. I was the newest young hire of about 120, and the year was classically heady—most everyone has such a year, ripe and unbelievable, the year you talk about the most and regret the least, destined to be written up and optioned for movie rights.

The first thing I remember about Michael is the morning that he walked into my office with a stray gray kitten loosely stowed in the breast pocket of his oxford shirt. I'm not really the cat-loving kind of lesbian, but it was cute, and I joined the crowd watching him feed the newborn with an eyedropper pilfered from someone's desk. He named her Hillary, after the soon-to-be first lady.

Less than a year later, he somehow convinced me to become his neighbor at his mid-sixties-era, cat food–colored apartment building on Hollywood Boulevard. After I moved in I met his friends, tried on his wigs and baby-sat Hillary when he traveled back east to visit his parents. In that building, I got a view of the Michael that was so carefully protected: the darling *faygehleh* boy who got on so well with Mother's friends, the pretty young thing fawned over by crafty older men, the angry infected faggot and the man, with all of his constant contradictions, searching for his bliss.

Co-workers teased Michael and me about our relationship relentlessly, demanding to know when the wedding was and taunting us when we sounded like an old married couple. One spring, a story appeared in the staff newsletter about our engagement—congratulations and questions abounded from folks forgetting that it was April Fool's Day. Friends occasionally would call us "Mr." and "Mrs." just to get a rise. Though we spent quite a bit of our free time together and alternated holidays at each other's parents' homes, our credentials as a lesbian and gay man, respectively, were bulletproof. The truth was, though, that I looked forward to my time with Michael as much as my dates.

We received a few promotions and continued to work, responding to the needs of the haggard terminally ill and the worried healthy obsessive-compulsives who tweaked through Los Angeles. Compassion for clients was our business, but during the off-hours we laughed about the plague, and I found that as the years passed friends and relatives became increasingly uncomfortable with my perverse litany of gallows humor—a staple of the coping-mechanism diet. But Michael infused it, understood it and, most of all, appreciated it.

Faithful was the constant anticipation of the end. Intermittently, we discussed Michael's final arrangements, because it was the sensible thing to do—though there were no indications that his health was worsening.

The only warning was the opinion of the physician who delivered the news that he *should* have been dead, making every day seem like a sweet, mocking gift. Meanwhile, I shamelessly talked about my future and made wry comments about the day that certainly would come when I would commute from hospice to hospice doling out chicken soup and comfort to my intimate group of friends. I delayed plans to "get on with my life" until those needs had been attended to. Michael hesitantly planned for the very near future—a man tonight, a visit to his parents in a month, work for another year, perhaps. I voraciously seized the complex fibers of love and insight he offered, threading them together to create an elaborate quilt that I could wrap around myself after he was gone. Eventually, emboldened by the silence of what had been a fierce but faulty alarm, he planned for a year, two, five and ten. I slowly unraveled the threads and graceless remnants, using them for other projects, and enjoyed the withdrawal of what had seemed like a daily encroachment.

Five years passed, and we slipped into a comfortable routine. We ate lunch together every day, and I took breaks from the demands of nonprofit work on the grubby couch in his office. We watched videotaped *Saturday Night Live* episodes on Sunday mornings, and I relied on him to counsel me on my family, my job and my own personal demons. After I left the agency where we met, there were emails and brunches and Wednesday-night *Star Trek* viewings, but I found myself craving the daily contact we'd had before.

I'd moved on to a job in academia while Michael moonlighted as a driver for the most exclusive limousine company in Los Angeles, which provided me with trivial but seductive information about the lives of virtually every actor in Hollywood and how well he or she tips. One Saturday morning, he dropped by in his uniform and we went for coffee. As usual, he railed against LA men. "Let's move," he suddenly sprang on me, as we watched a woman wearing a red cotton muumuu and an enormous pink hat preach to an equally eccentric congregation. I had been on and off with a psychotic ex-junkie ex-girlfriend for about five years, and getting out of town seemed just what I needed to be rid of her one more time. Besides, the other twelve lesbians in town were all matched up again. A new scene might present an opportunity for fresh drama.

As we emptied our paper coffee cups and walked back to the stretch

Lincoln Town Car that he drove, we continued our conversation. He held open the door and I stepped in, looking like someone of consequence. "Where shall we move?" I asked as I slipped into the sleek leather seat.

"I'd like to move south," he said, "San Diego, maybe."

Discussing our future energized me. Rather than working in the "AIDS industry" our entire lives, we decided we wanted to do work that involved less crisis. Our fantasy eventually evolved into the achievable goal of owning our own business. A quick discussion in a coffee shop prompted my putting my retirement savings into mutual funds and doing all sorts of other responsible things. He bought stocks and paid off his car. And to cut expenses, we reasoned, I moved in with him in April 1999. It was all very logical, very sensible.

Cohabitation was both a challenge and a very good thing. The apartment was a small two-bedroom with only one bathroom, and Michael guarded his privacy pretty fiercely. As an extrovert, I can be around people all day, every day for weeks on end and never crave privacy. I needed to spend time with him, even if we were just reading magazines or watching the news; he needed daily downtime after a full day of servicing the uber-rich or poor of Los Angeles. But compromises were reached early on.

Lucky for us was the fact that, after years of being out on my own, I had become the femme of my mother's dreams. I learned to bake awe-inspiring cakes and long for a ladylike glass of chardonnay while getting a seaweed facial. (Frankly, I don't know how I ever tried to pass for butch in the first place.) Michael, on the other hand, always has been handy with a power tool and tends to steer clear of the kitchen. And so it turned out that I'm the Woman and he's the Man, by preference. I take charge of shopping, cooking and laundry. He changes the light bulbs, takes out the garbage, cleans the kitchen, kills bugs, fixes stuff and deals with the auto-insurance claims adjuster.

When our discussion about starting a business began, it was a daydream, a little healthy denial. But the more distractions that the looming phantom of HIV presented, the less we joked and the more we planned. If Michael was going to quit his job to work on the business, he'd need health insurance. I could get it through my new job, but only if we were married. At first he balked, but eventually realized that it was the best way to get him quality health care and get us both closer to our business goals. Besides, we were going to live together, own a business together and buy a house together: Health insurance became just a symbol of how much we cared about each other.

The marriage proposal was all at once traditional and deviant, fairly calculated and decidedly unromantic. One night after we'd gone with friends to see Holly Woodlawn, the legendary torch singer and our former next-door neighbor, someone yet again asked in jest, "When are you going to get married?" Michael said something about its inevitability, scandalizing our entire party. Two days later, as he scrubbed the stovetop and we prattled on about some innocuous domestic issue, he suddenly poked his head out of the kitchen and said, "I suppose I should make this formal . . . Will you marry me?"

"Yes, Michael," I responded. "I will marry you."

The words sounded alien on our tongues. I felt a nagging pang of guilt knowing that marriage was off-limits to our friends in "traditional" gay and lesbian couples. It was truly, and still is, a foreign language to us. It is something we recognize; we speak it as if we grew up in this country but spoke another tongue at home. We used the strange and familiar speech of fiancés, brides and grooms—words like "nuptials," "wed" and "vows." But some expressions more easily rolled off our tongues, like "until death do us part." Those words have always rung true.

Most people are perfectly willing to accept the idea of a lesbian marrying a gay man for immigration purposes. Not a few of our friends are married for this reason, and champion this manipulation of the system (*Viva la revolución!*). Most people understand, even if they don't relish, the idea of a Hollywood-style or similar marriage of convenience. Finally, in the lesbian community, we have all cringed and sighed with resignation at the news of one of our own realizing she was "actually" straight, her girl-on-girl dalliances having been the folly of a "confused" young woman. But the concept of a practicing lesbian marrying a chronic gay man because they love each other and want to spend the rest of their lives together is too queer for most to comprehend.

Michael's late lover, Jeff, understood our relationship better than most, and he was never threatened by it. He took to calling me "Michael's woman" long before we even moved in together. When making introductions, Jeff would begin, "This is my lover, Michael, and his wife, Faith . . . "

Our parents understand our relationship the least. Though they met years ago and have been enjoying annual out-law brunches together, they are a little unclear on the details of our relationship and probably wish they knew less. We have redefined marriage to the point where it is virtually unrecognizable from their perspective, but we know we are re-creating it in a way that works for us.

Our day-to-day married life is about as typical as any. Michael wakes up and sits down with a mug of coffee to watch *CNN Headline News*. I leave for work as he gets into the shower. After work, I cook for us, and at dinner he patiently listens to my dramas and ravings. He cleans up afterward and takes his anti-viral meds, and then we watch some TV or rental movies until I can't keep my eyes open any longer and he says, "Go to bed." Later, he goes to bed, in his own room. The next morning, the routine begins again.

Initially, it was difficult for me to understand how I became so compatible with a man. Eventually, I realized we are well-suited in most of the ways that people search for in a partner. Yet the myth that a life partner, whether heterosexual or homosexual, will provide for every need is really a misguided construct of contemporary times. The actually-quite-new "traditional" concept of marriage and couplehood includes, but is not limited to, emotional and financial support, sex, intimacy, a constantly patient ear, friendship, fantasy fodder, meals, inspiration for creativity, ironing, encouragement, a soft lap to lay one's head on, a clean home and a well-made cocktail. My husband provides many of these things, at different times, but he never will provide sex. Michael and I accept that one person can't be the be-all and end-all who fulfills every need, and I feel truly lucky that my marriage lacks this particular delusion.

Because we do not share a bed, we also probably fight less than most couples. Arguing seems a little superfluous in our relationship. Moreover, death makes a grand mockery of trivial details. Viewed through the lens of mortality, time is precious and small. Call us arrogant, but we've agreed that arguing about laundry is pathetic.

And frankly, the sex in our relationship is great. I have my partners and Michael has his. Throughout our sexual lives, neither of us has been monogamous, so this arrangement works to our mutual advantage. We have a long-term loving relationship with the benefit of a variety of sexual partners, and I will keep my promise never to cheat on him with another gay man. We agree that this isn't bad for the beginning of a beautiful relationship.

Everyone always asks, "What happens if one of you meets the person of your dreams?" Our answers are pretty consistent. One configuration out of my many fantasies goes like this: If I met a person with potential, she would come to pick me up; we would have an evening or two out and inevitably end up at my place for the night. Subsequently, she would come for dinner and meet Michael. Eventually, three at the dinner table would be a regular thing. Soon she would have work clothes in my closet and a permanent toothbrush in the glass in the bathroom. The same circumstances would transpire for Michael. He would make scrambled eggs for four on Sunday mornings, and, eventually, we'd decide to take a vacation together. Our partners could move in. We'd split the bills, do the gardening, the cooking, the cleaning. It's romantic in a very unique way. I imagine that she would be lovely, with an easy smile and a thing for gay men. I imagine he would be friendly, warm and open to living with two lesbians.

Since I got married, dating has not been a great success for me, but I'm an eternal optimist, so I persist. I've been out with a few women recently. Some whom I have told about Michael just didn't work out past the first few meetings. On the other hand, I've dated a few women whom I have not told, and they didn't work out for any length of time, either. A few have stayed around, and others have not lasted long enough for breakfast, but I'm confident that the reason is usually unrelated to the spouse in the next room. I am certain there is a woman out there for me, and just as certain there is a man out there for Michael who sees the mutual benefit of a larger, queer family.

For the moment we're enjoying the journey, living for each day as it comes and planning for our future as rich and happy oldsters. So rather

Faith Haaz-Landsman   57

than finding Ms. Right Now, I'm exploring some possible Ms. Desirables while living with the mister. And she's just going to love him.

The Two-Body Problem

Georgette Chen

John and I have been together for ten years, which is a crazy enough idea to get my mind around. But there's more—we've never even lived in the same city, because my job and his job have never been in the same city. In academia, they call this "the two-body problem." If you added up all the time we've actually spent together, our relationship probably would be only two years old.

We met early in my freshman year of college. What was I thinking, you ask? The best explanation is that it seemed like such a good idea at the time. Looked like it might be fun to try out this older-guy thing so popular in literature and film, and the idea of easy, no-strings-attached sex was enormously appealing. (Oh, like it wouldn't have been for you, too.)

He, being so worldly—having just graduated from college and gotten into (gasp!) graduate school—also had not yet quite grasped the idea of, say, getting away from his college town: He made the four-hour drive from his new city every other weekend for parties of ill repute and cheap keg beer. Our first encounter was at an otherwise-lame soiree in his old dorm's common room. I deduced, in rapid succession, that this guy 1) was twenty-one, which was *so* old, 2) seemed interested, 3) had a car and 4) did not in fact live anywhere near me. Hot damn, I thought. I can have sex with this guy, he'll go back to his city, he'll be nowhere around, I can dog on him behind his back, I won't tell him anything: It's my chance at the American Dream!

I understand that the American Dream usually involves home ownership, amber waves of grain and a golden retriever. But this was my personal seventeen-year-old version. I had spent the vast wasteland of my adolescence desperately planning my escape from the oppressively small town I had grown up in and watching various female friends routinely fuck themselves over for guys. When I got to college I was in a big city for the first time—and isn't casual sex and heart-breaking what Big City Girls do? My whole college experience was all about independence and flight (and taking a well-balanced array of classes in the humanistic tradition, of course). It was about not being what I'd been for so long— boring, stable, completely out of it—and this fling seemed like a great way to break out. Plus, did I mention the sex? Very exciting for a girl of seventeen.

John and I started seeing each other whenever he was in town, which was about every two weeks. *Très* convenient for me—didn't cramp my freshman style—and very sophisticated and adult, like those French people who drink café au lait and wear berets and carry baguettes in their bike bags. I had plenty of time to make my own friends, do my own thing, be my own person. I didn't have to worry about the inevitable question all my friends seemed to be asking their freshman-year boyfriends: "Do you want me to move into your dorm room?" Sure, I'd have liked him to sit next to me in the cafeteria and stuff, but this was also the best of both worlds. I got to do the sex thing and have company at restaurants, but I was able to go out a lot and Find Myself and all that freshman-year crap one does instead of actually studying. I was living up to my feminist ideals—you know, "A woman without a man is like a fish without a bicycle." Plus, I was planning to get a lot of play from other guys.

Unfortunately for my oh-so-sophisticated independent-woman plan, the skeevy twenty-one-year-old perv hitting on girls who, goddamn it, weren't entirely out of adolescence yet (part of the appeal in the first place—I am Lolita, hear me roar) turned out to be a really nice guy. And I somehow never got around to playing the field. Sex with John turned out to be sufficiently . . . interesting to distract me, and it was much more compelling to talk on the phone with him than to go out and hook up with other guys. He was always good for an interesting adventure, he had intelligent things to say and—very important to me—he always, always got my jokes. Maybe I never got involved with anyone else because I didn't want to have to clarify my pop culture references. With John, I never had to explain, "Well, you see, I said 'like Jon Bon Jovi' because you said that he was wanted dead or alive, and remember, Bon Jovi had that song 'Wanted Dead or Alive,' which they sang on those little stools at the 1987 MTV Video Music Awards." Those conversations profoundly depress me.

By the end of the year, his weekend visits had tapered off because of school pressure and we were seeing each other on breaks, for about a week or two at a time. We were very, very into this newfangled email technology (it was 1991), exchanging ten to fifteen messages a day. Much to my dismay, I looked up one day and we were in a bona fide long-distance relationship. Damn it—I am really not very good at the planning thing.

What next? You can't have a relationship if you're four hours away from each other! Can you? So when we had what I like to call our first State of the Relationship Address, this was topic number one. I was not about to transfer anywhere. I was very pleased with my school and its home city. I was certainly not about to move out of my cool college town after only one year to go to the sucky, wasteland, middle-of-fucking-nowhere town that housed his PhD program. And he wasn't about to leave his boring city (it was an excellent program and his dream grad school). Good for the goose, good for the gander—if I wasn't moving anywhere, it didn't feel right to ask him to move, either.

The two of us are ridiculously stubborn. Neither would have objected if the other had appeared in town permanently, yet we weren't going to go out of our way to make that happen. While it would have been nice to be together, it was perfectly fine (and just as nice) to be apart. In a short-distance relationship, you have a date every Friday

night, frequent sex, lower phone bills and constant companionship—
but you also have fights about space issues ("Why can't you give me a
little room just to *breathe,* for God's sake?"), the elaborate check ins before going anywhere, and less time with your friends when you're with
your honey (and less time with your honey when you're with your friends).
In a long-distance affair, as much as those off Fridays can suck, you have
all the room in the world to do whatever the hell you feel like, the whole
bed is yours and you don't have to plan for anyone but yourself.

Our relationship was more about two individuals wanting to spend
time together than one organism referring to itself as "we"—and we
liked it that way. After I got out of college, the miles between us became
more of an issue. Let me trace you a handy-dandy geographic/chrono-
logical history.

Fall 1994
John is living in New Jersey, depressed because he didn't finish his dissertation on time and has to stay another year.

I am moving to Manhattan for my first year of law school. Great, I
think. We'll be one hour apart by train. Won't it be nice to see him
regularly? This turns into me taking the train down at random hours on
random days to weep about how much law school sucks ("Hi, I'm at
the train station, please pick me up; I don't care what you're doing, I
need validation of my self-worth immediately") and him taking the train
up on weekends so we can see movies and buy indie-rock CDs in Green-
wich Village. Cool, I think, we're getting into a regular relationship.
Maybe we'll just live in New York for the rest of our lives. I begin to
plan accordingly: cute Upper West Side apartment near Shakespeare &
Co.; I'll take the 1/9 subway to Fifty-ninth Street and walk across town
to work. For fun, we'll eat at cute restaurants and indulge in the New
York cultural scene. I get a subscription to the *New Yorker.*

Winter 1994–95
To my dismay, John moves to Michigan for a post-doctoral fellowship,
despite a long, tearful and in retrospect tedious conversation about how
we were going to "start putting the relationship first," and our first
priority was going to be "being together" now that I was out of college

and being hit by a tidal wave of domestic impulses. These "priorities" of mine are rejected with his (quite reasonable) statement: "But I thought we were going to put our careers first."

I am still in Manhattan, pouty. He tentatively floats the prospect of me moving to Michigan and is greeted by my Gary Coleman facial expression and the always-good-for-a-laugh "Whatchutalkinbout, Willis?" Michigan? Where they killed Vincent Chin? I don't think so.

Summer 1995

He's still in Michigan, applying for jobs in New York in an attempt to appease me; none is panning out. Academia: very competitive.

I still feel miffed about Michigan. (Hypocritical, I know.) I interview for a job in San Francisco. Distressingly, I really like everyone there, and think it might be a good place for me to work. Hmmm, I think. I see why people find this working thing so fulfilling. I accept the job, which will start after I finish law school in two years.

Summer 1996

He is in Berkeley, doing academic research.

I am in San Francisco, doing a summer internship at my law firm. We're living in the same place, but we have different area codes so it's not so unsettling. Satisfying, but weird having him around all the time— "Why can't you give me the common courtesy of calling at 10 P.M. if you're going out?" "What do you mean, where are we staying tonight?"—and strangely fulfilling for both of us to be working, instead of one of us being on vacation with the express purpose of visiting the other (who is usually working). An interesting experiment, one possibly worth repeating in the future.

Academic Year 1996–97

He is back in Michigan, getting all into academia as a career.

I am back in New York, getting all into law as a career (and eagerly awaiting the end to the law school torture).

Summer 1997

Him: Michigan, natch.

Me: Berkeley, studying for the bar exam. I spend a lot of time weeping in frustration about California law and am thus too distracted to discuss the distance in any meaningful way—no doubt to John's relief as well as that of my friends and family.

Academic Year 1997–98
He is applying for jobs in San Francisco; none is panning out. Academia: very competitive.

I move to San Francisco for good to start working at my law firm. Being three time zones away is the hardest part, with me resentful and socially edgy because I have to come home early to talk to him, and him resentful and tired because he has to wait up for me to call.

Fall 1998
After looking unsuccessfully for jobs in San Francisco, he gets one in Los Angeles. Well, about an hour outside of Los Angeles. The cultural highlights are the Olive Garden and the Old Navy, both located near his apartment. One hour and seventy-five dollars away from San Francisco by plane if you book two weeks in advance.

I toil away for "the Man" in San Francisco. As I can't book anything two weeks in advance because of job constraints, I must convince him to come up more often. The new post-school, same-state paradigm is quite pleasant (dates on Friday *and* Saturday night! no need for either of us to flee to do work!), except that post-visit Sunday evenings feel melancholy and barren.

Spring 1999
He tries—and fails—to get an academic job in San Francisco. He does, however, get an offer to stay in Los Angeles for two or three more years.

I try—and fail—to persuade him to take a job at a dot-com and move up to San Francisco.

I'll spare you the gory details of the emotionally trying three-month fight that ensued, but basically: I am not very good at compromise. He is not very good at compromise. Both of us are now pretty much ridiculously committed to our careers. It is much, much harder to get a job in academia than at a law firm. I really, really like being an attorney—in San Francisco. He really, really doesn't want to give up teaching. We do still love each other.

Around this time, I found myself starting to resent the questions from well-meaning people: "Well, why don't you just move down there? You could go anywhere, and he can't." (To his credit, John has never asked me to move for him. I won this concession when he went to Michigan. He said, "Please don't break up with me; just let me have this for my career and I promise I'll never ask you to move for mine.") I'd gotten a lot of these questions before ("Why don't you transfer colleges? Why don't you transfer law schools? Why don't you get a job in Michigan?") but my reasons were always so plain that even the people asking seemed to recognize their interrogation's futility. I mean, clearly I'd picked a college based on the strength of its programs. Clearly I'd picked a law school based on the strength of its programs. And come *on*, even John didn't want to be in Michigan (though I must say that Michigan was always a good place to visit, and I do have a very fabulous oven mitt with a picture of the state of Michigan on it). I don't know if I get subjected to this line of questioning because academia is less flexible than law or because I'm a girl. John instead gets "Why are you restricting your job search to the Bay Area? Why can't you just make her move to where you get a job?" from his more piggish friends. I have made the unilateral response of cutting those friends from our joint social circuit.

It is a fair question, though. Why don't I just pick up and move? Yes, yes, we all understand that a job can be fulfilling. But if you can't give up your career for love, what kind of relationship is it? Of course, I respect everyone's lifestyle choices, but let's turn that question around: If you can't give up love for career, what kind of a career do you have? Puts a new spin on things, doesn't it?

That isn't entirely fair, I concede. Career and love are not always mutually exclusive. But right now John and I can't have both on the terms that we both want. So we talk on the phone almost every day and see each other almost every other weekend (though the dozen emails a day are over; we email each other only if we see something truly ludicrous on the Internet).

See, I like work—and I derive a pretty large portion of my self-esteem from doing well there. If my entire adolescence and early adulthood grrl-power years were about anything, they were about realizing that I do *not* derive my self-esteem from having a boy around all the time. I mean, I love John and all that, but I don't risk crippling depression without him—and how unhealthy it would be if I did! (Although it also seems unhealthy that both of us *would* be cripplingly depressed if we weren't at our current jobs. Self-knowledge is important, I guess.)

So what's the plan now? My friends have been asking if we're going to get married, but I kind of think we should try living in different places in the same city first. He's applying for jobs again, and maybe he'll get one up here. Maybe not. Maybe one of us will be ready to make a career compromise one of these days—and maybe not. I only know that we'll try our best to work it out and stay together—on our own terms.

Table for Three, Please

Ellen Anne Lindsey

"Are you married?"

It's the question my students inevitably ask me. Almost all of them are young wives and mothers who have decided to attend college now that their children are safely out of diapers and in school.

Marriage was an early decision for these women. Most decided to marry long before they even thought about coming to college. So when I answer "No" to their query, they usually raise their eyebrows in shock and follow up with, "Well, haven't you ever been married?" At this point, I generally say "No" again and then quickly revert to the course syllabus: how to avoid comma splices or how to use MLA documentation.

It's natural for my students to be curious about my personal life, and for them, the question "Are you married?" is not a hard one. For me, it is. And when I answer, I always feel dishonest, because while "No" is the easiest answer, it's not really the right answer.

I am married in my heart, though single according to the laws of church and state. And while my relationship has lasted longer than many of my students' marriages, I know that most of them would regard my long-term relationship as immoral or simply inconceivable. I adore my students, and I sometimes envy the legally married teachers who can speak casually about their personal lives during class, but I simply cannot face the challenge of explaining my complex love life to a roomful of women whose understanding of romantic love was inspired by Harlequin romances and romantic comedies starring Meg Ryan.

These heterosexual romance novels and so-called chick flicks construct a dangerous myth for women. In essence, these books and movies say, "There's only one man out there for you, honey—your Fabio or your Tom Hanks. And you'd better get your hooks into him, because he's your one chance at happiness." Obviously, this myth is disturbing for both its sexism and heterosexism, but it is also troubling for another reason: It asserts that, because of fate or some other unseen force, there is only one person out there for each of us.

Yet it's easy to prove this assertion false. If the cosmos decrees that there's only one "right" mate out there for each woman, then how do I explain my eighty-four-year-old friend, who has outlived three husbands and describes each marriage as happy? How do I explain my younger, happily single friend, who does not sit pining away for that special someone, but who instead enjoys numerous casual relationships with both men and women? And how do I explain my life? It certainly contradicts the idea that there has to be just one special someone, or even one special someone at a time. For the past ten years, I have lived in a three-way relationship.

I first met Michael and Samantha when I was an undergraduate at a university in a mid-sized southern city. Ten years older than I am, Michael and Samantha were married and completing their PhDs at the same university I attended. They were settled into a long-term marriage and were not looking for a third person to add novelty to their sexual relationship. I was introduced to them by a mutual acquaintance, and the three of us quickly became friends. Our friendship had a level of intensity I had never experienced before.

Their interests overlapped with mine. They were happy to talk for hours about books (Charles Dickens to Erica Jong), movies (Ingmar Bergman to Woody Allen) and music (Mozart to Loretta Lynn). Because they were older and more sophisticated than I was (despite my bohemian pretensions at the time, I was still a small-town girl), their knowledge about nearly everything exceeded mine. Unlike some intellectuals, though, they were not selfish with their knowledge. They were happy to share it with me, without playing the Pygmalion role. In return, I let them look at the fiction that I wrote compulsively but rarely showed to anyone.

The previous year, I had gotten up my nerve and entered one of my stories in a contest sponsored by a university feminist organization. When Samantha read it, she said, "Oh, this is the story that won the W.C.C. award." I asked her how she knew, since the story was unpublished. She answered, "I was the judge." In another coincidence, Michael and I discovered that we had attended the same Catholic high school in rural Appalachia, although years apart. Our lives were filled with overlaps, coincidences and those rare moments when you can say, "I know exactly how you feel," and mean it.

As our friendship intensified, the romantic relationship I was involved in stagnated. Although I already had declared myself bisexual, I also had saddled myself with a fairly conventional straight relationship, which, at the time I met Michael and Samantha, had been going on—yet going nowhere—for nearly three years. My life with my college boyfriend involved drinking beer, having rather workmanlike, drunken sex, drinking more beer, listening to old Rolling Stones LPs and talking about the people we knew. There was safety in the sameness of stagnation. I knew that while my college boyfriend might irritate me, he would never cause me to have feelings that were intense to the point of being frightening. Michael and Samantha, however, stretched my mind and heart to lengths that were quite challenging for an emotionally immature twenty-one-year-old.

Eventually, perhaps inevitably, Michael and Samantha's and my relationship became sexual. Since I'm striving to write a somewhat serious essay here instead of a letter to *Penthouse*, I will leave out the lurid details (which I selfishly prefer to savor for myself). I will say, though, that we didn't just automatically fall into being a threesome. The first sexual encounter was a pairing.

Samantha and I had been out to dinner one night, and a friendly goodnight hug turned into what couldn't really be called a goodnight kiss because we didn't say goodnight until hours later.

Afterward, we both felt guilty and conflicted. While we had acted completely spontaneously on our strong feelings for each other, we still felt that our act of love constituted a betrayal. Samantha felt terrible for cheating on her husband of ten years, whom she also loved. I felt guilty and confused because I had strong feelings for both Samantha and Michael and knew that I could just as easily have fallen into bed with him under similar circumstances.

The next day, with our tears, fears and insecurities on display, Michael, Samantha and I sat down and talked. Since we all felt the way we did, we probably should have agreed right then to form a partnership of three. But we were afraid. There was no blueprint for the type of relationship we were contemplating. Determined to do "the right thing," the three of us spent several months as very virtuous and very frustrated people, until the dam broke one New Year's Eve when the three of us shared champagne, strawberries and a bed. That night, we opened a door we could never close again.

Sex with Samantha caused me to acknowledge passionately, both physically and emotionally, the lesbian side of my sexuality that had been within me but unconsummated for years. And while sex with Michael wasn't my first experience with a man, it was still revelatory in how radically different it was from the drunken fumblings of a college boy.

I wish I could say that after the night of champagne and strawberries, everything magically fell into place. But, of course, it didn't. Instead the three of us wallowed in jealousy, anxiety and insecurity. At various points, each of us threatened to leave so that the remaining two could be together, but no one who made this threat ever stayed gone for more than an hour or two. When we were all three together again, we'd sit and try to figure out if it was possible to make a relationship among the three of us work. Michael and Samantha had a whole decade of marriage behind them, only to be blindsided by their feelings for a third person. As for myself, compared to what they knew about long-term relationships, I was still a little girl playing house.

We weren't helped by the fact that we live in a world largely oblivious to the possibility of successful long-term relationships involving more than two partners. Restaurants don't offer Valentine's Day specials for three, and film depictions of threesomes show them ending in tearful separation (*Henry and June*) or death (*Jules and Jim*). Except as a short-term sexual novelty, the threesome barely enters the popular consciousness at all.

Confused by our feelings, we finally decided to see a therapist. This decision could have been disastrous had the therapist been too conventional or judgmental. Thankfully, our therapist was a smart, plainspoken older woman who said that she never had seen a successful threesome before, but she saw no reason why ours wouldn't work if we all wanted it to work.

And it has. Michael, Samantha and I have been together for a little more than nine years, five years of which we've been living together. We have overcome the jealousies and insecurities that plagued us in the early days and have stayed together longer—and more happily—than many of the "committed" couples we have known. Although we have never felt the need to have a formal commitment ceremony, I am given equal status as a wife to both Samantha and Michael. Our marriage has even borne fruit in the biblical sense. Our son (their biological child) is a happy, inquisitive kindergartner who pities the deprived children who only have one or two parents instead of three. He lists Michael, Samantha and me as his parents on all school-related paperwork, and his five-year-old friends don't bat an eye when he mentions his "moms and dad." In the near future, we plan to have a second child. This time, I'll perform the childbearing duties.

As a young girl growing up in the shadow of the women's movement, I swore I would never marry. The conventional marriages I saw around me—while some of them, such as my parents', were good—placed too many limits on women's choices and freedom.

But even as a child myself, I found the idea of bearing and loving and mentoring a child appealing; however, the thought of having a husband I would have to care for like another child and a house I would be responsible for cleaning was not. As I could not imagine my ideal as a reality, I constructed a vision of my adult self as an independent, single writer with numerous cats. If I had known as a girl that relationships such as ours were possible, I might have pictured myself differently.

Obviously, a three-way marriage offers more sexual freedom than a monogamous two-person marriage, but it has other, equally important freedoms to recommend it. Three people sharing childcare responsibilities makes for less frazzled parents. Theoretically, three people sharing household duties makes for less work; but since Michael, Samantha and I are all unrepentant slobs, I can't say that three people always make for a cleaner house. We do share cooking duties equally, however, and on the rare occasions when we feel the need to tidy up, there are three of us to sort through the rubble.

The three-way marriage has distinct economic advantages. Three adult wage earners make for a higher household income than two do, and three people working allows for more flexibility in schedules as well. Because the third income provides a cushion, if one member of the household needs to cut back on his/her work schedule, it can be done without disastrous financial consequences. For example, we all agreed that when our son was born we wanted him to stay home the first couple of years instead of going to daycare. At the time I was fresh out of graduate school and wanted to devote more time to my fiction writing, so I stayed home with the baby while Michael and Samantha worked—a situation that was emotionally beneficial to me because of the fulfillment of both parenting and writing. Since then, I have returned to work while Samantha has reduced her workload to a part-time schedule in order to attend professional school. In the future, if Michael ever wishes to take time off for study or writing, he can do so knowing that we will still have a stable household income.

I realize that such freedoms do not mean that three is a magic number, and I don't think that polyamorous relationships are always more equitable. I seriously doubt that the old-style Mormon polygamous marriages offered women much in the way of choice and freedom. Our relationship works because Michael and Samantha's marriage was an equal partnership from the start, and when I entered the relationship I was accepted as a third equal partner. A threesome not based on mutual respect would offer women no more freedom than a two-person marriage.

The majority of the difficulties we have experienced stem not from our relationship, but from people's reactions to it. Many people who were friends with Michael and Samantha as a married couple were horrified when they took me in as a third partner, and several of my college friends couldn't understand why I had ditched a "perfectly good" boyfriend to take up with "an old married couple." Some straight friends were uncomfortable with the lesbian aspect. A few gay friends could understand Samantha and me but couldn't figure out where Michael fit in (who, just to confuse matters further, identifies as bisexual and has had relationships with men in the past).

Some friends got over their shock and stayed in our lives. Others we lost forever. Over the years, though, we have made many friends—some gay, some bi and some straight—who look at our marriage as a fact, not an "issue." One of my personal rules is that in order for a person to be considered a real friend, he/she must know about and accept our relationship. People who don't know—either because I feel they couldn't handle it or because, for whatever reason, I've decided it's simply none of their business—are only acquaintances.

And of course, we are surrounded by acquaintances—people who wouldn't understand our relationship even if they did know about it. Although we're out to our friends and to the members of the Unitarian Universalist church we attend, we're not always public about our marriage.

I'm out as gay at work (I never want to be accused of trying to pass for straight), but refer to Michael and Samantha only as my friends when talking to co-workers. Michael's work situation is similar. He is out as bisexual but is known to be married to only one woman, Samantha. Samantha is the most secretive, partly because of her natural reticence, but mostly because she fears the reaction of her family of origin. While Michael's mother and my parents know, Samantha is tight-lipped about our relationship when she deals with her conservative, conventional parents, who we fear might try to take custody of our son if they knew about us. To them I am simply an "old maid" who lives with their daughter and son-in-law and helps with childcare.

Even though the nature of our relationship isn't known to everyone around us, Michael and Samantha and I have taken steps to ensure that my rights as their spouse are protected. Since I don't have the automatic privileges that come with a legally recognized marriage, we have worked with our attorney so that I have the same rights of inheritance. After the birth of our son, we visited our attorney again, this time to draw up papers to give me legal guardian status. Since our society does not provide protection for any form of marriage it deems "abnormal," we have spent some energy making sure that our relationship has as much protection as possible.

Because of the number of acquaintances who might judge or even punish us for our supposedly abnormal relationship, in writing this essay I've chosen to protect our privacy by using false names for all of us. Also, over the past few years I have made a small name for myself as an author of lesbian fiction. I am by no means famous, but my novels have been reviewed in the gay press and have appeared on numerous gay bestseller lists. I feared that some of my lesbian readers might feel betrayed to know that one of "their" writers is in a relationship which includes a man.

I certainly don't feel the need to recruit people into the world of polyamory, because I don't think it would work for most people. I don't hope for a future where three-way marriages are the norm. When I do think of the future, though, I hope for a time when the definition of marriage will be broadened to include more options. I hope for the disappearance of the myth of the "one special someone," an idea that leads only to disappointment. I wish for the word "marriage" to apply to lesbians, gay men and bisexuals . . . and to trios, quartets, quintets and so forth, instead of just duos.

Since I am a person who strives to live in the present instead of the future, however, I spend a great deal of time being thankful that I have been lucky enough to find myself in a marriage with all the necessary ingredients: love, respect, freedom, great conversation, domestic tranquility and hot sex. I wish all women the same luck regardless of the gender or number of their partners.

Oh Baby

Erin Aubry-Kaplan

A friend called recently to announce she'd had a baby. I knew it
was in the works, had known it for months, of course, but there
was finally that dead-air period of silence between the approxi-
mate due date and the official birth announcement, that span of
several days in which you don't know if everything went according to plan. I had thought only briefly about it in the entire nine
months, to tell the truth, when Lana called sounding more
content than she ever had in the twelve years I'd known her. I
hardly knew her voice. She professed to be permanently altered,
enlightened, liberated yet bound to a person as she had never
been bound before. She bubbled like a brook, fairly sang, thought
that her relationship with the man who'd fathered the child was
looking up by the hour. Already the baby was sleeping in bed
between the two of them: Lana couldn't bear the thought of part-
ing with the girl for a night by putting her in a crib. Life was
strange but splendidly different. "I'm so in love with this child,"
she sighed. She couldn't explain it to me, quite, though she
delicately hinted that I would understand by and by, when it
happened to me, when I too would be seized with a baby yen
and be carried along by its current, helpless but happy, magically

fulfilled at the end of the journey despite any expectations to the contrary.

I hinted right back, not so delicately: Thanks but no thanks. It's very unlikely I'll ever have a baby. I never wanted one; I was probably the rare little girl who didn't mind playing with appliances and tea sets and helping out in the kitchen but never, ever imagined herself a mother. I didn't really want to hear about Lana's little one, awful as that sounds, much as she had wanted this. I like babies but think they should be experienced, not talked about. When they're talked up they start sounding like acquisitions, things to be held up, admired and envied by those who don't have this limited-edition model. Mothers especially start sounding smug, which I guess they can't help but I can't tolerate. Their babies start sounding less like love bundles and more like expressions of a female hubris that's tied, like male hubris, to powers of reproduction. Beneath their coos and gauzy talk about the oneness of humanity is naked triumph: "Look at what my ovaries, my womb, my cervix, my nipples can do! How about yours? See how I sacrificed, how I suffered! Like a Roman citizen for the gods! Not everyone can do this, you know." Madonna had done it all, and knew of only one way to top herself: have a baby or two. The Material Girl finally got all the goods.

True, not everyone can have a baby. But maybe some can and don't want to. What I hate most is that milky, patronizing response: "Oh, but you will—give it time." Well, I've given it my entire lifetime, and I'm pretty certain. My ovaries don't decide things for me. Read my lips: The locus of my brain isn't my uterus. It's interesting—women are constantly accusing men of having a dick for brains, which means he's about as Neanderthal as they come, but a woman who thinks with her uterus is perfectly noble and natural. Say what you will about choice and freedom and how far we've come, but the litmus test of womanhood is still motherhood. Ask any celebrity what she considers to be her greatest accomplishment, her finest creation, and if she's a mother she'll invariably say, "My kids." I resent that kind of reductionism, the implication that a woman's life is best utilized in service to somebody else's.

Of course, whole generations of women, including my mother, did exactly that by staying home and tending to the house and children. Motherhood was simply an incontestable part of the marriage package, and marriage was the best way they knew to get out from under their own parents' roof and claim some independence—independence that was severely compromised, of course, by becoming parents and caretakers themselves. These women knew motherhood and its million small ironies and tradeoffs intimately, and for that reason were likely to advise their daughters against choosing such a lot, at least right away—my mother did. I remember her opinion on marriage, which I solicited as a child and which she delivered with remarkable equipoise: "Don't do it until you're at least thirty. Do something with yourself. See the world. As for kids, unless you really want them, don't even think about it. Once you have kids, there are simply things you can't do." She certainly knew. Then she'd go on ironing.

My resistance to motherhood is not purely ideological. I've been pregnant a total of five times; I was miserable five times. I had no business being pregnant, no business taking any sort of uncalculated risks because, first of all, I am a lousy gambler—the biggest pot I ever won in Las Vegas was $250 on a nickel slot machine, and believe me, I took the money as a gift from the gods and ran. Another inexcusable thing was that all five pregnancies were with the same man, a very long-term boyfriend with whom I had a terribly stormy relationship, to put it mildly, a heated but fitful spark that was always shorting out, recouping, shorting out again. Despite the longevity, we didn't bring up marriage once— we at least had that much sense. He was a pretty boy and an emotional wanderer who made me more sexually reckless than I was used to being, and I threw much natural caution to the wind—good for my underdeveloped sense of carpe diem, bad for consequence. I was bewildered to discover that I was pregnant the first time, hearing a nurse intone, "The baby's due in June," in a carefully trained voice that betrayed neither satisfaction nor reproach. I never debated what I wanted to do. He expressed some remorse that first time, even though he had a teenage daughter by a woman he said tricked him into fatherhood, a woman—and child—he was so eager to avoid he wound up checking into the military for several years. I was essentially feeling sick and terrified, most eager not to be pregnant anymore, wanting to reclaim myself. Still, though I was always relieved afterward, I was never proud or satisfied about what I did; I didn't want motherhood, but didn't entirely expect the remains of a certain sadness that I carried around in my palm, or under my arm like a newspaper, or somewhere out in the open because I really had no private place to put it. It didn't lacerate me, but it didn't leave me either.

Over the course of other pregnancies I settled on feeling like I could recommend nothing—not unplanned children, or abortions, or hasty marriages, or marriages that might bring children you didn't want. My boyfriend steered wide of all these musings, as he had steered wide of musings in general, because he ultimately had no real interest in divining me. For him it was more about sex, availability, a warm body of certain dimensions with skin a certain shade of nutmeg, a particular length and curl of hair. This I gave him, gave myself, because it seemed such a welcome counter to the dark complications of pregnancy, the fact that our coupling simply didn't work and that the string of thoughtless and unrealized pregnancies was symptomatic of the failure.

He grew tired of me and my irresolution, and I grew tired of his callowness. The third time, I think, he came over and gave me his half of the money for the abortion; the fifth, he loudly asserted that he couldn't be the father, not this time. In our worst fighting moments, when I was in the midst of one of my frequent depressive fits fueled partly by brain chemicals and partly by our unworkability, he would accuse me of being unnatural and unspiritual because I had opted out of having children—a pact with the devil that was now extracting its price in depression. "See what you hath wrought," he would say loftily, as if pregnancy and badly measured chances were entirely my doing and as if children could have rescued us or imbued us with a depth and meaning we did not have. Yet I also felt he was right—this was my choice, in the most critical sense. I was plotting direction for the both of us, wayward as it was, in a way that he couldn't. I was failing, utterly, and I felt it. What he would not say, and what I also felt, was that my choice not to bear his children diminished him; though he didn't want children, it tampered with a base male pride, which he had in abundance. Kids were an extension of his own narcissism, which, among other qualities, made him a miserable candidate for fatherhood. But the larger concern was that I simply didn't want to be a mother, not with him, likely not ever. He took that as an affront and finally, after more false endings than I can count, broke it off with me after nine wholly spontaneous but truly fruitless years.

My bouts with pregnancy did not leave me any more sympathetic to prospective mothers, except in the most superficial sense: Yes, I knew the warning signs, the lethargy and perceptibly altered consciousness, the feeling of your body being overtaken by an invading creature. Such feelings only confirmed for me that pregnancy is something to be avoided. I never connected with the joyful mystery or a more quotidian sense of fist-pumping victory—I did it!—that I'm sure Lana, Madonna and countless other women have experienced. For me it always connoted failure, a mistake, bungling, death in the metaphorical sense, sometimes more than that. I never believed motherhood could give my life shape and purpose I couldn't give it myself, though I might struggle with that purpose until the end of my life; maybe that view comes from being a writer and inculcating a certain artistic arrogance that may be no less damaging than the female arrogance I decry. As women, perhaps we all must have our babies, our issue, and perhaps we will all stop at nothing to nurture that, no matter what. I like to think that a baby that springs from my mind like Pallas Athena sprang whole from the head of Zeus is morally preferable to one that is carried dumbly, unknown in the womb. I like to think, perhaps, that my baby is the better legacy, a greater addition to humankind than simply another body needing another quarter of a million dollars or so to raise, clothe and feed.

In the end, I don't know; I feel about it sometimes like I felt about being pregnant—that no option is the right one. And here is a bit of a coda that is probably more of a prelude, bigger, but anyway: I would do just about anything to avoid that life-meets-death descent into the maelstrom known as labor, an understatement so gross it borders on etymological evil. The thought of my body wringing itself out over and over, tighter and tighter, like a wet dishcloth that can't get dry, while I look on, dazed—I can think of nothing worse. This imagining steels me against sacrifice and makes me certain that as much as I am grateful for my mother's willingness to endure labor for her baby's sake, I will not. I am also certain that I must *have* something, that something must work its way out of me at the cost of great pain, and my writing must suffice as a birth. In the end I can get away from babies, but not birth, and whether or not I resolve to write a book out of guilt, or whether gestation and birthing and cultivation are parts of a larger female instinct, I don't know. I do know that I need evidence that I lived life with some valor, that I stared a few demons down and won. Having a baby might take you to hell and back, but I want the freedom to choose a hell of my own. The triumph can be greater.

I am now newly married, to a man who feels about children exactly as I do: He loves them, is very good with them, but would rather not have them because he prefers to accord the leisure time in his life to guitars, movies, us. Our pairing has borne fruit neither one of us ever tasted before; we feel a miraculous lack of any lack at all. He says if I must do the deed, he is willing to discuss it, though his willingness is less about children and more about love for me and cooperative spirit. Do I want that? I have considered children only because, despite lifelong resistance, I feel I'm supposed to before officially dropping the possibility altogether. In the back of my mind I'm counting on time making that decision: I'm thirty-eight and counting. There are points, flashes where I suddenly don't know if the reluctance is based on prudent self-knowledge or on an unwillingness to take a risk that just may be worth it. I don't know then which voice is speaking, mine or the culture's, whose has ultimate authority.

Yet even as I say this I know I'm splitting hairs—who, in this age of instant and ubiquitous media and ad campaigns, acts on pure impulse anymore? The point is simply knowing what you want and what you don't want, and learning to let everything be and refrain from trying to torture one thing into being the other. What I do know, as a writer and a seeker and aspiring albeit schizophrenic mother of some kind, is that my own mother gave up the most so that my voice would sound as loudly as hers did not. She instilled in me not baby fever, but a bigger burning that is more voracious, and rewarding, than children might ever be. That is the fire that will mark my universal place this time.

A Suitable Union

Bhargavi C. Mandava

There aren't many conversations I recall from my elementary school days more clearly than this one: I was completing the sixth grade at Public School 122 in Queens, New York. The sidewalk trees were budding with pink blossoms. It was nice enough to eat ice cream, but too cool for shorts. All the sixth-grade classes had gathered in the playground to practice for the annual Maypole dance. Ever since first grade I had watched older kids do the Maypole dance, excited to know I'd be there someday myself.

We were milling about, waiting for someone to call order to the assembly, when a few of my classmates, two girls and two boys, got to talking about dance partners.

"Maria and Dino. Marilyn and Frank. Ming and Jim. Bhargavi and David. Andromeda and . . . "

It didn't take me long to understand that they were pairing up people according to shared characteristics, mostly ethnic. Maria and Dino were both Italian. Marilyn and Frank were the class clowns. Ming was Chinese and Jim was Korean. David was Puerto Rican and I was Indian.

"Wait a minute, how come I get David?" I asked.

They were speechless.

"Who says I have to be with a brown person because I'm brown?" I said.

They blinked at one another and realized if there was such a rule they had no idea who had made it.

"Why can't I be with Frank because I like to laugh or Donny because I like freckles?"

"Yeah," they all agreed. "You're right."

Then an adult shouted into a megaphone for us to line up, and we had to adjourn council.

I looked over at David. He was very handsome and good at basketball.

The adult with the megaphone began explaining how the dance would be performed, and I realized what we had all forgotten in our excitement: No one has a single partner. We would all be dancing with one another, together, skipping round and round, alternately ducking with our ribbons and braiding the Maypole in a kaleidoscope of colors.

When I turned sixteen, there was talk of arranging a marriage for me. I obstinately voiced my desire to remain single. "No way, I want to go to college," I said.

I stood there for a long moment, not saying anything as my parents continued their arguments, until I found my voice again.

"Look what happened to Akka," I said, my older sister's recent marriage passing before my eyes like a bad dream. They fell silent. The marriage arranged for my older sister was annulled almost immediately when cultural differences (he was too "old-fashioned" and she was too "modern") could not be reconciled.

"That was because your mother's father rushed us," said my father.

"He never gave us any thinking time," my mother added.

But I felt the injustice I had felt with David and the Maypole. It was wrong of my classmates to pair me with him because we were both a shade of brown. And it was just as wrong of my parents to pair me with an Indian guy just because he was Indian.

"I'm never marrying someone I don't know," I said.

They gave in then, but I knew we'd be having a similar conversation as soon as I graduated from college.

During my freshman year at New York University, I returned from a

Depeche Mode concert to discover that my father had died of a heart attack. After that, "arranged marriage" was never uttered again. My brother married an Indian classmate. My sister started dating. I started waitressing to put myself through school. I became increasingly vigilant and adamant about keeping the possibilities open and my freedoms limitless. I had the right to 1) eat curry sandwiches and hamburgers, 2) speak Telugu and English, 3) enjoy ragas and rock 'n' roll, 4) wear saris and Levi's, 5) keep my hair long or shave it off, 6) date no one or anyone, 7) get married or stay single.

Seeing my mother's suffering as a widow filled me with sadness that eventually became optimism about staying single. I decided it was the only way I could succeed as a writer. Unless I met someone similarly devoted to a creative life, I promised myself, I would never marry. Unless I met someone who wouldn't be threatened by my independence and my need for solitude . . . and so the list went on.

I was on a business trip to Los Angeles in 1991, unwinding with a co-worker at a bar, when I met Mark, an artist. Rather than the start of a wonderful friendship, it seemed to be the continuation of one. When I returned to the East Coast, we kept in touch, and soon our phone conversations and visits became more frequent. We clicked on so many levels—creative, spiritual and physical. I made the move from New York to LA and eventually we moved in together.

Though we both mistrusted institutionalized religion, we had explored religious texts in search of some structure on which to hang our faith and philosophies. We began intermingling books on one big shelf: the mysticism of Sri Aurobindo with the Taoism of Lao Tzu, the zen of archery with the zen of tea, metaphysics with homeopathy, existentialism with feminism, his painting with my writing. If there were duplicates, we kept them side by side . . . just in case.

Mark and I discussed the works of favorite authors, poets and philosophers and the gamut of religions and spiritual practices. Our verbal investigations often continued independently—he painted in the studio and I wrote at my desk. Though we never found any concrete answers, we did have a clearer, truer understanding of ourselves and each other.

Mark and I both have fractured religious and ethnic histories. His mother's family was predominantly atheist, while his father became an atheist, breaking away from Judaism. My parents' families were both Hindu, though my maternal grandfather dropped out of school as a young teenager and went on a spiritual quest that led him to Buddhism. By seventeen, he had written a treatise on Buddha's life in our region's native tongue, Telugu. My maternal grandmother respected his decision, though she continued to practice Hinduism. Together, the two fought with fervor for Indian independence, my grandfather as an orator (he was fluent in seven languages) and my grandmother as an advocate for equal rights regardless of caste. They went to jail many times for their political ideology. (That these two pressured my mother into an arranged marriage seems a glaring contradiction.)

While growing up, neither Hinduism nor Buddhism was forced on me. Of course, numerous statues of Hindu deities stood on the *puja* altar, and vibrant images of Parvati (the goddess of courage and war), Lakshmi (the goddess of prosperity) and Ganesha (the god of obstacles) had been torn carefully from old calendars and tacked to the walls of our Queens duplex. As my mother performed special pujas on sacred dates, my siblings and I were rarely bothered, left to do our homework or watch television. Sometimes we'd be asked to go to her bedroom, where, while holding a flaming spoon of camphor, my mother would murmur mantras in Sanskrit and fan the black smoke over each of us with her open palm. On our birthdays, she made certain the first food we ate was something sweet to ensure the coming year also would be. At that age, I never questioned whether her practices were rooted in religion, tradition or superstition. I respected them, and whenever I was blessed with the sacred fire I felt good.

Still, I did not gain a clear, comfortable understanding of Hindu rituals. They were pleasant memories when I grew older, but should I carry on any of that ritual as an adult? Was I a Hindu because my parents were Hindus? Could I be a Hindu without being actively religious? Did I even want to affiliate myself with any single religion, and, if so, which?

During my final years of college, I persistently chose religion-related electives—Taoism, Islam, Buddhism, Jewish mysticism, Zen Buddhism and, of course, Hinduism. I read scriptures in their entirety and discussed them with unbiased, generous professors. This study not only allowed me to see the beauty, truth and wisdom in religious texts, but also led me to believe that the many paths cut off from each other will, at some point, merge back into one. The transformation of my spiritual understanding, however, did not affect my religious practice, which generally consisted of lighting an incense stick while studying in bed and the occasional exclamatory prayer whenever the subway was exceptionally late.

When Mark and I decided to get married, we found ourselves whirling down a limitless corridor of symbolic and spiritual possibility, our options spread before us like our colorful library. The combination of Mark's atheistic upbringing and my polytheistic roots left us in a philosophical tangle. Until then, our religious investigations were speculative; the wedding would be our first major opportunity to put theory into practice. With what kind of ceremony would we both feel comfortable? Should there be a ceremony at all? Should we skip the formal wedding and just have a huge party?

Mark's mother had gotten married at Manhattan's city hall, while my mother had an arranged marriage to my father in rural southern India. Their Hindu ceremony was preceded by a Buddha puja, which my grandfather performed in a private room with the bride. And since he did not support the caste system, a Sanskrit pundit (rather than a Brahmin priest) performed the marriage rites. My mother tells me there were thousands of people sitting on mats spread before the *mandap*, or canopy, and that the entire village was welcomed and fed.

Surprisingly, our mothers gave us similar advice about the ceremony: "Do what you feel comfortable doing. Do what feels right." The day had come for Mark and me to get off the fence and render a genuine, clear verdict about religion's place in our lives.

Our first decision was to keep the business aspect as just that: business. So a month after Mark proposed, we were at the county clerk's office in East Los Angeles, sliding our paperwork through the glass window as if we were at the DMV. The deputy commissioner led us into a room with a little arch twined with silk flowers and asked us if we were ready for the seriousness of marriage. We were touched by the humanity with which she conducted the ceremony, which took no more than a couple of minutes. As we left, she said, "I have to tell you, you're the least nervous couple I have ever married."

Going home, we realized the office was in a neighborhood once called Brooklyn. There was Brooklyn Market, Brooklyn Hardware and Brooklyn Street. Brooklyn, New York, is where Mark's paternal grandparents had immigrated to from Russia and Romania. His father was born there, and the place held some of our most precious memories. Happening on the word itself seemed like a serendipitous gift, and we were instantly overwhelmed by the magnitude of our decision. Nostalgia and the childhood optimism of taking on the world with your best friend by your side swept over us and we arrived at our next decision: There would have to be a meaningful ceremony. There would have to be a celebration. After that, there were no more Vegas jokes. We refused to be impostors at our own wedding. Mark didn't want to pretend to be Indian, and I didn't want to pretend not to be.

I found a program from a cousin's recent wedding detailing the rites of the Vedic ceremony. Mark and I read and discussed the basic principles. Did they feel right? If not, could they be changed? To our surprise (and I was the one itching to veto it), we discovered that much resonated with us in the Vedic vows. They strike a fine balance, seeing the bride and groom as two halves of one whole—as necessary and interdependent as earth to sky, as *purusha* (the true eternal self) to *prakriti* (primal matter from which the physical and mental universe evolves). They also include sensible elements: "Help each other in all good deeds," and "Bring up children in such a manner that they are strong in mind and body."

The Vedic rituals also excited us; they are universal enough to be infused with our own meanings and include actions representative of our feelings for each another. One of our favorite ceremonies begins with the element of water (to purify the time and the place, as well as the minds of participants and witnesses). It culminates with Agni, the element of fire (around which the bride and groom circle, taking seven steps representing seven vows) and concludes with the cool glow of the Arundhati star (the priest points out its location as part of the symbolic oath to always remain faithful and firm). Both Mark and I are avid stargazers, and we looked forward to the fact that long after our wedding the Arundhati star would serve as a small yet brilliant reminder of our love.

We still insisted on some important changes—specifically, instead of the typical eight or so hours, we wanted the ceremony to last only ninety minutes. With determination and patience—and support from my brother and mother—we pressed the issue until we received the firmest "I'll do my best" from the priest. We wouldn't know what this meant until after the ceremony. We also decided to forgo the rituals that seemed redundant or outdated (for example, the bride's parents washing the groom's feet). Research revealed that Hindu ceremonies differ in India from region to region and even from village to village. For example, during some affairs lasting from evening until dawn, a groom is accompanied by a young girl, usually his sister or niece, who ensures he stays awake by rattling a metal pot containing coins in his ears! Comical, yes, but we wanted to avoid such arduous effort and fatigue.

The next issue was our attire. With the recent popularity of Indian culture in the United States, we became self-conscious. After all, these days it's not unusual to see trendy types flaunting yoga mats and Kali lunch boxes, sipping their chai espressos and yogi teas in such a way that other equally hip customers can admire their hennaed palms. Boardwalk shops on Venice Beach were offering skintight silkscreened tops with images of Durga and Siva. Even museum shops were selling *mehndi* kits and jeweled *bindi*.

It wasn't so long before that people were staring at me, wondering where I was from and thinking I was odd. But rather than feeling liberated by all this modish attention, I felt cheapened and exploited. Capitalism had turned me into the ethnic woman du jour. Now, I suddenly didn't look Indian enough, and I was being bullied at the hair salon. "Hey, where's your bindi?" asked the guy trimming my hair. "They're so cool."

I didn't resolve my feelings until I remembered a trip to India I'd made at age fourteen. Shortly after we arrived, I hung about the veranda eating mango in my favorite cutoff jeans and complaining about the heat. "She's half-naked—she doesn't have anything to wear," my grandmother had complained. So off I was whisked to the town center, visiting textile shop after textile shop. The fabrics—chiffon, muslin, poplin, silk, *khadi*, voile, tricot, crepe—in every imaginable color and pattern made me giddy. Shopkeepers brought us chai and soda in little glasses and tailors began fussing over me, taking measurements and noting preferences. I was thrilled.

With this memory, I realized how much I didn't want to hunt for pre-made white dresses that fit, or shoes, or veils. I wanted to lose myself again in the possibilities of texture and color, with golds and purples and ivories and pinks.

"I want to wear a sari," I told Mark.

"So, what are my options?" he asked nervously.

"How about a dhoti?"

He gave me a skeptical look.

"It's a silk . . . sarong type of garment that's tucked—"

"It says in the dictionary that it's a loincloth worn by Indian men," he said.

"It's not a loincloth. It's very elegant. Trust me. It's not a loincloth."

"Maybe I can just wear a suit."

"Should I wear a wedding dress, then?"

"No. But if I wear a suit and you wear a sari, that doesn't seem right either."

The negotiations went on for weeks—until I tried on my white sari bordered with orange and Mark tried on his white dhoti piped with gold, and we stood side by side and looked in the mirror. We were stunned into silence. The clothes were beautiful, but more important, they felt right for the ceremony. We decided that we would wear the dhoti and sari for the ceremony and change into a suit and dress for the reception.

We resolved other questions, such as the menu, in a similar way. Tugs-of-war over food went deeper than preferences for cold salmon with capers or chicken curry. It was as much about cultural loyalties as making certain everyone would have something palatable to eat. In the end, we favored a meeting of East and West and included dishes such as curried couscous salad and vegetable rice. Why shouldn't it be a wedding in every application of the word?

Mark's artist and photographer parents designed and printed the wedding invitations, my brother procured an open-minded priest, my mother shopped with me in India for my sari, my sister-in-law and cousin fashioned the flower braid for my hair. The list goes on.

The night before our wedding, Mark was putting the final touches of mehndi on my palms. Mehndi is traditionally applied to the bride's hands by female members of her family for adornment and to ease the tension of an arranged marriage. It can slow things down and provide a topic of conversation for the bride and groom, who have most likely never met before that day. Obviously, this didn't apply to us, but the ritual proved just as valuable. As I studied Mark drawing on my palms, cradling my hand in his, time seemed to stand still. Though we had known each other for eight years, the moment was so uniquely intimate and original that it was as if we were looking at each other for the first time.

The day of the wedding I woke slightly disoriented, thinking I was back in India. It was exceptionally hot, the air humid and scented with incense. I saw my sari laid out on a chair by the window. I felt something strange on my fingers, and when I looked at my hands I saw the dried mehndi paste. I started rubbing it off and saw Mark's intricate designs had taken to my palms in the deepest red.

We completed the final preparations: I finished the flower arrangements, Mark finished constructing the mandap, my aunt brought the puja cushions, and the Orissan leaf puppets on which I had inscribed the date and our names were placed at the table settings. My mother was helping me wrap my sari, and Mark secured his dhoti. I peeked out the window and saw some guests had gathered around the wishing well sprinkled with rose petals. My heart was racing. As the ceremony began, we still didn't know what to expect. There's no such thing as a rehearsal in Indian weddings. My mind flooded with questions: Would the priest stick to the schedule? Would everything be beautiful?

The ceremony began with Ry Cooder and V.M. Bhatt's *A Meeting by the River*, a favorite record of ours whose blend of Indian and American traditions made it perfectly suited to start us off. Mark and I took our places under the mandap before our family and friends. In a gesture representing purity and fertility, Mark began dripping milk from a silver spoon as I drizzled rose petal after rose petal on our intertwined wedding necklaces laid out on a green coconut. The priest recited prayers in Sanskrit.

After Mark and I exchanged necklaces, rings and garlands signifying our union, I was given a sari by his family and he a *kurta pajama* (tunic and pants) by mine. As we hurried upstairs to change into them, we heard the priest quip to our guests, "They gave me forty-five minutes to do what normally takes days, so I'm doing my best." Everyone laughed and commented later that they liked him for his honesty. The ceremony went over our one-and-a-half-hour limit, but it didn't matter.

When we returned in our new clothes, which symbolized our familial union, it was time for Talambralu, a ritual that represents long life, prosperity and happiness. A large vessel of turmeric-stained rice and rose petals was placed between us, and Mark and I dug in, showering handfuls over each other's heads. Talambralu often turns playfully competitive, as it's believed that whoever manages to dump the last scoop of rice will rule the house. Some of my relatives were shouting their encouragement that I race to be the last. As Mark and I caught each other's eyes through a curtain of rice and petals, we were reminded of the importance of laughter . . . and balance. We split the last scoop of rice between us, pouring it over each other simultaneously.

In one of the most important Vedic marriage rites, Saptapadi, the end of my sari was tied to the end of his shawl, and we prepared to take seven steps around the sacred fire. Each step represents one of the following vows: 1) Let us live with honor and respect, let us walk together so we may be nourished; 2) Let us be happy and enjoy life, let us walk together so we may become strong; 3) Let us share joy and pains together, let us walk together so we may prosper; 4) Let us not forget parents and elders, let us walk together so we may be happy; 5) Let us observe all acts of charity, let us walk together so we may have family; 6) Let us live a long and beautiful life, let us walk together so we may have joy; 7) Let us be friends with love and sacrifice, let us walk together so we may have friendship.

We circled the fire holding hands, neither needing to walk first. As I stared into the flames, I was filled with the same peace and reverence I felt looking into a campfire in the California desert. Mark had taken me on my first camping trip there. As we repeated prayers and vows in an unfamiliar but ancient language, our wedding in the material world began to reflect our deep, wordless feelings for one another—the mysterious abstraction of love itself.

After the ceremony, Mark changed into his suit and I changed into a beaded dress. Everyone seemed to be enjoying the string quartet, the food and the wedding cake (next to the plate of *laddoos* my mother made). Although the sun had been beating down all day, toward the end of the celebration it began to pour. The priest rushed to his car, the vermilion and sandal paste markings on his forehead and bare chest washing away. My mother stood on the porch, spinning one of the purple Orissan puppets in her hand.

I remembered when I had handed her the Maypole dance invitation I'd made in art class. She had told me, "Oh, we do a similar thing in India."

"Our teacher said it goes back to the Druids, Egyptians and Romans."

"Well, you can tell her some Indians also welcome spring with a similar dance," she had said. "It's just a little different."

When the performance day finally arrived, an ample audience of parents, students, teachers and passersby had assembled. We were excited, clutching red, blue and yellow ribbons in our hands. Someone put the needle on the record player, and we all stood, breathless, listening to the crackle of vinyl.

The music started and we started, too, skipping in opposite directions, crouching under each other's arms, laughing as we added another plait of color into the weaving. It was a blur of bodies as I passed—Dino, Marilyn, Frank, Maria, David, Ming, Jim, making round after round, Dino, Marilyn, Frank, Maria, David, Ming, Jim—whirling faster and faster, catching glimpses of my mother looking on in the crowd and so many colors.

Omnisexual for Life

Sabrina Margarita Alcantara-Tan

"I hope now that you're married it doesn't mean you won't kick ass anymore," a friend of mine remarked offhandedly.

When I got hitched, many of my single-lady friends assumed that once I got married, I'd become so domestic that I wouldn't continue all the work I loved, such as writing, putting out my zine, doing performance art, making video shorts, organizing and networking within the Asian Pacific Islander and women of color communities, and producing stickers and T-shirts with fun, empowering slogans. They thought I'd fall off the face of the earth and stop being active within my surrogate family, the queer Filipina community. That couldn't have been further from the truth. But I felt that I had to prove to my peers and to readers of my zine that I would remain a loud, proud, queer feminist activist whether I tied the knot or not.

I'm used to struggling to fashion my identity. Traditionally, Filipina women are supposed to be very femme—they're expected to wear dresses and preen themselves for beauty pageants when they're young. I never conformed. Homosexuality is still a taboo subject, even though lesbian and bisexual Pinays (slang for Filipinas) are common. (In fact, most Filipinas I've met, even if they consider themselves straight, have admitted to being attracted to, or having a relationship with, a girl.) The Philippines is a strongly Catholic country, so same-sex unions are prohibited and thought disgusting. Being an Americanized Pinay in the U.S. made it easier for me to come out and allow my sexuality to be a key part of my identity. Five years ago I co-founded a queer-identified Pinay collective in New York, and it became a place where I could grow and come out at my own pace.

But many queer, feminist and young women I know seem to believe you lose all sexual, proactive and progressive identity once you're married. Since I am a young queer feminist, making peace between my queer politics and the straight lifestyle of marriage is a challenge. But rising to that challenge pushes the boundaries of the way people think about queerness. I believe in the fluidity of sexuality; many categories, including "bisexuality," are too limiting and narrow for me. Bisexuality implies that I am only attracted to men and women, which isn't true. I've found transsexuals and transgendered individuals attractive as well. That's why I call myself omnisexual. (The term "queer" also embraces that wide range of attractions.)

People in both queer and straight communities tend to define sexual identity according to whom you're having sex with at the time. But being queer encompasses everything from whom you envision as your life partner to appreciating the loveliness of the gender(s) you find attractive, respect and love. Though I'm happy with Rom, my biologically male significant other, I still revel in the beauty of women and wonder what certain ones are like in bed, what they may smell like. Ever since my first date with my husband, I've been up-front with him about my love for women, men and transgendered peeps. Even though he was brought up in the sexist and male-oriented culture of the Philippines, he is open to my orientation and at ease with the resulting politics. He knows that my attraction to women is going to remain, and it doesn't faze him. (In fact, I've found we have the same taste in girls; when we catch each other checking girls out, we can laugh and say, "She was cute, huh?")

When I was going out with women, I felt very comfortable in the queer community. My identity as queer was accepted easily, and I knew where I stood with my friends. I also knew to expect hostility on the street from homophobic jerks who felt the need to express their hatred of lesbian couples. I was part of the struggle; I was going through the same hardships and homophobia as my fellow queer galpals.

When I started dating a guy, the queer community still accepted me. But everything changed when I got married. It was okay to date men, it seemed, as dating is temporary—but settling down with one made a permanent statement. My husband's gender wasn't important to me— we got married because it was the right time for us. (I would've gotten married to my girlfriend years before if the time had been right.) So, while I was confident about my marriage, I worried about the aftereffects within the community.

For many months before the wedding, I was apprehensive: What does this mean? *Am I still queer?* Will my queer friends treat me differently? Will they look at me weird at queer functions? Will they be rude to Rom? Are they gonna be passive-aggressive about it and do a lot of *tsismis* ("gossip" in Tagalog, the national Filipino language) behind my back? I was fully aware, too, that some of my lesbian and queer sisters had a strong dislike for anyone who claimed queerness yet slept with men. The authenticity of my identity was going to be in question.

Since my marriage, my lesbian sisters seem to struggle with their language: The term "lesbian" no longer includes me. Their body language shows discomfort; their eyes dart, their bodies get a little rigid, they stammer a bit. Our conversations are peppered with comments like, "Well, you know, I have some straight friends, so I understand what you're saying . . ." Even my ex-girlfriend, who used to consider me a lesbian, said, "I don't know what it is with me and bisexual women," referring to me and her present girlfriend. I'm the same person, but all of sudden I'm lumped in as straight (with a patronizing tone, to boot) or labeled as bi even though I reject that categorization. My peers in the queer community also assume that, because I now have some measure of heterosexual privilege—the availability of legal marriage, no homophobic reactions in the streets—I no longer understand their struggles. They assume that I don't know the depth of queer identity, that I can't fathom what queer women endure every day.

I think people label me as straight (or bi) because they're uncomfortable with the range of sexual identity. But even though I have experienced the variations within myself, falling in love with a man did make me question my queer identity. For years, I envisioned myself married to a woman, thinking only another woman would understand what I was truly about. She would be in tune with my feelings. We would have certain unspoken understandings. I still think that women can have a sexual and emotional bond that being with a man can't equal. When I chose to marry a partner of the opposite sex, I feared that the relationship would not be as fulfilling—that I would lose the familiarity I felt with women. But the differences between my relationship with my husband and those with past girlfriends are due to the differences between people, not gender. Being married to a man right after such active involvement in the lesbian community didn't mean that I changed my sexual orientation like a pair of clothes. I became more settled in my skin and more at peace about my sexuality; as Larry-bob, of the zines *Queer Zine Explosion* and *Holy Titclamps,* says, "Nothing should be assumed about anyone's sexuality, including yours."

Accepting this gave me the strength to stop caring what other people thought. Those who distanced themselves from me because of my choice to marry ("marriage is just an institution that does not honor the relationships of queer love and is therefore meaningless") and those who were ready to write me off as bi, as straight, as previously bi-curious and now hetero, were not going to be as important in my life. I traded my overly concerned "Will they accept me as queer even though I'm married to a man?" mentality to "I really don't give a fuck what anyone says anymore."

The process was painful, but I ended up finding out who my true friends are and learning about myself. I can choose not to put myself in situations that make me feel uncomfortable, misunderstood or belittled. I don't have to obtain a queer merit badge from my peers, because I know who I am. What matters is that my husband and I are comfortable with our relationship and who we are. My identity is for no one else to decide.

During this time, I made a point of going to queer-related events with Rom. He often felt out of place, but he came with me anyway. He knew it was important for me to be visible as a proud queer woman married to a man. It felt good to break a silence and force people to recognize the wide range of queerness.

I have continued to be as vocal as I can about my identity, talking about it publicly and writing about it in my zine. I experienced the first attack from a stranger when I was on a panel discussing queer identity in the Filipino American community and a gay man asked me, "How can you call yourself queer when you're married to a man?" It was a tense moment; some audience members clearly expected drama. But I was ready—after all, I was used to the question. I answered that being queer doesn't mean sticking to a certain set of rules, that sexuality isn't either/or or easily labeled, and that this is just the way I am. "It's like asking me, 'What makes you think you're Filipino American?' That's a silly question. I just *am*," I declared. I don't know if he was convinced, but later that evening a fellow Filipina approached me. She seemed about to break down in tears, and she thanked me for speaking up. She told me that she, too, was a queer Filipina woman who loved men, who loved women and who was seeing a man. She told me how hard it had become to tell her lesbian sisters that she was dating a guy (and a white guy at that, which provoked negative reactions from some Filipinos). I felt great: That guy may not have understood me, but my conversation with this woman made all the difference to me—and to her.

I'm going on my third year of marriage, and, though it's been a difficult process, it was one of the better choices I've made in my life. I've grown more calm and peaceful. It's strengthened my resolve, convictions and intuition. It's helped me act more loving toward myself, as New Age as it sounds: I listen to myself more, and I keep up my boundaries so I don't feel as violated when people attack my stance on marriage and sexuality. My opinions on the topic have become much more solid.

When I feel unsure, I remind myself of my struggle in getting both the queer and straight communities to accept my marriage and sexual identity. I'm proud of how far I've come. I will always speak out about queer and feminist issues. I will always consider myself queer. I will always be a fierce woman, a lover of women, a lover of men, a lover of third sexes. No one can take away what I won't give up.

Teenage Army Bride

Bee Lavender

We met in criminal court. I was charged with a misdemeanor count
for being in a park after hours. We shared an attorney, but he
wouldn't say why he was there. We sat together on a wooden
bench and started talking. He had freckles and blond hair sticking
straight up; in five minutes he told me three outrageous stories
and the attorney told us to be quiet. He smelled of sawdust and
sweat. When they assigned his case I understood the source of his
reticence; the charge was communicating with a minor for immoral purposes. I laughed out loud. We were both eighteen. Jay
was an archetypal juvenile delinquent, always under suspicion,
couldn't walk down the street without a cop stopping him to look
at the bottom of his shoes. He had felony convictions, a stash of
weapons, stories about raids on businesses. He was trenchantly
funny, a certified genius and a dropout. He didn't know how to
drive. I responded to his lawless behavior, the depth of his disregard for social conventions. Everything was up for grabs; he didn't
respect any authority or respond to any punishment, and he did
not have plans for his future beyond the immediate pleasure of
each day.

I had a car and an allowance and stayed up all night watching television, then spent my days wandering around town wearing peacock sunglasses and men's silk pajamas. I was recovering from a car accident that took the health (spinal columns, intestines) of my best friends. My psychiatrist said I had survivor's guilt and a tendency toward magical thinking. I had broken bones, a vicious headache and sensory hallucinations. My plans were vague, though scholarship offers stacked up in my post office box.

We lived in a small town on the Kitsap Peninsula, across Puget Sound from Seattle. We were bored and restless. He devised elaborate and dramatic pranks, and I worried about political ideas. He stole a boat and played chicken with a state ferry, developed plans to launch a paramilitary attack against nearby Bainbridge Island, cultivated his anarchistic image. I wrote and distributed zines calling for procedural changes in the school system and community, started a youth liberation group, went to protests, won citizenship awards. It was a scandalous match and all the more amusing because it shocked our friends and families.

Our courtship was conducted around his work at the lumber yard and a grueling court schedule. I had complicated legal problems related to the car accident. He was implicated in many crimes, at least two of which were murder cases. His judo sensei's wife turned up dead in the trunk of a car, and suspicion was redirected to Jay by an anonymous phone call; we suspected the sensei. The other was an act of patricide by my neighbor, a boy who had been beaten bloody for years before ending the situation. Jay had advised him on the best weapon to use.

We took road trips and experienced natural phenomena. We sat on top of my car in the Yakima desert, listening to Led Zeppelin as a lightning storm played around us; saw a lunar eclipse over Seattle; watched the aurora borealis over Olalla. We interpreted these things as cosmic directives, a romantic confluence to encourage our passion. At the end of the summer I went away to a progressive liberal arts college.

The campus was situated in a forest and cut off all views of the mountains and water, and I was deeply homesick. From the first day, college life seemed boring and pointless, my classmates immature and foolish. My life was defined by physical pain and continuing grief from the accident, and I nurtured my resentment by writing essays that shocked my seminar group. I refused to live in the dorms or make new friends. I went home each weekend to pick Jay up and we walked on the beach at night, drove around in my car, visited friends locked down in the county jail or mental hospital. He taught me how to ice skate and how to shoot a gun. We started to create a mutual mythology of safety, and earnestly believed that our friendship would sustain us through any challenge.

We helped each other avoid the frightening intrusion of adult choices by pretending that we could make a new and better family. I didn't have to worry about making new friends, and he didn't have to worry about the future. I could forget the accident when he made me laugh. He could depend on me to provide a schedule and direction. Each of us reflected only the better and more amusing aspects of the other. We had fun. When his parents accused him of selling methamphetamines, he came to live with me near the college, and we conceived a child on ten shots of rum.

He joined the Army to support his new family, against my wishes but with my consent. I respected his right to his own destiny and was willing to accept being alone for an unspecified length of time. Our friendship was more important to me than any other concerns about myself or a potential child. I thought it was funny and contrarian that he would make the choice, and we strategized how to deceive the government so the Army would take him despite his juvenile record and lack of education. But what started as a semi-serious prank proved his master, the one force that could give his life structure and change him in tangible ways. Within weeks he was no longer a criminal; his willful ways were superseded by discipline and physical activity, and his interest in weapons was sanctioned and controlled.

The pregnancy was, to many around me, my ultimate failure; faculty members and counseling staff advised me that it was antifeminist to parent as a teenager and that I would not be supported in making that choice. I was told to drop out of school for the duration. If I had been a more gentle and loving teenager I could have found peers through the co-op or midwifery community, but I was too bitter and odd. I forfeited my scholarships and went home.

I leased an apartment near the naval shipyard, living downstairs from a woman who kept three dozen cats. I suffered through a complicated and fearful pregnancy, the ruination of the accident still dictating my health and habits. I wrote thirty- and forty-page letters each day, baked cookies, waited for brief phone calls from training camp in Georgia. The baby was born just before his two-week leave, and we married in order to increase his paycheck and qualify for health insurance. I wore a white gown and flowers in my hair, he wore his uniform and we stood up in front of an assembly of friends and family to promise our devotion. We invited thirty people but 150 showed up, surprised to find us both alive and out of jail.

Having a baby young was the norm in my family; we were all products of teen marriages, and the cousins produced a dozen infants that year. My family understood and supported my choices, and lavished me with support and help. I moved back in with my parents. After the baby and wedding I realized that I would have to do something to occupy my time. I was not domestic and failed at even the most simple tasks. I couldn't care for a pet, let alone cook meals, clean clothes, manage bills. The baby was as loved as any child could be, and entertained me endlessly with her strange and interesting behavior. But staying home with an infant was not satisfying for me, and good jobs outside of the shipyard were scarce. It was clear that I would need to find a career, fast.

As I recovered from the birth I also gradually recovered from the car accident. My headache and sensory hallucinations vanished and a cash settlement arrived. It occurred to me that leaving school was a foolish choice, and that going back was the only way to improve my life. I reasoned that the accident money was mine to spend, and could justifiably be invested in an education. Many other people disagreed, particularly Jay, who wanted me to follow him to an assignment in Alaska. My parents wanted me to buy a trailer and learn how to keep house. The choices open to me were phrased in either/or terms; nobody believed the cinematic fiction that I actually could choose to exist in both worlds. Defying the wishes of my extended family, husband and college advisor, I enrolled in classes that fall. The baby would stay with a grandmother during the day, and I would commute hundreds of miles each week. Jay moved to Alaska and our relationship consisted of letters, packages, occasional phone calls.

College life was still difficult, due mostly to my bad attitude. The college was peopled by the young and idealistic, the newly radical children of the middle class. It was a very particular place and time with a defined costume and values. It was the Pacific Northwest in the early nineties, and my college town had a fervent music scene covered by the mainstream press. My preference for local indie music, vintage clothing and zines placed me in a social category with people who were striving to popularize new approaches to academic and cultural discourse. But early marriage and parenthood were neither socially acceptable nor understandable. For the most part, people were puzzled by me, by my unapologetic choice to marry a convicted felon and breed. I wasn't a girl any longer, but something entirely different, a "mother," with the attendant responsibilities and change of perspective. I had no patience with the standard late-adolescent exploration of values and philosophy, because I had bills to pay and a child of my own to think about. At age eighteen, I had settled on a permanent commitment that would control all other life choices.

I didn't want to look like the people who rejected my choice to be a mother, so I cut my hair and packed up my beloved clothes and bought a new wardrobe. I wore shirts that said "Kill 'em all and let God sort 'em out" or "One Shot, One Kill," and then denied they were a joke. As my peers moved forward into their maturity, explored ideas and had independent experiences, I withdrew further into the family and social values of my hometown. I didn't want to talk about body image or go to feminist encounter meetings. I didn't want to know anything about nascent third-wave feminism, no matter how much I agreed with the rules of the canon. I didn't want to be part of the revolution, especially when it became a media phenomenon. I was not a riot grrl; I was a working-class teenage Army bride.

I considered following my new husband to his post in Alaska and flew up to look at schools and housing. His friends all lived in rows of identical pastel houses with equally identical wives. The heat was centrally controlled, the weather was dark and dreary, the post isolated from the city. I visited the bowling alley, the movie theater and the mall. I saw myself reflected in the person of a smart girl from New Orleans, with a baby the same age as mine, amusing herself with alcohol and bargain shopping. I met other wives who seemed to have no particular husband of their own—they just swapped around every few months. His friends were all our age, the wives occasionally younger, and it seemed as much a game as college life. It wasn't real or authentic in any compelling way. They were all playing at being adults, and getting paid to blow things up suddenly seemed no more valid than studying creative writing or cultural anthropology. I started to understand that perhaps everyone else was right, that it was impossible to combine our two worlds, and that I might need to choose one or the other.

We both wanted to make the family work. He requested a transfer but was refused. Years passed while I attended classes, worked, took care of the baby, worried my way through a war. The words "husband" and "wife" came to mean nothing more than the credentials on an identification card, health insurance, tax returns. I was so busy with school and being a parent that I was happy enough with this simple arrangement. We still provided each other with an immediate cover story, a convenient definition of our plans. Being a wife and mother made me different and protected me from the social pressures of college life, and presumably being a husband and father did the same for him in his travels. I listened to his funny stories long distance, and he returned the favor. We were pen pals with marriage vows. Our choices created geographic and emotional distance so profound, I forgot what he looked like. My husband seemed less a person with real emotions than a cartoon action hero.

Jay moved home after our daughter's second birthday, and we rented a basement apartment on the peninsula, two counties distant from his work and my school. We chose to stay on the peninsula because we shared a sentimental connection to the landscape and depended on family for childcare. There were three Dobermans and a high chainlink fence around the property; our idea of gun safety meant keeping them on top of the fridge. Our surviving high-school friends were still living in town, going to community college, working as janitors, commercial fishermen, waitresses. We had a hand-me-down sofa and table and bed, a signed and framed "Hunter S. Thompson for Sheriff" poster, a playroom full of toys and a storage room full of guns and knives.

Jay had no hope of promotion within the military because he had never finished high school and could not drive, both of which were minimum requirements to join in the first place. I refused to participate in the wives' club, the unit parties, the culture of his work, all of which might have helped his position. His life had become disciplined, totalitarian, entirely masculine, and I found it disgusting. The relentless training schedule, injuries and lack of advancement had changed him. He was still charming and intelligent, but his criminal tendencies had been channeled into the work of the government. He didn't share his thoughts with me, but even a casual observer could tell that we suffered from loss of innocence. Instead of a frantic, funny boy, he had changed into a tense and tired man, and one who no longer recognized or appreciated the girl he lived with. We didn't change for each other, or resent the fact of our family, but the circumstances we created together proved intolerable. His last, small rebellion was to wage a fight to have "Discordian" listed as the official religious choice on his dog tags.

I had given up the frivolity of dress and dramatic manner, the compulsions and fears, the need for him. My concerns were now entirely practical and rooted in desire for a stable family life, and this included the right to pursue an education and career on my own terms. I was a mother, and one accustomed to setting the rules and standards of my small family. We quarreled about how to parent our active, loud, smart child; it was disruptive to have another perspective insinuated after making my own choices for so long. I wasn't interested in knowing his thoughts about sleep schedules or potty training. I wrote short stories and essays in the morning, studied in the afternoon, took naps on the floor of the play room while my toddler played on top of me. Five days a week I drove hundreds of miles back and forth to take Jay to work, pick him up and drive myself to night classes. I refused to do more than my fair share of housework, and he thought he shouldn't have to do any. I went on strike and stopped cooking or cleaning. The long drives finally broke my confidence in a shared future, and daggers misplaced under the sofa cushions eroded my trust in my husband. We could not compromise, and our friendship ended.

During our final weeks together we went on a road trip, and I taught Jay how to drive. Our progress around Washington state was erratic; we missed all the major landmarks we had planned to see. It was a frivolous plan, an attempt to break away from routine and remember the qualities we liked in each other. During the trip he risked our lives with a careless driving mistake, and the ensuing argument killed any shred of interest I still had in the relationship.

I wanted to know an all-consuming passion. I wanted to be with someone who was lawless and forceful yet embodied principles of justice. He wanted a true and romantic love, a reflection of his own best self, a partner and friend. Somehow, in our impetuous rush toward adulthood, we found that our mutual admiration was not enough to make a marriage. We could not figure out how to give in to another person before the effacement of self became an effacement of the point of being together. I can break out the details and say that I was raised to be an independent woman, and he was raised to be a patriarchal man, but that would be false and also too easy, because it exempts us both from blame. The truth is that we were too young and too stubborn. We could not handle the mundane obligations of married life, of a world where rules were necessary and advantageous. Real adults are not outlaws, and good parents must be adults.

I was offered a place at graduate school, and he was notified of a transfer to Louisiana. My first and only response was to make the right choice for myself, which meant staying in school. His essential, implacable anger caused him to break out in hives whenever he talked to me. He hated me because I had the freedom to go to school, because I would not follow him, because I disregarded his opinions on every critical life decision. I simply did not care. We were no longer exquisitely strange; we were just normal and stressed and trying hard to grow up, with a child of our own to raise. We had a final, brutal, disastrous argument. The marriage was over, and our parents came to sort and pack. He kept the ironing board, a few books and the Hunter S. Thompson poster. I took the household goods, all my letters, the child.

My Best Friend's Not Coming to My Wedding

Jennifer Maher

We are standing in the stairwell of the English department hallway. The walls are institutional orange, a color recently hip again. As Astrid is on her way down the stairs to receive an academic award, I pick the worst of times to break the news. I do this because I am afraid that in the few minutes before the awards ceremony someone will pull her aside and refer to it casually, in end-of-semester banter. After all, many people will be at this celebration, as there always are when you combine graduate students with free booze and food.

"I have to tell you something," I say, panic rising in my throat like a wave full of jellyfish tentacles.

"What?" she says, picking up on my nervousness and setting her jaw tighter.

"Gareth and I are getting married this August." I do my best to smile, because after all, this is good news. At the same time, I know how Astrid feels about marriage, and also that many of her political beliefs about it as an institution are dead-on. So I try not to smile too much. I don't want her to think of me as one of those women with a fat issue of *Bride's* under one arm and a gleaming layaway mall diamond on my finger. However, I know that if I do not smile enough, act appropriately happy and excited, I will be subject to even more intense questioning about my motivations. I will be asked over and over again if this is something I really want to do, or if it is an unconscious attempt to control my future when so much—the dearth of academic jobs, the uncertain future of ad-hoc college lecturing—is out of my control. I want her to be happy, but I know she will not. She will be angry, and I will act surprised and even angrier back. Astrid is one of my closest friends, yet right now I feel as if I'm driving a borrowed car: Though I know how it works, the seat is too far forward and I'm not sure how to turn on the headlights. In order not to crash, I must pay close attention to everything I do. I think all this in a few (nervous) seconds.

"I *knew* you were going to do this," she says, as if she finally caught me trying to pocket her favorite M.A.C. lipstick, or as if I had broken her heart for good this time, which I suppose in a way I had.

Astrid's reaction, though she might argue with this interpretation, is based on equal parts politics and emotions. A real sadness arises when you formally declare your decision to make one person (especially a person of the opposite sex) your chief life partner. I sometimes think "forsaking all others" has more to do with your female friends than it does sexual fidelity. For women, at least, marriage signifies (among other things) an end to careless girlhood. Right or wrong, in this culture marriage communicates maturity, a giving up of lighthearted youth in order to hunker down and take the next step, one that involves mortgages and sleeping in your own bed before midnight on weekends. As is the case with many cultural myths, this isn't necessarily true. My marriage, for instance, includes the unstated provisos that I will still attend the band performances of friends and that, as a part-time bartender, I will be out later than midnight at least two nights a week. This has caused people to remark, sometimes in awe, sometimes just in surprise, "You don't act like you're married." Mind you, I don't spend these evenings making out with strangers or dancing on tabletops—it is purely that I am out telling stories with a cocktail in one hand and no husband holding the other. Gareth is similarly taken aback when people act surprised that I go out at night on my own (he has a far lower tolerance for indie rock than I do). Questions are asked, often including words like "allow," as if "spouse" were a synonym for "Dad" and getting married means you lose all desire to do anything other than stay home and order candles from the Pottery Barn catalog. Thus, my husband and I both conform and do not conform to the marriage = maturity proviso. We have no mortgage payment (as recent humanities PhDs, we have little money), and though we sleep in the same bed every night, from time to time I am crawling into it in the wee hours and waking him up because I smell of smoke.

At the same time, though, it would be insincere to suggest that others' expectations of what marriage means have nothing whatsoever to do with how we perceive our relationship. An actual giving up of personal freedom comes when you claim couplehood so officially. Though I think this is the case in any committed monogamous relationship, being married seems to signify something stronger to third parties whom you don't know very well, like acquaintances and extended-family members. When I went out alone before I was married, people flirted with me much more, though I feel the same about my husband now as before we exchanged vows. Suddenly, it's as if I were surrounded by an emotional invisible electric fence, one activated by the ring around my finger.

This assumed distance from people other than the spouse is even built into a father's traditional disingenuous wedding toast: "I am not losing a daughter, I am gaining a son-in-law." But, as the polite laughter indicates, no one actually believes it. It is a culturally agreed upon cover-up along the lines of the high school graduation caveat/cliché that commencement is not an end, it is a beginning. Sure and bullshit all at once. Let's face it, graduation is the end of believing that you can be a famous journalist and a pop star in the same lifetime. It's the end of getting stoned with your best friend in a clean and quiet house at three-thirty in the afternoon, a house where all the food in the refrigerator is paid for (and not by you). Similarly, after you are married, you will never lie so comfortably again on your single bed secretly smoking cigarettes and waiting for your laundry or a phone message. You will no longer automatically give your parents' address on forms that ask for emergency contact information. You can't take home the lovely boy in the black sweater who's been eyeing you all night. You can't decide to drive with your friends to Chicago at 11:30 P.M. because someone else is going to be wondering where you are. When you get good news, or when you feel so bad even expensive lipstick doesn't help, you will most likely turn to him, not to one of your "pussy posse."

It's not that losing these things is all bad—I mean, who wants to sleep in a single bed forever? And remember how much you actually *wanted* to leave high school? The guy in the black sweater might very well be a lousy lay, and a psycho besides. So goes the sweet loss, the choice that makes other choices unmakeable. Marriage-inspired monogamy is a kind of synecdoche for the whole end of possibility that marriage ushers in. I wouldn't want it any other way, but it's tough to face the facts head-on. Never sleeping with anyone else for the rest of my life seems hard to believe, but when I lie next to Gareth on our lumpy futon and he pulls me closer to him like I am the most interesting book he could ever wish to read in his sleep, I could believe anything. Whenever you choose to spend the bulk of your time and energy with one person, you are to some extent closing yourself off to that intensity with others. I believe this to be a valuable path to a deeper self-understanding. But where does it leave your friends?

Marriage, for all its celebration of love, is also about broken hearts. I know, I know, we are all told that marriage is about a bringing together, a mingling of hearts and families. While this is true, it leaves out what such a step signals for friendship, especially female friendship. Long the subject of feminist analysis, female friendship is of central importance to any understanding and/or change young women might bring to the institutions of marriage and feminism. Indeed, I found the reaction of three of my closest friends to my impending marriage—Astrid and my two former roommates, Anna and Sarah—to mirror current feminist debates about the meaning of marriage, couplehood and friendship. While Astrid's tone was one of chagrin and anger, Anna and Sarah wholeheartedly supported whatever I wanted to do. They teared up at the thought of this imposition into our threesome, but they decided at the outset to be there for me in whatever capacity I needed.

But first, an introduction. When I moved to Milwaukee from Los Angeles for graduate school in 1991, I had no idea that America's Dairyland would provide the kind of experiences I had only dreamed about in my terribly geeky teenage years in California's San Fernando Valley. I spent my adolescent years compulsively watching MTV, spraying my hair with Aqua Net and planning what poem I would quote when I met Sting. Being two thousand miles from home and in a community where you can meet most of the interesting people within a few months allowed me to reinvent myself. I met Anna and Sarah—best friends who looked like the coolest girls at every gathering—fairly quickly and was immediately besotted. On the afternoon I finally sat down in their big pink kitchen, drinking lemonade spiked with cheap beer and sprigs of mint, with Liz Phair playing on the crummy boom box in the corner, I knew I was home.

I couldn't believe my luck to have met these fantastic, beautiful girl-artists who dressed extravagantly, cooked four-course dinners on a whim and listened to Leonard Cohen (even the new stuff!). They had won a dance marathon at eighteen and gone to Jamaica on the prize money. Once Sarah got so angry that she poured orange paint all over Anna's bed. Anna was locally famous for making silver headless-mermaid jewelry and for hand-painting designs on her tights. One night when I was particularly anxious about something so meaningless I can't even remember it, the girls distracted me by sneaking us through the backyards of the lakefront mansions to go swimming in our clothes. All this glamour and fun was mine for the taking, and with a few adjustments in my old-fashioned need for a full night's sleep and the Valley Girl conviction that shoes and purses should match, I was living a life I thought existed only in mid-eighties Bananarama videos. Anna and Sarah had been a support system for each other for more than five years. When I joined them, they became my second family. They offered a wonderful chick-positive environment, where—though we were all boy-crazy—our alliances were first and foremost with each other. Their house was, no doubt about it, Girl Central. I soon moved in.

I remember awakening from one of those three-hour midweek naps in which only students, the ill and the unemployed can indulge. As always, I awoke startled, with my heart pounding: Am I late for a class? Is something due? What day of the week is it? Where am I supposed to be? Soft laughter and the sounds of Joan Armatrading entered my consciousness as I kicked open my door a crack to see Anna and Sarah treating the wood floor in the kitchen. The kitchen opened out onto a slanted roof garden covered in tarpaper and Astroturf, lined with sunflowers planted in toilets painted in psychedelic swirls of color. The sun was setting, and the light coming through the leaded glass kitchen window bounced off Anna's thrift-store collection of state souvenir pottery and the glass marbles on the windowsill. Though I would come to hate having this room (it's too near where everyone congregates drunk at parties), I felt a rush of thankfulness and pleasure so intense that it almost immediately made me sad. I call it pre-nostalgia.

Anna and Sarah constructed this house as a girly paradise. Almost every flat surface was painted. The house was huge, pink inside and out, and stretched long and wide. A former dance hall from the twenties, it had a sprung wood floor, elegantly curved walls and a living room accessible only by walking through the mint-green-tiled bathroom. Its attic was stuffed with vintage clothes and a ten-foot-tall table of elements from an abandoned warehouse downtown. The main living-room furniture was a large bed on an iron frame, covered with pillows. Common activities during my time there were spending hours dressing up to go out (always the most fun part of the evening); spending an entire afternoon ripping up magazines to make a mix-tape cover for a new crush; and taking part in elaborate ceremonies like the funeral we held for the house's blue Japanese fighting fish, who finally had given up his lonely life after one too many ash-strewn parties. It was 1993, the height of Northwest grunge, but it might as well have been the Jazz Age to me.

The pink house was magical, no doubt about it, and adamantly girl-centered. But, although Anna and Sarah wouldn't hesitate to call themselves feminists, the house was not outwardly political. Rather, it was instead gender conscious. In "Fear of Feminism: Why Young Women Get the Willies" (*Ms.*, November/December 1994), Lisa Maria Hogeland defines gender consciousness as, among other things, "our self-awareness as women . . . an appreciation of things pertaining to women." She argues that feminism, on the other hand, politicizes gender consciousness, cutting through girl-power marketing strategies, and "inserts it into a systematic analysis of histories and structures of domination and privilege." Though the differences between gender consciousness and feminism proper are very subtle, and indeed, the two bleed into each other, I can still say that the pink house vibe was more about female alliance than feminist analysis. Even though we spent more time with one another than with the men in our lives (which contributed to the end of one of my relationships), the feminist connection was implicit but not explicit: We all knew, for example, how much being judged by our appearance was wrong and patriarchal, but we still took pleasure in modeling outfit after outfit and raiding one another's makeup bins.

But Anna and Sarah and our Bananarama lifestyle made up only half of my identity. I was, and am, an academic, and my friendships outside the pink house were chiefly with other graduate students. My first meeting with Astrid embodied this collision of cultures. I was a few minutes late to the beginning-of-semester meet 'n' greet. I rushed in, breathless and carrying my belongings in a red, cinnamon-scented plastic bag, the only one I could find in the pink house that morning. I don't remember much about my first impression of the other students at the meeting, but I noticed Astrid right away. Befitting her name, she was very Danish-cool, with her long, thick blond hair pulled back, tasteful silver rings and oversize man's watch. My hair was curly at the time, and dyed a gorgeous shade of eggplant that unfortunately had faded into a pinkish, dry bird's nest of a mistake. I think I had to ask to borrow someone's pen. Later, Astrid told me that when I dashed in with that big bag and that hair she felt like she was in a scene from *Desperately Seeking Susan*. An enduring and often cantankerous friendship began.

No stranger to pink-house shenanigans herself, and a fan in many ways, Astrid pinpointed what would later become a pressing domestic dilemma. At one gathering there, she leaned in to me and, between giggles, said, "This place is so great. But how do you ever get any work done?" The feminist-studies work she was talking about, as alluded to earlier, had everything to do with our subsequent fights about my decision to marry. Anna and Sarah considered (as I do to a certain extent) deciding to marry (or not) an individual choice predicated on the freedom of individual choice that itself forms the basis for feminism. But the feminist belief system Astrid and I share would not let me off so easily; it instead demanded theoretical inquiry into the very notions of freedom, choice, politics and individuality. She would just as easily say something like, "So why do you think you're buying so many clothes you can't afford this week?" as she'd say, "Nice jacket, is it new?"

I needed, and do need, both kinds of feminism—and both kinds of friends. Feminism allows me to say "fuck off" to patriarchal expectations of behavior and bearing, as well as to dress as I want (in spike heels or a wedding dress, or both). Feminism also prods me to analyze what it is about spike heels and wedding dresses I find so compelling, and where the cultural constructs undergirding my desire for such things come from. I can't just view feminism as offering me an out to do whatever I want without the accompanying analysis of the influences and pressures upon that want. It's exhausting, but I couldn't imagine it any other way.

Of course, these categories of playful girl-centric feminists versus those committed to rigorous analysis are to a large extent artificial. After all, it's not as if you can't wear platform shoes and fishnets while reading *Ms.* on the bus. In fact, I'm sure Astrid has. I am by no means trying to imply that as a feminist one has to be one or the other—although people often expect it. As with the surprise that people register with the way Gareth and I live—not acting appropriately "married" according to their conventional definitions of the term—so too could I be called out for not acting appropriately feminist, according to one limited definition. Getting married meant, depending whether you asked Astrid or Anna and Sarah, that I was either a "bad" feminist (apolitical, engaged in the worst elements of heterosexual privilege) or a "good" one (believing that feminism is above all the permission to make individual decisions apart from anyone's expectations of you to do otherwise). Rather than feeling like it was more complicated, and that I was being both good and bad in differing ways, choosing to get married made me feel as if I had to align with one side or another. Through my friendships, I saw these feminist conflicts in exaggerated relief.

However, my internal struggles with the pink house and feminism (in addition to my ideological wranglings with Astrid) started long before the marriage plans. Certainly, the house was perfect for me before I began writing my dissertation, when I was dragging myself to a bookstore job that started at 10 A.M., full of embarrassing memories and a killer hangover. It was heaven before prelim exams and independent study sessions, when I felt as inclined to build a kite on a Saturday afternoon as to finish a paper. Sarah and Anna were not frivolous by any means; the discussions we had well into the night around that kitchen table were about loss, one's place in the world, the pain of affairs, the fucked-upness of family. But we didn't spend much time delving into the connection between gender and politics, and I never felt like my serious academic side, the one that was writing papers about this very thing, was adequately recognized. Saying "I have to work on my essay today, so I can't go with you on the picnic where everyone will be dressed as Frida Kahlo and there will be a talent show" made me seem more like a spoilsport than the girl-power feminist I (also) was. I was more inclined to get extra sleep so as to get some serious reading done the next day than to stay up 'til 3 A.M. making a surrealist film about the *Challenger* explosion.

I met Gareth at the time when my need to focus on academics over pink-house projects was intensifying. I don't profess to know anything about fate or if I even believe in it, so this confluence of emotional readiness and circumstance remains unexplained. I do know that I began hanging out with Gareth, a recent grad of my PhD program, because he was wickedly funny, sarcastic and smart. I liked how his shaved head, dark eyebrows and chlorine-blue eyes made him look like a cross between a science-fiction villain and a Wim Wenders angel. He is as much a fan of *SportsCenter* as of Zora Neale Hurston. He likes Bioré strips almost as much as I do. His favorite movie is *Reds*. His second-favorite is *Clueless*. How could I not fall in love? But while he liked and respected the Pinkies, he was very clearly a foreign element (literally, being from Wales). Quiet, shy and inclined to bursts of silly rhymes in his underwear only when alone with me, he struck Sarah and Anna as slightly cold, not at all spontaneous and fundamentally uninterested in films about space travel made in the wee hours.

It's not that Gareth and I didn't, or don't, have fun, but rather that we share a serious pleasure in intellectual inquiry and good writing. We get off on philosophical debates and entire days in bookstores. As my relationship with Gareth developed, I was more than ready to leave the pink house. I wanted to indulge my quiet, serious side. I wanted to live with the person I slept with most of the time, not with my best friends and three other people who might crash out on the floor after returning from a sailboating trip in Australia. I was embracing the giving-up of girlhood that commitment to a partner necessitates. I wanted a higher ratio of stability in my life.

Astrid supported my need for a different environment and, I might add, my relationship with Gareth (before the wedding announcement). However, after her reaction to my impending nuptials, I spent less time with her, instead viewing myself as more of a gender-conscious girl-power feminist. In the face of her criticism, it was simply easier for me to be on the side of personal choice—the same kind of argument used to support breast implants or a stripping career unequivocally.

Couple my own political ambivalence about the institution of marriage (though not the man with whom I was entering it) with Astrid's uncanny inability to let sleeping feminist dogs lie, and there's gonna be trouble in Friendship City. My ambivalence goes back not only to my own experiences as a child of a divorce and a bitter (is there any other kind?) custody battle, but also to effective feminist and gay rights arguments against marriage. Though I believe, as do other lefty married friends, that avoiding something (marriage) will not effect political change of that thing (e.g., legalizing marriage for gays and lesbians), it still brings up some sticky ethical issues. Would those of us having alterna-Unitarian ceremonies with vows taken from Thich Nhat Hanh feel as comfortable toasting everlasting love with marijuana brownies by the beach if interracial marriage were outlawed? How about if adopting a husband's name were still a prerequisite? Why would anyone want to take part in a ritual originating in the notion of women as property to be passed from the father to the husband?

The logical objections to marriage are many, and I am not willing to answer those objections with an "I did it because I love him" non sequitur. Although marriage is an ethically shaky proposition, I was going through with it anyway. At a practical level, we had to do the legal thing to stay together. (Without citizenship, Gareth's visa issues would have constrained our mobility—of central importance in the academic job market.) This puts me in a precarious position. Marriages that have as their *only* purpose a green card can pass feminist analytical muster because they are a trick on the legalized system of heterosexual privilege. I didn't have this excuse, because I do love Gareth and am committed to sticking to this relationship through poverty, illness, boredom, temptation and differences in decorating tastes (there's still a bit of pomo pink-house hippie girl in me that wants to paint each wall in our apartment a different color). Gareth is my partner, the person with whom I see myself raising a kid and growing old. Though he is cynical and sometimes awkward in social situations, he loves me with a patience and joy that still knocks me out. I knew how easy it was to leave an otherwise good relationship because of boredom or crushes, and frankly, I was tired of that. I didn't think Gareth would make all those feelings go away (a mistake I think a lot of serial monogamists make), but he is someone I want to force myself not to run from when the going gets tough. I like the idea of a covenant, a promise that makes it just a little bit harder to walk away from something so good. So while I can say that I got married for legal purposes, I still did it for love.

Thus, I had no rejoinder to those who might criticize marriage, except for a version of "I agree, and I don't want to talk about it." I like to debate issues, not personal dilemmas, which always seem beyond the grasp of much theorizing. I don't strive or expect to understand other people's decisions, but Astrid almost always does. I sometimes find myself feeling like a flabby and overly ambivalent feminist around her. She is a difficult-to-attain ideal of feminist ethics—a supermodel, if you will—whereas while I know very well why I spend too much money or make out with a local band member in a rusty Toyota Tercel at two-thirty in the morning the week my dissertation proposal is due, I do it anyway. It's not that Astrid doesn't understand this; she just expects me to theorize it when the only thing I want to do is bury my hungover head into the pillow and pretend everything is fine. Or go shopping. Or get married.

With Astrid, I couldn't argue my way out of a paper bag and began to resent that I even had to try. When we would go out, we tried to talk (albeit awkwardly) about other things, until she found some way to insert a questioning of my motives in what often felt like an entirely roundabout way:

ME: I think I'll have a cinnamon roll with pecans; God, two-fifty for a roll seems pricey.

HER: Yeah, these alterna-cafes are just as pricey as Starbucks, but they think because they sell additive-free cigarettes and hang up photos of motorcycles that they're actually different. Kind of like people who rewrite marriage vows to pretend they're not really participating in a system of heterosexual privilege, dontcha think?

Such confrontations continued off and on for months. I would argue that as a friend she had a responsibility to accept me unconditionally; she would argue that I couldn't expect her to accept something so clearly against the political beliefs we shared. Plus, she would rightly point out, I had almost all of society on my side, from *A Wedding Story* on cable TV to bridal registries, which encourage you to shop, shop, shop without paying for a thing.

It became harder and harder for me to spend time with Astrid. I was angry, of course, and I was also tired and conflicted about the decision. So it became a circle as vicious as a diamond-encrusted wedding band. See, not only was I getting married, but I was proving one of her main points: Marriage is designed to keep women at a distance from each other in favor of a more "serious" heterosexual bond, one you can't have with "just a friend." At the same time, Anna and Sarah became a refuge. Though Sarah had decided to move to San Francisco later that year, and Anna was forming new alliances with a group of community artists and performers, there was no doubt that they would attend the wedding and be supportive in every way. Sarah and Anna came up with a girly ritual to send me on my way involving alcohol, flower petals, three cut strands of my pubic hair and a version of "light as a feather, stiff as a board" where I was ceremoniously carried out onto the balcony in the middle of the night and accidentally burned on the back of my thigh with a curling iron (don't ask).

In the three years since the wedding, Sarah has moved, and she recently came back to visit with her baby son in tow. Carrying on the pink-house tradition, he is a fifteen-month-old bundle of smiles and flesh, completely dedicated to laughter and the appreciation of shiny and brightly colored objects. When I hung out with her again, it was like no time had passed. Just last weekend, Anna and I spent a wonderful Sunday repainting the pink house's window frames a dark forest green. The only argument we had was about color choice. "Isn't pink and green kind of, well, an eighties preppy thing?" I wondered. She stamped her yellow rattan platform–sandaled feet and said, "Why should we give those colors to the preps? Monet invented this color combination at Giverny, so fuck that!" I still miss my time with them, and I hate getting older. It's not pre-nostalgia anymore.

Astrid and I still struggle along, our friendship combining awkward and angry moments along with intense and incredibly fulfilling confessions about our lives and our emotional motivations. Most recently, we went out for a drink after not seeing each other for a few months (due to geographic rather than emotional distance). I told her I was writing on this subject and that I couldn't remember when we stopped arguing about my decision. I couldn't for the life of me recall a final blowup, a door-slamming discussion. She said, "I think we just stopped arguing after you did it, after you got married."

My experience shows how intense female bonds embody a continuous struggle, rhetorically and emotionally—to get at the heart of being a feminist, and a friend. This piece began as an argument about marriage, but I realize it has ended up as a dedication. At its worst, marriage and its accompanying valorization of the heterosexual bond makes you take your friends lightly. We still have no official legal bonds or rituals honoring our commitment to friends. But at its best, marriage foregrounds how the self is identified in relationships to others, and not just with husbands and boyfriends. I bless my conflicts with these women and hereby dedicate my marriage to them. Though I don't know if marriage is a politically justifiable act, I am sure of how indelibly my friends make up the strange ball of desires and convictions that is me. My life with Gareth is a living monument to them, more vital than any dress wrapped up in cellophane. If I actually believed in such things, I would toast them with pink champagne and personalized matchbooks with the words "Anna, Astrid, Sarah and Jen, June 25, 2000."

Pillow Talk

Maria Raha

In the middle of a beer, in the middle of the night, in the backyard, on the first clear night of spring, when we are waiting. Waiting to climb into bed and draw maps of desire on each other's waiting breathing laughing stomachs and chests, when there are still globes and worlds left to explore. Comfortable but not too comfortable, still excited, still staring at each other's lips as we speak. As always, I'm trying so hard to tell you in some way other than letting it fall to the table in a clump of mud or clay or a heavy ton of bricks you can't possibly elevate or diminish.

I want to explain myself without using the words. I want you to instinctively know, so that we can move on and get in bed and marvel at our flesh and not think about it. But I've not thought about it before, and have ended up with lovers telling me I use it as an excuse; that with me, sex is miserable. "It" is always thought about. It is why you can never direct me. It is why I can't fall asleep without the sound of noxious sitcom reruns, to keep me from jumping at every little shift in the trees outside my window; why I slide a switchblade into my beat-up black boots; why I wait in anxiety for everyone to abandon me. It is why friends tell me I'm distant; why I can't confront your sour moods and sandpaper words. I'm always anticipating a confrontation too deep for me to handle; in fact, it is why I know there are things too deep for me to handle. I've visited those oceans and they've dragged me under.

It is why I am always suspicious of drinks bought for me, compliments, gifts, favors and anything that makes me in some way submissive. I'm suspicious of smiling, strange men; of any man who walks behind me; of the military; of men in groups of any kind. It's why I can never tell the difference between sarcasm and cruelty; why I think my writing is terrible; why I will always relay the ugliest stories I have about myself; and why I prowl like a panther instead of merely walking, to reassure myself and smiling, strange men that I am the hunter and not the hunted, and that I will never be the hunted again.

It is also the reason I pay attention to the struggle of women worldwide. It's how I learned that my own strength and love and compassion might just conquer the world. It's how I taught myself to rely on my own sense of self-love and beauty rather than on the approval of someone else; it's helped me become a pacifist and a lover of the struggle. For all the ways it puts me in a box, it's created a sea that carries me, too. I learned to build a life out of anguish. Maybe that's the most important lesson a survivor of violent crime can learn. Of course, the other lesson, the more immediate lesson for survivors, includes forcing ourselves to salvage roses from the fire for the rest of our time on this planet.

Even now, in all my empowered educated kick-ass feminista womanista enlightened glory, the dread still sits in my stomach: that you'll ask me how it happened, and inevitably I'll feel as suffocated as I did ten years ago. As if I asked him to shove me to the floor of a cold, rocking van; as if I asked him to cover my mouth with his arms and talk to me about my virginity. Talk me out of my virginity. Beat me out of my virginity. Steal away in the middle of the night with my used, beat-up, ripped underwear shaking like a Jell-O casserole on the cold metal floor. My big fat scarlet letter *A*, my own personal witch-burning. A trial I put myself through every time, uninvited by you or any of the other men I've had to come out to. My mouth still chatters insistently with what I was wearing, how much I had to drink, who he was, where he came from and how hard I worked to fight back, without knowing how to, until I couldn't fight anymore. I still have to convince you, convince myself, convince anyone who knows me that I wasn't asking for it.

I'm tired of having something to reveal. As a Catholic-school girl, I always hated confession. I never really took it seriously. I was always searching for something to tell the red-faced priest who looked as if he had held his breath for the last twenty years. I would sit in the church and choke on the incense and think really hard of some sinful things that would really wow him. All these years later, I wish I could sit just once in this backyard with my legs wrapped around you and the moths moondancing above us, spinning like halos, with the stereo blasting, and really have to think hard to remember what was the biggest, most earthshattering thing that's ever happened to me. I want to be able to search for something and not have it sitting there on the top of my skull and all over my hips and all over these pages, one by one, that all seem to fall back to the night ten years ago that becomes more vivid with each confession, each coming-out story, each dream, each time you climb on top or under and let me go; each time I won't let go all the way because I can't lose that much control, not with you or anyone.

I wonder whether you understand what this means. I'm suspicious of your wide embrace around the cool air that sifts from my eyes and across the invisible walls between us. I can't let go of you right now, as you apologize for another man's agonizing anger and destruction. No apology is good enough, even the one that would come if my little bad-girl kick-ass feminista dream came true: the one where he is underneath my beat-up black boots, bloodied and unrecognizable and really, really hurt, writhing, pleading for forgiveness. Even if all that materialized, I don't know that any apology would be good enough. So I'll just sit here and hug you, feeling once again wrapped in a short spurt of safety, and not say a word after I tell you he raped me, only explaining that I was in so much pain, in a house full of guests, that I didn't tell a soul. I was in so much pain and disbelief and misery, lonely at seventeen, lonely with my cunt pounding like a heart, with my heart broken, that I wound around my drunk, oblivious, sleeping friends who were scattered all over that summer house like dirty laundry, and walked up a flight of stairs that seemed to go on forever to find a place to lay my body down. I'll stop there, to let you hold me and kiss me and apologize for another man's hatred for me and for women and for himself.

But there's more and more and more to it, the way wine spills on clothing and spreads itself out like oil or blood or floods from a river. It snakes out like veins into everything else I've been, in good ways and bad ways and all the ways in between. And every layer of this mess must be revealed to you. To make you understand. I still can't understand why I have to do this every time, why all the words in the world aren't enough to really get to the bottom of this. I think I keep telling you as a test, although every man I've ever told has reacted initially in this very same way, and eventually has needed comforting of his own. I have comforted men in bed, explaining that when my thoughts crawl deep, deep into the back of my mind, I can't stop to catch them, and I can't continue lying there, underneath a heavy body drilling into me, insisting that my reaction has nothing to do with them.

It doesn't happen very often—only once in a while, really—but when it does, no man will ever come get me from that place, set miles into the back of my mind. I've become used to that. You will pick yourselves up and roll over onto your backs, huffing, staring at the ceiling, wondering out loud if you did something wrong: wondering out loud if I equate you with the gritty animal maleness I've seen before. Sweating and hungry, you lie there trying to encourage me to admit aloud that you're not him. But when I'm gone to that place so far away, a place I can't even describe, where there are no doors and no light and no talk, I get stuck there, in a maze of thought and empty, screaming, bursting tears. It's not like dangling from the lip of a well, where a man's white-knuckled grip might be able to keep me from hitting bottom.

I know you're not the same as he is. But when you're huffing and puffing and wanting to be cooed at like a child or a kitten, you make me feel as if I have to take care of you. And, damn it, I'm fucking *tired* of having to explain it, of having to go through this over and over and over again, in every bed, with every lost body, in every set of deep and beautiful brown or blue eyes, in a soft voice that needs to be *heard* instead of encouraging. "You didn't do anything wrong, baby, it just happens sometimes." Not once have any of you asked me to express anything beyond that. Not once has it, from that point on, been about me—as if it's harder to be the man dating a survivor of rape than it is to be the survivor. Poor things. What you're really dating is a kick-ass little bad-girl empowered goddess feminista womanista who doesn't have time to climb all the way out of the holes I've been pushed into to chase your egos around. Instead of saying, "You didn't do anything wrong, baby, it just happens sometimes," I want to be saying, "Don't let the door hit you on the ass on the way out." That's really how I feel, when you lift your sweating pounding skin off me and start sighing, because I was in some place I couldn't control, some van, ten years old now, thinking of alien fingers and coercive grunting and hands over my pleading mouth. So don't make me take care of you, 'cause to be perfectly honest, I don't have the time. I'm too busy sorting all of these moments into piles of "to be remembered" and "to be forgotten" and "to be determined" to help you work through my past.

I'm willing to do that, you know. I'm willing to take your hand and lead you over the small rocks that traipse across the middle of a deep creek; move the prickly briar bush out of the way so you can find your way through the woods without hurting your face and eyes and arms. But not now, not in bed, not when I'm stuck in a big, gaping black hole in the dark, naked and close to losing control and feeling so much like I could climb into that embrace that sits in the space between you and me and live there. And maybe this is a truth I should tell you straight away: In the end, you better believe I will always make myself comfortable and safe first, even if it means you get hit in the face with a few briar bushes, or that you sink to the bottom of the creek without a hand to guide you across. I will always take the time I need to escape the black spaces in my sometimes-heavy head, to walk away from the discomfort, to let myself feel the discomfort and the ache and the isolation without having to mother you at the same time.

I have done this all on my own, you see. I left the van alone. I lay down alone. I woke up alone; nursed my aching cunt alone; let my body become the dumping ground for food, alcohol, semen, cocaine, marijuana, crack, LSD, crystal meth, Ecstasy, cigarettes, caffeine. I washed myself out alone; I rehabilitated myself. I described that night when I was ready. I educated women about that night when I was ready. I've been educating ever since, everyone I know, every man I love, every man I let see me all bared down and weak and still, somewhere, naive. I kicked most of my dirty habits alone, live alone, write alone, love alone, clean alone, think alone, eat alone, cook for one, sing for myself, go to the movies alone. I've done this by myself. Which is fine—I like it. It's the best education I've ever gotten. When I do it alone so often, though, it's hard to tune out the hum in my skull once it has begun. And having done this whole let's-lie-in-the-dark-until-one-of-us-lets-the-other-feel-safe thing over and over again, I can promise you that I have learned my lesson about that first reaction, the one I've seen one hundred times.

When you opened your arms and covered me, I realized that every one of these embraces feels the same—like I want to stay in that one heavy and brooding and passionate moment forever, safe and away from the haunting fear he's created and time has nurtured. I thought I needed you boys to validate me, but maybe what I really crave is proof that you're not all like him. Maybe that's why I can't know one of you for more than a few weeks before I tell you. Before I go through it, again and again. I need you all to actively prove to me that he is not inside you.

I have to tell you, straight away, that with a few exceptions, I can see him in many of you, when you huff and puff and roll over and don't take the time to understand that earth will not stop its rotation because you didn't come. I hate to break it down like that, so bluntly and so unrefined, but that's what I see. I see boys who didn't get off, turning their blue balls into blue boy who needs the attention of a woman whose attentions can be so unreliable. She's busy nursing the lost, lonely aching girl she is trying to put to rest, like she went to rest ten years ago, after he wrestled her to the ground and dug around inside her until his fear of getting caught stopped him. All the attention some boys need when they haven't gotten laid because their lover is injured and exhausted are pieces of him bleeding, sweating, panting through and showing me their face. I can't give him any part of me anymore. If he shines through in some part of your reaction, I'm going to have to cut you off.

Turning over in the midst of horrible pain and anguish to face a man in my bed is something I've always done. I've always taken the empty parts of me and filled them with a companion. It's easier and quicker and, of course, safer to take care of something outside of my own chest and fluttering stomach on the brink of disaster than to face myself, my empty bed, my silent apartment. As a western, middle-class woman, I have always been taught to be accommodating and nurturing and loving, as long as it's not for myself. That, we say of women, is selfish. So I'm just setting it out on the table for you, like all of this other stuff I'm laying on you, like sour milk. I'm selfish. I can't roll over and swallow the burn of tears in my throat and ask you if you're okay. I'm way beyond that. In the scheme of things, taking care of you would last a few minutes, but I will have to live forever with the knowledge that I sacrificed myself again for the body next to mine.

When I'm there, by myself, with my mouth paralyzed and my back up against the wall, let me be a sad, battered and confused seventeen-year-old again. Let me sit in bed with a pillow between my legs and have my hair stroked and the seemingly endless faucets of tears wiped dry. Make me a drink, paint my toenails, braid my hair, read me a story. Read me the story I wrote—the one about the cleaned-up, strong and careful woman who attends her rapist's wedding, punches the groom and takes the bride out for a beer. Read me any story, because when the hurt sets in I want to retaliate with these muffled, strangled, hiding, incomprehensible thoughts. I'm paralyzed because there are memories I can't reach and feelings I can't define. The less I talk, and the more I seem neglectful, the more I am trying to climb into these crashing and burning moments and spaces and chasms. The more frustrated you become, the less clear this garden of madness becomes. Half of me feels estranged, unable to listen to her crying little sister when I can see the landscape of your back out of the corner of my eyes and feel your glare bouncing off the eavesdropping walls. I would much rather see your eyes, silent and open and caressing, than feel as if I'm on the edge of an avalanche of distracting, detracting questions.

Just let me know I don't need to figure this out alone and that I don't need to figure it out for you, too. Let me know it with whatever creativity you can find for a sad, lonely, confused, angry and afraid little girl who's dying to be let out. And maybe, with a guide—one who will let her wander around in bed, in the dark, in peace—everything that's wrapped and bundled will explode with joy all over these sheets and this room. And then I can take you to those black spaces and show you around. We can trade secrets in the dark.

I'm proud to be a strong, self-made, self-sculptured woman. I'm proud of the mind that can entertain me for days, months, years, minutes. As with anything deep and long and brilliant, there are many, many sides, angles, complexities, widths, breadths, dimensions. And as with anything human and living and struggling, the sides, angles, complexities, injuries, flaws and weaknesses aren't pretty and perfect and built just right, discrete. I can't pretend they are. I will never again deny myself the right to run into the corner of the room and curl up like a fetus and let myself go in a torrent of anger or bile or terror, because that's exactly what makes a woman deep and long and brilliant, like me.

Raw Material

Sonya Huber

Twice in the past four years I have sat with a man and talked about the food to serve at our wedding. Once it was going to be catered with smoked barbecued ribs; the other time it was going to be a buffet of Chicago's ethnic fare. Once I got a diamond ring, and once I got a ten-dollar silver band from a cart in the mall. Both times I bolted, earning sympathetic smiles from my friends and comparisons to Julia Roberts in *Runaway Bride*. I felt like a failure announcing both breakups to family and friends, as if they would all think I'd nearly snatched stability from the jaws of bohemian aimlessness only to screw it up.

When I wake up from dreams where I am married to either man, I sigh with relief, feeling the weight of their troubles evaporate as I remember where I am. I took on both men as if they were projects, convinced I could help them become what I needed. I didn't believe in finding true love. Men are just too problematic, I thought, so I've got to start with a basically decent male and help him to mature.

The first time, the proposal—delivered over the glass-topped table of a Thai restaurant in Boston—was casual. Patrick wore jeans and took the white carnation from the vase on the table. I

126

said yes and meant it 100 percent, overwhelmed with a giddy, picked-for-the-school-play feeling. The relationship took a year and a half to fall apart. With Mike, the proposal was romantically choreographed, a surprise with a diamond ring and a dozen red roses in the front hall of our apartment. By the time we arrived at the fanciest Thai restaurant in Chicago an hour later, I knew with a flutter of panic in my chest that I had screwed up—we already had discussed a breakup and this was no way to resolve it. Within four months, we were living in different states.

Aside from the fact that Thai restaurants play an ominous role in my love life, what have I learned? Those four words—Will you marry me?—represent a major commitment, but they can't magically transport a relationship to a new level. Both times "yes" flew out of my mouth, I imagined I was being promised a new view of my man, like marriage was a little door we could step through and everything would change. He'd start to deliver on all those promises and expectations I'd been socking away like extra twist ties and paper bags. While I never idealized men, I idealized the transformation that marriage would bring, without any evidence that it could occur. Girls—if you don't have your dream relationship by the time he asks, say no. Let's practice. "Oh, Howard, thanks . . . but no thanks." Because it might not get better—you'll probably just get more of the same.

I believe in feminist revolution, in fighting for an ideal world. Yet with individual men, I have clung to fantasies of deliverance and slow reform, taking what I can get and trying to make it livable. Even though I'm all for fifty-fifty, mature relationships, I tossed that goal out the window in practice, figuring it was ridiculous and unattainable. I did retain some litmus tests for my raw husband-material: He needed to have good politics, be an organizer by background. He needed to be able to make me laugh and make me come. And I needed to fall in love with him. Any other problems, even if they were obvious and he wasn't taking steps to fix them, were not important enough to hold me back.

I didn't really believe a guy could make me happy as he was—I had to make him, fight to create him out of the frightening soup of testosterone and bacon grease and skin that is a man. I grew up in a world where men sometimes expressed their creativity through chaos, broke things and fathered children here and there. They dragged their emotions after them like broken legs or bombs with lit fuses. Secretly, I wanted some cheesy fantasy like Eric Stolz's character in *Some Kind of Wonderful,* an eighties teen movie about a soulful painter with a good heart who realizes he wants the drummer chick, the weirdo who's devoted to him, instead of the airbrushed high-society babe. I wanted to be that drummer chick. I wanted a strong man who was the creative type, who had a heart and did impulsive, kind things. I wanted a man who would pay his bills and also buy me flowers, whom I would be able to trust with a child and who could hold his own in a conversation about feelings. Are there men out there like that? Yeah, right, sure—in the movies. And in my attempt to be realistic, to avoid being alone and to protect myself through cynicism and practicality, I ended up settling for, and saying yes to, a man I was intending to change or help. Twice.

When I was four, I played bride, slinging my ratty blanket over my head for a veil, walking down the aisle in front of the TV in our living room. I knew I'd find a husband, because that's what happened to little girls when they grew up. By junior high, I was devoted to the show *Family Ties.* Michael J. Fox's fictional parents, the ex-hippies Steven and Elyse Keaton, seemed to have an ideal marriage. They wore blue jeans and got perplexed when their kids did something wrong. They struggled with issues, one episode at a time, and worked through them all. I had never met a hippie or an ex-hippie, but Mr. Right would be relaxed, a nice guy with a distinct personality. He would have passions and his own life and would have things he wanted to do. He wouldn't leave you holding the groceries or the kids. He would respect his woman always, would shoulder half the burden.

When the closing credits rolled on *Family Ties,* I didn't want to admit that I'd never witnessed a Steven and Elyse relationship. My parents have a loving but traditional marriage. When crises hit, my mother carried the emotional weight of us all. I burst into tears one day in seventh-grade gym class, standing in the grass behind Oakview Junior High trying to shoot an arrow at a target. My dad had taken me on a drive to Kmart the night before and had asked me what I thought about him leaving for a while, going down to Florida to sort out his head, escape from money pressures and from us. I cried not because I didn't want him to leave but because I hated the adult responsibility that went with that question, and the idea that he couldn't handle things.

My mom then threatened to take the RV and leave, like a game of chicken. Neither of them did, in the end, and they worked it all out in some way that I don't remember. The way I understood it, my mother and her iron will forced the issues; she made the threats and succeeded in pulling my father back from the brink. It seemed to me that he was a less crazed and more aware person afterward, because she'd threatened to leave and won. My mother's advice for her daughters in relationships is "You have to make compromises." That, combined with the example of her actions, meant "You have to work like hell at this." That's great advice if you're in an eighteen-year marriage with three kids. But I took it as advice on dating and starting a relationship, in a world where my options were much wider than hers had been.

I also learned about marriage through family stories that fascinated me, told at wakes and late at night over wine or beer: spouses attacking each other and husbands nailing rooms shut with wives trapped inside. In my family, women seem to have two choices. One is to become a nun: Three of my dad's sisters are in a convent, and the fourth used to be. Or you can get married, bite onto a scrap of leather for strength and wait for an explosion or several, which might or might not culminate in him leaving you a few kids later. I developed the opinion that every man has a fuse which can be lit to create chaos. Even though there are calm, cooperative men in my family, I focused on the wild ones. I thought you had to say the vows, then plant your feet firmly, hands spread apart, ready to wrestle with a bear.

We did not have enough lentils to make a cold salad, and the floor of the co-op where I lived was covered with black, brown and blue sleeping bags, flowered pillows. I ran up and down stairs hunting for duct tape for flyers, trying to find permanent markers and wondering who else could house the extra anarchists. It was 1992, and I was missing the main discussion in the Midwest Eco-Anarchist conference I'd helped to organize, because there were practical problems to attend to: food and shelter. The two guys I'd organized with were sitting in the conference room. I'd bowed out, playing the martyr and little anarchist wife, replaying the practical problem-solving role I'd learned (even though we were trying to make a new society).

In the year before the conference, I shaved my head, got a tattoo and left school, which provoked screaming fights on the phone with my mother. I lived in Minneapolis with an older political activist and her eight-year-old son. I worked in a coffee shop and was inducted into an anarchist political collective. We planned direct action, street theater and public plays to share our views on abortion on demand, Columbus Day and nuclear-waste storage. I was busy rejecting every controlling part of society.

Anarchism and the Minneapolis political scene of the early nineties taught me that we could create a new world by opting out of the mainstream and making our own institutions. If you didn't want to pay your money to some corporation, shop at the anarchist-run co-op. If you didn't want to support the entertainment beast, go to the performance-art parade in the park. If you didn't like the Gulf War, go and set fire to dumpsters, march in the street and spray paint and yell. All the women with whom I organized were kissing each other, and I did too, even though I always ended up on the floor in a sweaty knot with one of the anarchist boys at the end of the day. I never figured out an alternative way to set up a man-woman relationship, though.

I went back to school that winter and took a course on radical feminist philosophy. The key to a new nonsexist relationship seemed to lie in reformulating men. The best students in the class all seemed to be men intent on changing their gender identity, wearing nail polish and dressing in drag. They were interested in becoming something so different from traditional men by manipulating and rejecting the symbols of manhood. I struggled through the readings and stayed quiet in discussions, working with the abstractions of philosophy that didn't seem to apply to my daily life. If I wasn't willing to become a lesbian, to challenge and flip gender, no alternative seemed available.

I knew then, as I got serious with an anarchist boy and moved to Boston with him, that I wasn't going to get trapped in any marriage. When his mother gave us napkin rings for Christmas, I almost hyperventilated. I thought that we might get sucked into a marriage, as if it were a huge streetcleaner that would mow us down and wipe away our personalities. I figured it started with the napkin rings, and then I'd find myself at the altar. I ran away from that relationship, crushed when I saw us replaying traditional roles I thought we'd worked so hard to weed out.

In 1994, my friend Brooke and I sat at the Someday Cafe in Somerville, Massachusetts, drinking coffee and picking apart recent breakups. Whenever we got to the point where we felt, for a second, like we understood ourselves and had talked ourselves into believing things would get better, there was a silence. We'd look at each other, smile and shrug.

"But someday we'll have an anarchist school for girls, out in the country," she said, smiling.

"And we'll have cows. And we'll grow vegetables to make money," I said.

"And we'll write and do a magazine and have a studio where you can weld," she said. We kept adding wings to the anarchist school for girls. We talked about opening the Chaos Cafe, a place to meet folks, drink coffee, talk politics and build a new society.

"I think we should have a sperm bank with the cafe," Brooke said once. "That way we won't have to deal with men, but we can still have kids." Brooke was a lesbian who wanted a family, and she knew I worried about trying to find a man I could stay with. The sperm bank would solve the problem for both of us.

"Great," I said. "We'll call it Jack in the Box." We told all of our friends about that one, but nobody else found it as funny.

Around that time, I was dating in a frenzy: guitar boys and club boys and boys with cool accents, whomever, and making just enough money to cover food and rent. I fought myself into a major rift with my parents. Nothing in my life—not friends, job, relationship, city or family— was the same as the year before. I'd torn everything apart, and it had started to scare me.

The Jack in the Box idea, however funny, reflected a serious concern. The first of my friends got pregnant. I wanted kids, but it didn't seem possible on my income or with my solo lifestyle. On the other hand, it didn't seem possible to stay with a man.

Later that year I met Patrick, a thirty-six-year-old socialist, at an organizing meeting for an anti-Klan demonstration in Boston. I thought it was hilarious, at first, that the father of an eight-year-old would call me, pester me to meet him for a beer. I agreed to go because I was trying to be open-minded and because his disagreements with my anarchist politics challenged me. Then he appeared in a bar one night after the man I was in love with had stood me up. So we had a few more beers and I took him home.

He seemed stable compared to the anarcho-boys and band boys. He had been a carpenter, could put up drywall. He cleaned his apartment and his car meticulously, and he knew how to cook. His scarred hands could fix and break things. He was getting his PhD in history. He knew all about Marxism. He'd been politically active in the eighties, for God's sake, when I was in grammar school. He had history and lots of good stories. He had bright blue eyes and a cocky self-confidence, a terrible Irish accent when he was drunk. When I think of him, I remember him raising a pint of Bass in a hole-in-the-wall south Boston Irish bar, urging the other drunk Irish guys to sing along to folk songs on the jukebox. He was one of the fiercest, most intense men I'd ever met. Unlike the wishy-washy anarchist boys who didn't want to be men, this guy was a Guy. It seemed like another attractive rebellion to prove that I was tough enough to handle and mold this big-shouldered man.

I learned so much from him, but couldn't win an argument. He didn't believe in feminism; he said it was a middle-class fixation that divided the working class. He liked women's bodies and pushed me to wear things other than huge sweatshirts and my brother's old jeans. I felt sexy around him, physically desired. Because he'd been wild in his twenties and early thirties, I believed he'd already spent the chaos inside him and broken a few women's hearts, so he wouldn't break mine.

There were warning signs I chose to ignore. He borrowed gas money from me on our first date and often forgot or refused to pay his bills. On Valentine's Day 1996, after a year and a quarter of dating, he said, "I have something to ask you." He couldn't look at me.

What I thought was, Oh shit, he's going to ask me to borrow a lot of money. It had become a pattern, and I'd swallowed increasing resentment about it. When he asked me to marry him, I was shocked, and then thrilled. Now, I thought, it will get better between us. As if a few words could lay a foundation.

Patrick's proposal made me feel secure, real. Being able to tell co-workers and people I hardly even knew that I was engaged made me feel like a regular adult, despite all my crazy activism and my sailor's mouth and my wardrobe of clothes from high school and the thrift store. I assumed that marriage would help us achieve the stability I wanted. I don't think he agreed.

He was still married to but legally separated from the mother of his daughter. I had to tell him, eight months after he proposed, to hurry up and buy me a ring already—just something symbolic around which to build a little more of the dream. Even if he was a socialist, I was entitled to a little romance. I got a thick, scrolled ten-dollar silver band from the mall. Not that I'm into ostentation, but his choice of ring just added to the degradation of having to nag him for it. It should have been enough to clue me in, if I had been paying attention. When you have to nag, you're not going to get some heartfelt token of love. You're going to get something from Charlie's Discount X-treme Silver Cart.

I worked so hard to turn our little situation into the seeds of pre-wedding bliss, editing out of my memory all the nights I waited frantically for him to drive home drunk from a bar at two or three in the morning. I tried to play twentysomething stepmom to his daughter, but he didn't seem to care that she cut up my sweaters with scissors. She and I had a contentious, love-hate relationship, as only befits a preteen and her dad's young wife-to-be, but he seemed completely uninterested in our difficulties. I would slip into post-marriage fantasies when I found our financial and emotional chaos too overwhelming. Someday, I thought, if I just hold on, things will get better. This suffering is an investment in the future.

I tracked him down one night when he was three hours late to meet me. He was drunk out of his mind in an Irish bar, and we had a screaming fight in the doorway. I took off the ring he'd given me and drew my arm back to throw it at him, but I didn't let it fly. I walked off crying, unable to catch my breath and wondering whom I could call for help. I felt something break inside me—that stupid dream of joy. The look of hatred he gave me, standing in the doorway of that bar, had finally gotten through.

When we broke up a few months later, friends came out of the wood-work to say, "Thank god." I looked at them over coffee, hurt that they had not stepped in earlier to rouse me to consciousness, but almost all told me I wouldn't have listened anyway. I was deep in the throes of a desperate fantasy: Here was a man with problems, a man who drank too much, who didn't even try to manage his finances or plan his life in any way. Yet I was going to take him on, build a family around him, because he was good enough. It became an ego thing: I was as tough as other women in my family. I could handle shit and come out on top. I had started out wanting to escape from wild men, and I had come back to find my own.

My next lover was Patrick's polar opposite, a quiet, funny man who could have played Steven Keaton, a man who listened to me. I was mak-ing progress. Mike and I met as co-organizers for a political nonprofit devoted to national student organizing. We had great discussions about the civil rights and women's liberation movements, neither of which I knew much about. A strong group of feminist organizers in Florida had given Mike his political education; he gave me books on women's liberation as Christmas and birthday gifts, opening up my mind to wanting more from men. He owned a minivan, which screamed "dad material." He wanted to have kids, had a strong commitment to poli-tics and owned a thrilling library of books.

Around him I felt articulate and strong, because he pointed out my strengths constantly. Our first date was a student meeting at which we were the featured speakers. I almost puked with nervousness, but he supported me and then described everything I'd done right. Four months later, we declared our love for each other during a break in a frantic student activism conference that we organized in Washington, D.C. I slept on the floor of a dorm room in a sleeping bag next to his and kissed him after the students had fallen asleep.

I thought, okay, now I've got it right. This guy hardly drinks at all, is too young and gentle to even *want* to hurt anyone. He did tend to shut down in crises. He couldn't talk to me about what was going on in his heart or his life. That, I figured, was something I could help him fix. Here was raw material of a much finer grade. My work wouldn't be quite as demanding as it had been with Patrick. Within six months, I asked him if he ever wanted to get married. I was clear that marriage was my ticket to stability; I just needed the right guy to build it around. Mike, however, just shrugged, not ready to tell me what he dreamed about. That pattern continued.

We moved to Chicago together for a job I'd gotten at a political magazine. He was depressed for many reasons, including his heartbreak over the collapse of the nonprofit where we'd met and trouble with his family. I didn't know it—I just knew he seemed uninterested in me and in life. After nine months of trying to get him to talk to me, I gave him a deadline—"I'm leaving you by September 1, 1999." During a few months trying to hash stuff out, I wrestled with a quiet state of constant panic, not knowing how to fix my unhappiness. I had tried everything in my bag of tricks.

When he engineered the elaborate proposal, it broke my heart. Things were bad between us, but hey—here he was being enthusiastic about something. He went ring shopping all on his own. It was what I'd been working for, right? A real diamond ring from a good guy, a guy I loved. And he was a nice guy. A catch. He didn't hit me, didn't drink and wasn't married with a child. So, without being able to resist the static in my head, the image of a good guy down on his knee made me say yes. Once again, I figured that even if he wasn't pulling his weight I could take up the slack until I was able to educate him. In the months after the proposal, I was shocked to find that our problems didn't dissolve. He seemed, if anything, more complacent and less willing to address them—I'd said yes, after all.

Feminism and other political ideals gave me a clearer sense of myself and my own abilities, but these ideals could do little to shake my fundamental belief that men, no matter what political verbiage came out of their mouths, were still the weaker sex, the ones who would let women down. The separatist feminism I encountered at school only encouraged me to develop my "men as inevitable assholes" theories, feeding the rage and fear with which I'd grown up. And the only way, it seemed, that men could be feminist was to adopt new ways of talking and interacting, to get all sensitive, to put on a show of being saved and reborn.

It seemed fake. What for a lot of people may have been liberatory only confirmed my cynicism: There was no such thing as a good man.

Feminism could have given me hope of an alternative, a real-life Steven Keaton, but it didn't, partially because I got "feminism" in dribs and drabs, in half-digested chunks heavy on theory and light on real life. I didn't want a guy who talked softly to me because he thought that was "feminist." The feminism I ran into focused on changing yourself; it didn't address concrete, structural things that feminist men and women could do to build alternatives, to change society. Maybe this was a function of the time in which I became politically active: Young women were reaping real benefits from a previous generation's feminist organizing while no visible movement advocated anything beyond reform. Revolutionary feminism of the nineties variety was a between-the-ears and between-the-sheets experience, rather than a wave of women mounting the barricades to demand free childcare and complete equality.

In a nineties kind of way, with a broadened set of standards rather than a list of new ideals, I focused on trapping a good enough man, and failed—thankfully. I declared myself a strong political woman who wasn't going to take any shit; in fact, I was so competent that I would sigh and pay off the gas bill when my man forgot to do it, to prove I was stronger than he was. My feminism had identified the material and cultural restrictions that make my life—and the lives of other women worldwide—the way they are. Maybe this attitude reflects the weaknesses of our movements today: We can list everything that's screwed up, but when it comes to articulating what a better, just society would look like, people shrug, embarrassed to be thought of as pie-in-the-sky dreamers. The list of goals gets vague and fuzzy.

Our main struggle has been to unite our million factions and develop some common goals, but how do we do that? We've had to concentrate just on bringing everybody to the same table. Never mind a new society and don't say revolution because that's too radical—too scary. Mention something concrete, like the Canadian health-care system. We don't want to change society, we want to tinker with it. We're on the defensive—just like I am in my personal life.

In political organizing, asking people to imagine what they really want results in a rush of good ideas. In my personal life, asking myself what I really want results in things I am too cynical to believe I can have. I want kids, a garden, a circle of friends, a community in which to do political work and the chance to get paid for my writing. I want a man who will stick by me, whom I don't have to coddle. I have more faith in a revolution.

Allowing myself to dream of this man is confusing. Believing in men is a well-trodden but dangerous path. My cynicism is a powerful departure from that path, but it's only the beginning. I am still struggling with what I really want, how to let my guard down and build a relationship with a real live man without assuming he's going to break my heart. That idealism and imagination intimidates me, because I have few models for it. My revolutionary imagination falters and fails when visualizing an excellent relationship with a man.

Last year I fell in love with Rob, a thirty-year-old rock 'n' roll artist-skateboarder-carpenter I met in the grocery store. He fits none of my listed requirements for what I thought I was supposed to find. He isn't an organizer anxiously seeking his next nonprofit job, and he doesn't have a big shelf of left-wing books to attest to his political authenticity.

He and I share the habit of picking pieces of rusted metal off the ground and bringing them home. He needs to stay in some nights to build things, the same way I need to get up and write. He asked me how I felt about kids well before I'd thought to go fishing for that information. He's eerily psychic, one of those premonition guys who occasionally can feel things before they happen. He knows if I've had a good or bad day based on how I say hello on the phone.

We're so different, too. I'm fundamentally a country geek, and he's a badass with five tattoos and a big beard (who misses his cats when we leave for the weekend). With an open Sunday morning, I'll read the newspaper and he'll go jump hills on his bike. But we both have punk rock and coffee in our veins, and our personalities are similar in strange ways. We both figured out during our twenties how to build lives over our own boiling pits of anxiety, how (mostly) to manage our hypersensitivity and worry.

But I've worn out some of the illusions and dreams of the future that sustained me in past relationships. I am tired of playing the strong woman, the one who brings order to a chaotic boy's life. If something goes wrong, I have to stay pretty hands-off and wait for the solution, because I can't step in and fix everything. For the most part, Rob has figured himself out.

When I feel the need to fix a problem, I walk around the block and talk myself into refusing. It sucks, but it's the only option left. If you want a strong man, says my latest theory, let him be strong on his own. I'm trying to be "weaker," a version that isn't weak at all, just less willing to shoulder the weight of a whole relationship. I'm trying to freak out when I feel freaked-out, to bring up things that piss me off before I've solved them, without putting them into neat packages so that he doesn't have to do any emotional work. It's terrifying and uncomfortable. I'm trying to complain more and lean on him, even though I hate the thought.

The only way I can tell I've made progress is the fact that Rob's not raw material. I have not had a single impulse to think, He'll mature nicely, because I want him exactly the way he is right now, with his weird days during a full moon and the sculptures he builds in the woods and his huge amount of affection and heart. It's frightening, because I have a crush on him in addition to being in love with him. I enjoy just being with him, and that makes any old day together feel like one of our first dates, rather than an investment in a far-off future where things will be better. Yet I'm much more comfortable when I'm playing the therapist and paying the overdue bills and controlling things for a man out of control, when I'm writing a fairy-tale ending to this latest development in my love life. I struggle every day not to do that, to take things as they come. I do want it to continue working, just like this—knock on wood.

My visions of marriage have gotten a little worn around the edges. Having busted up that fantasy twice, I approach the idea now and crack my knuckles, knowing that if it happens, it will still involve work—but not just from me. In a man, I want to see some muscle, some sign that he is not afraid to get dirty and fix things that get broken between us. I want someone who is aware of life's ugliness, of the fact that, if we don't patch these holes as they appear, the water will keep rising and we'll drown.

I still want marriage, though, because I want that legal commitment for my eventual kids. More important, I like the idea of having someone to be with, a best friend who knows me better than anyone. I want to try to make it work, to put into practice a dream of marriage as a tool, like a universal joint that helps you move in directions you couldn't reach by yourself. It's something you use to build a life. I want to use this tool to build something better than what I've seen, to get beyond where I am now. I want somebody who's able to wield this thing as well as I can. I'm willing to sweat for it, because I know now that it doesn't come with a button for automatic liftoff.

Sex and the Shacked-Up Girl

Stacy Bierlein

Let's say his name is Ned. A perfect name, you think, for the lover of a woman who spent a disproportionate percentage of her girlhood absorbed in Nancy Drew novels. Nancy Drew and her devoted, fast-driving, windblown Ned Nickerson. You are a sleuth and he is your preppy lover man.

Let's say you meet through friends. A relationship begins when you're a student in Chicago and Ned is leaving a dead-end job in Denver. You exchange letters and daily and nightly phone calls for five months. He arrives at your apartment one night, and neither of you wants him to leave. He's the one, you think. You can't explain how you know it. You just do.

In the vibrant chaos of your first years with Ned, you stop seeing this living arrangement as a precursor to marriage. The things that you'd been looking forward to, the elements of your childhood marriage fantasies—loving a man, sharing a commitment and then creating a home and life together—have already happened. And you like your life together the way it is.

Enjoy excuses others make over the years for your unmarried status: her hippie-era parents, his repressive Catholic upbringing. Her wanderlust, her reading list, their commitment phobia.

Lilith Fair. Argue or laugh it off. Hold to your beliefs.

Later you'll be able to ask them: If my wanderlust is to blame, why have I been here for eight years?

Embrace your so-called badness

Notice single friends opening up to you more about sex, calling you for advice on things you didn't know you knew. For the first time you're the one "getting some" on a regular basis. Somehow you've become the sexpert. Enjoy the idea that you've become the sort of woman who says things like "Yes, there is a male G spot." In a spa locker room your girlfriends tell you that you have perfect nipples. It's official, you think. You've been sexualized.

Perhaps your friends admit that in college they said this about you: "She looks like she doesn't, but we know damned well she does." "Well, yes, I do," you say that day in the spa locker room, your perfect nipples moist with eucalyptus steam. I do, I do, I do.

Note that your college relationships went bad when you tried to be "good." You told a curly-haired management major, then an Irish fraternity boy, then an edgy anthropology guy, "No, I don't want to sleep with you." Not true, of course. That's exactly what you wanted to do. There were times when you said yes and things got bad anyway, but at least then you'd had a good time.

Feel happy now that these moments are behind you, that you've found a real and adult love, in all its wonder and complexity. Go on a date, and wear your great leather pants to a badass concert. Laugh when your lover man calls you Tiger. If you notice other women checking him out at the concert, remind him that you love like a lion. You've found a man worth fighting for, with no battles required. So monogamy is an enthusiastic choice you make together, not an assumption, not a mandate.

Establish your own rituals

Think, Yes, there are many brilliant ways for lovers to live together. Leave goofy notes for each other in drawers and cupboards. (This may cause some confusion when you have houseguests.) Quote silly, sappy love songs. Write "You're everything I've hoped for. And I love you more today than yesterday." Read to each other. Share recipes, novels, comics and poems.

Read *Shelter* by Lisa Glatt. Marvel at the way she compares a lover to walls, windows and a stucco ceiling. His toes to beams, his eyes to skylights and his lips to doors.

Take separate vacations. He skis and rafts with his friends, you hike and spa with yours. On the nights of your returns, he fills the bedroom with candles. He is not your vacation; he is your home.

Perhaps your apartment features several hugging stations: places where a step occurs, where you can stand taller and for a short time, equal your height to his, then kiss and hug. Use these stations every day. Arriving home after long stretches of work, hear Ned say, "Let's lie on each other." Race to the bed, peel your clothes off as fast as you can, jump under the sheets and take turns on top as you discuss your days.

In the outside world, dress up and dance as often as your schedule and budget allow. Celebrate your partner. Order your favorite wine and toast monogamy. Celebrate the anniversaries of when you met, moved in and the first time you experienced sex together. (French waiters dig this: Request a bottle of champagne and explain that it is the anniversary of your first intercourse.)

Live five hundred miles from his mother

Add five hundred more if he is the favorite. (When the initial shock of your living situation wears off, your mom mellows better than his.) Be patient with her at first. Perhaps, in an attempt to be cute, she calls you "outlaw" because you are not an in-law. Finally lose patience with her disapproval. You love her son with everything you have. You've created a beautiful home with him. You've cared for, inspired, tolerated, supported and encouraged him. Those are not the activities of an outlaw.

Remember that he cannot take responsibility for his mother's words and then blow up at him anyway. "It's the sex that bothers her," he tells you again. You've heard this a thousand times. To her, living together is like announcing to the world that you're having sex.

"Yes," you say. "*We're having sex.*" You're having beautiful, healthy sex. You are fulfilled and waking in his arms, not running home in the middle of the night with your bra in your purse. He is waking with a smile and making you breakfast, not begging for a corner of your drawer in which to hide an extra pair of boxers. Your intimacy is valued and complete—not something you need to cover or hide. So continue to express yourself. Encourage him to communicate with his family, and eventually the lectures end.

Perhaps his siblings fail to be supportive during these events—they're too busy being amused. Try not to hold this against them. They'll be entertained again when his mother refuses to give aromatherapy oils for Christmas, fearing you'll use them as some sort of sexual aid. With sex fiends like you and Ned in the family, the siblings' quiet lives look pretty good to Mother.

Love the energy of love

You have always known and believed that a woman does not need a man. So sometimes it proves difficult for you to admit that you *want* one; that you want to share your life with this male partner; that when you started seeing him, you were so giddy you nearly burst. You called your grandparents to tell them you were dating a wonderful man. And because you'd always been so guarded, so private, they might not have known there were less-than-wonderful men before him.

Feel thankful for the energy Ned continues to bring to your life. Consider that this is what draws people to love stories—the energy of love, the way lovers can be relentless, the way nothing stops them. With Ned in your life, the world seems less heavy. You tend to take everything so seriously, but his humor and sense of adventure remind you to relax. You once heard an editor say that people in love think of themselves more lightly and fondly than ever before.

When you share with a friend the short fiction you're writing, she says she loves your lusty female characters, the way they fall so absolutely, so physically and beautifully for their men. Realize this is a big step for you in writing and in life—the understanding that loving makes women stronger, not weaker. And Ned is the man you love, the one who loves you back.

Cherish the swirl of passion, the joyful rush of sex. Really, really enjoy sex. Get a book if you run out of ideas—you probably won't—and experiment. If you haven't already, try talking dirty to see if it turns you on. Disregard stories about sex becoming less exciting with years. While sex may change—developing an instinctual quality, growing so you suspect you've come to know his lips as well as your own—passion can be like breath. Or sometimes you think of passion like this: It is love's chauffeur. It drives you onward and hurries you home.

Let kissing be your favorite form of communication
Laugh with Ned about your first kiss, how it took you by surprise. You were in a van he'd borrowed from his parents; snow was falling on the windshield. He'd parked outside the party you'd be attending. You sat talking, waiting for friends who had followed in their own car. And mid-sentence, in the midst of your nonsexual conversation—you don't recall the topic now—the urge to kiss you struck him, and he couldn't wait a moment longer. There it was, a long and sexy kiss, filled with his intentions. Of course, you kissed back, and this kiss is where the intensity of your connection began. (Yep, in a van.)

Six weeks later, you spent your first weekend getaway together and had intercourse for the first time. It amazes you now that you waited six weeks, a circumstance you attribute to the fact that you lived in different cities. The things you remember most are how in sync you were, how you seemed to crave the same positions at the same time, how playful you were, how you laughed. How your intercourse, like your kissing, was a gorgeous exchange of energy, passion and spirit.

Use both to express your attraction, to recognize this endless supply of longing. Kiss earlobes and fingers, knees, the bellybutton. Kiss on balconies and beaches, in elevators and parking structures. Kiss in front of the television, the washer and dryer. Have sex in every available space of the home you share. Allow yourself to feel lucky. After all, you have someone to kiss, someone to love. Remember how kisses send the most basic and honest messages, whether they—and the sex that might follow—last four seconds or forty hours. Notice the way you sleep together, the way his lips rest at the back of your neck, the way your limbs drape over one another as you dream.

Above all, keep it hot
Perhaps your sister gives a dinner party. You overhear a friend from San Francisco say, "Every woman should own a vibrator." She's right, you think. Suddenly, you can't believe you've never owned one. Share these

thoughts with your sister the next morning. Plan a trip to the Pleasure Chest after breakfast.

Notice that walls are placed around the parking lot, so that people in passing cars won't find cars they recognize. The owners have thought of privacy. It's entirely possible they've thought of everything.

The first aisle you stroll down has gigantic, flesh-colored penis statues. "Why do vibrators have to look like penises?" you say. Realize they're extra-large butt plugs. A blond wearing leather and chains hears you, laughs and leaves his post behind the register. "I can't believe you," your sister says. "You're being political, even here." "Especially here," you tell her.

Leather and Chains says, "Are you two sisters? That's so cute!" You leave the Pleasure Chest with three female condoms (they might be interesting), a pink torpedo vibrator, three tickler attachments, Astroglide (really the best, Leather and Chains insists) and, from the candy aisle, a Strawberry Penis Pop with testicles. Tell Leather and Chains you're a writer and watch him throw in three pencils with penis erasers. "On the house," he says.

Perhaps the mere news of your purchase excites your lover man. Maybe, at the writing of this essay, the pink torpedo sits in your nightstand like a gift, waiting for the night you'll unwrap it together. And recently you heard of nine foot strands of freshwater "sex pearls" that wrap, drag and drape around your bodies as you make love.

On an anniversary of your first date, Ned asks, "Do you ever look across the room at me and think 'What? How did he get here?'" Tell him that most often, you look across the room and think "He's so beautiful, and I'm so glad he's here." Then remember this: You've got eight years of sizzle under your belt. And there may be eighty more inside you.

The Lesbian Baby Dance

Diane Anderson-Minshall

It's 2 P.M. on a Tuesday afternoon. I have the house to myself and I'm surging. Well, I *could* be in my most fertile time. For eight days now I've been urinating on ovulation predictor sticks and arguing with the dog over whether my test line is getting darker.

After nearly ten years of talking, stalling, crying and "processing" (a term we use to describe incredibly long talks that involve alcohol and lack of sleep), we've decided to have a baby. I never thought I'd have kids. I thought they'd be a ball-and-chain, detracting from my career and my jet-set lifestyle. But, at thirty-two, my life isn't as jet set as I expected. I don't even think I want it to be jet set. In fact, by most accounts it's pretty domestic, and the older I get the more I envy the women who spend time dashing between soccer games and PTA meetings instead of power lunches and board meetings. I've started reading *Parenting* instead of *Cosmo* and *Vogue,* and I'm happy with that. But I still struggle. What will I tell people? What will my parents think? Can I still be my graduating class's most likely to succeed if I eschew a career for kids? Am I, as I would have thought at sixteen, a sellout? Very recently I watched *Baby Boom* and finally got it.

For so many years we assumed we weren't ready to parent. We

kept waiting for the perfect situation—the job my wife would be in forever, a big windfall for my magazine, a city we could envision growing old in, a man who could be more than just a sperm donor. And we were waiting for us to be committed to a lifetime together—a no-divorce option in our worlds—and to have our families accept us as potential parents of their grandchildren.

Then after I turned thirty the tick-tick-tick of my biological clock got a little louder. Not that we needed biological encouragement. Straight friends began to pull us aside and discuss my waning fertility. Rugged, blue-collar co-workers would discuss ovulation and fertility with Suzy. Folks bogged down with children of their own began to tell us that no time is ever "perfect" for having kids. I wanted to make sure Suzy wasn't going to leave me when I was forty weeks pregnant, crying constantly and demanding to name our child Twinkle Bell.

I think I've got the answers. Well, not really, but I do have a burning desire to experience something beyond my career, beyond my own life. The other morning one of our neighbors came running out of her house with her hair in rollers, wearing enormous glasses and no makeup and sporting only a robe. She was a frightful mess, but all she cared about was getting the kids to school on time. I want that ability to think about something outside of myself, the ability to put my life's energies and passion into caring for a life. I desire that weight, that urgency. And, well, I also want to know the happiness that parents seem to have—and maybe I want the chance to create for a kid the childhood I didn't have.

So, I'm done talking. We're done talking.

For the longest time, my wife Suzy (my partner, my lesbian lover, my copilot—who knows what to call her?) and I considered adoption. The environmental and ethical aspects appealed to us: Plenty of kids need homes already. But adoption is an incredibly difficult process for working-class lesbian couples who don't own their own homes and haven't lived in one state longer than a few years. Could we ever pass a home study? Would any parents want us to adopt their child? What would we say when little Timmy screamed that his *real* mommy wasn't a dyke? The home study was the most daunting. Everything we read offered encouragement: You could pass if you don't own a home, if you're a single woman (which we're considered), if you don't have a high income. Whoa, what if you're all of those things *and* a dyke?

We didn't care about looks or race or even having a brand-spankin'-new infant. For years, I would surf the web and look through the huge databases of kids available for adoption. I learned all about "special needs" kids—sometimes labeled thus simply because they are African American or Latino. But more often than not, the kids in the foster care system—some forty thousand strong—have led disenfranchised lives. Many have been physically, sexually and emotionally abused. Some have learning disabilities or are differently abled. Many have multiple siblings. The majority are too old to be attractive to your average (heterosexual) couple.

But most of that didn't matter to us.

Adoption is common in my family. My father and aunt were adopted after my grandmother's first child died. In 1946, everything was very hush-hush. When Oregon recently opened up the birth records of thousands of adopted kids, my father went in search of his birth mom. My aunt refused to do so. As young adults, my mother and one of my aunts gave up children for adoption; they have both had pleasant reunions since. I'm probably related to more than a dozen adopted kids—some yearn for their birth parents, some resent their birth parents, some are steadfastly loyal to their adoptive parents. But, since private adoption is out (it's simply too costly, too biased against folks like us), what would special-needs adoption mean for us—two lesbians? Would we be offering an adoptive kid yet another disadvantage? What if we adopted an African-American child and moved back home to be near our families? That would mean two lesbians raising a black kid in a not-so-politically-sophisticated state. And how can we uproot this kid whose life is already so uprooted?

Many legal and financial issues are central to our concerns. We might not be able to afford the lawyers' fees. We might not stay in a state where two women can adopt. More important, we asked ourselves how we would handle the challenge of a kid who had been abused. A boy who had been molested. A girl who now acted violently. Were we prepared for that kind of responsibility?

○○

Eight years ago we adopted Free, a dog who has been only a joy—smart, loyal, friendly. Probably the best dog this side of Lassie. We were so pleased with our girl dog that four years ago, outside the grocery store, I let myself fall in love with a puppy so tiny it shouldn't have been separated from its mother, much less sent to its death at the pound. Within months the dog, Rivers, was enormous. And he also had very specific needs of his own. He's easily traumatized and aggressive, and he won't allow visitors in the house. He requires constant medical care for a variety of conditions.

Around the same time that we were nursing Rivers and coping with the lifestyle changes that he demanded (no more dog sitters, no more long nights in the city, no more sleeping past 6:00 A.M. ever), one of my co-workers was staying up night after night with her sleepless baby. Robin and Pam were great lesbian-parent role models—together for a decade, Pam had given birth to a boy seven years prior and Robin gave birth to their new infant. But after a week of sleepless nights, Robin walked into work ashen and puffy, saying, "We just had no idea." Robin and Pam had such an easy time with their first child that they assumed the same would happen again—but their second son really put them through the wringer. I knew what she meant, in my own way, because our second dog was nothing like his canine sister.

But when our friends and co-workers began to ask why we didn't get rid of the dog, we were appalled. We felt a lot like Robin did about her son. You get what you get and you deal with it.

Certainly being a biological mom doesn't mean your child won't have special needs—Suzy's younger sister has Down's syndrome, and we've learned a great deal from her parents about dealing with a special-needs child. But adopting for us most likely means adopting an older kid who might not be able to attach, who might be aggressive, who might have been physically and sexually abused—all things we hope to prevent our child from ever experiencing.

After seemingly endless discussion and investigation, we gave up on adoption—at least in the short run—so we don't have to deal with the home study, the legal investment, the wait and uncertainty, the questions we weren't sure we could answer.

But the decision to go for biology brought up the next huge question: Could either of us bear children?

Suzy's thirty-three now and has been riddled with medical problems since childhood—allergies, stomach problems, bad joints. Yes, she's got the genetic code people in the area are paying thousands for (she's a blue-eyed blond) but she's not exactly a girly girl, she can't handle pain and her eyes are so bad even her toddler photos show her wearing thick spectacles. There is her sister with Down's and another who is almost legally blind. And, most important, I don't think she's ever wanted to bear children. She's always been more gender-identified with men (after all, she plays nature-cop by day in her job as a forest ranger), so pregnancy brings up more issues than we can possibly resolve by talking. Also, what would happen to me if she gives birth? If she got pregnant, gave birth, nursed the child—what role would I play?

Yet I have problems of my own. First, I may have childbearing hips but I'm also over the recommended weight. My own mother had terrible birth experiences—including a child who died and several late-term miscarriages. During her pregnancy with me, she was given a drug called DES that has been found to cause infertility and other health problems in female offspring. Neither one of us would win any genetic prizes.

Plus, I was the breadwinner for years. While she wandered through a laid-back natural resources career, I was a hard-nosed journalist and editor who spent 24-7 on the job. I have invested eighteen years in a career—and I hadn't ever considered stopping it, even long enough to get pregnant. I already had a "baby" in my new magazine. I did love my career. I thrived on the stress and rush of it. It sometimes demanded sixteen hours a day, and I could jet off across the country at a moment's notice.

So still we stalled. We kept waiting and worrying and promising ourselves it would be okay if we didn't expand our family. And we know that relationships change—what if ours changed? I like things the way they are; I don't want to mess it up. Suzy feels it, too. Sure we're afraid—afraid we'll lose ourselves in parenting, afraid it won't be as glorious as we hoped, afraid the minute I'm pregnant something will go wrong and I'll lose my life instead of my freedom. Afraid that we'll have made a huge, irrevocable mistake.

But soon after I turned thirty-two, we spent the summer in a secluded cabin nestled in ninety mountain acres. Suddenly, I could think of nothing but children. Back in the city, babies were leaping out at me from every magazine cover. Every celebrity on the planet seemed to be reproducing. Those crying, screaming, snotty little things in the supermarket that for so long I had resented started to look more appealing than my little circle of post-feminist publishing cronies. In fact, to those on the outside, I was suddenly Martha Fuckin' Stewart.

I began to cook and bake constantly. I'd look at the computer and look at the kitchen, and for the first time in my life the kitchen won. Each day Suzy would come home from work and there'd be an apple pie or homemade marionberry preserves. Dinner was on the table, oven mitts were on my paws and four hundred urgent emails sat unread on my computer. I turned into a lesbian Donna Reed, minus the kids. I can't explain what happened, and it sounds crazy to my friends, but I think one day I just gave myself the freedom to be domestic and realized that I liked it more than I ever could have imagined. I made fun of the girls who took home ec ("I'm going to have a *career*," I would sneer), but I'd never realized how many years I had stopped myself from doing those things because they were for "those" kind of women.

Obviously, the desire to have a child wasn't all that turned me into Betty Crocker. But it's part and parcel of the whole shift in my life. Another woman might have ignored these feelings and pretended they didn't exist. But I don't want to have any regrets when I'm ninety.

So I'm trying to let this change take over, let it direct me where I'm supposed to go.

Fortunately, Suzy began changing as well. Over the decade her self-identity has changed: Her definitions of what it means to be a lesbian have evolved beyond what they were when we married at twenty-two. She began thinking of children and roots as good things—instead of something from which lesbians were saved. And, in some ways, maybe for the first time, she began bonding with straight people—people who had kids, loved kids and, most important, seemed to provide a new and somewhat unexpected support network for us—when and if we finally did have a rugrat of our own.

Within weeks our day-to-day landscape had shifted so dramatically we wondered exactly how it happened. We were suddenly watching baby movies—*Nine Months, Baby Boom, She's Having a Baby*—even the insipid ones. My lunchtime indulgence of watching trash-talking transsexuals on Jerry Springer gave way to the Learning Channel's medi-docudrama *A Baby Story*. We began hanging out with friends with kids—and discovered that we'd spend most of our time playing with the kids. And our bookshelves, once filled with erotica, pop culture punditry and identity politics, gave way to books on fertility, conception and parenting.

The books, though, presented yet another trauma. Dr. Ruth offered great advice for getting pregnant—if you're straight. I loved reading about all the wonderful positions you could have sex in, but after three hundred pages I still couldn't determine whether oral sex was safe or not.

Finally we found the perfect book: Rachel Pepper's *The Ultimate Guide to Pregnancy for Lesbians*. A dyke-specific book about getting knocked up! Delighted, I read it cover to cover seven times. Suzy read it halfway through and stopped. Unlike us, Pepper isn't married, and the focus on being single made Suzy uncomfortable. But within days she had a new dog-eared book under her arm: *The Expectant Father*. She read it three times.

And we began to research our alternative conception options. We had to find a father. We fretted over everything about the potential donors. We wanted someone who would be in the child's life, but many of our closest male friends are HIV-positive. We had long wanted to ask our best male friend, but he turned ashen when we spoke about it and we shelved the idea. We joked about sending me out for a one-night stand after I surge. We thought briefly of calling old boyfriends and asking for one last favor. We scoured our roster of friends: Suzy's co-workers (too messy), some married older men (may not be fertile) and even guys we'd known for two months. But suddenly the image of knocking on the door with a jelly jar and asking for a cup of sperm seemed absurd.

Of course, it's not just absurd, it's risky. If we go through a sperm bank, we have legal protection, but through any other arrangement it's virtually impossible to guarantee that our rights as parents will be protected. We could get a donor we know, draw up legal papers and five years down the road find ourselves in court defending our custody rights.

After scouring a dozen or more sperm banks, including lesbian-friendly ones in the Bay Area, we discovered a small, intimate cryobank in Missoula, Montana. Our friends scoffed when we signed up, but we felt confident that going with a sperm bank in the Montana-Idaho region would ensure that the child's father would share our geographic roots. As folks with unusual regional pride, we felt good about this choice.

We made a few agreements about donors: must be healthy with no major diseases or early deaths in their family history. But questions remained: Should we get a Native American donor to keep my bloodline going? Should we find a German donor—a blue-eyed blond like Suzy—so the child looks like "ours"? We knew we didn't want someone whose donor essay used the line "The eye of God will be upon you." (A surprising number of essays tipped us off to the donor's religious and/or political feelings.) Suzy wanted someone who resembled me, I wanted someone who resembled her (or Brad Pitt). After endless discussion, we decided on a mixed-race man—white and Native American—whose hobbies and education matched my wife's and whose bloodline mimicked my own. Finally, after endless days of screening men, we had found Mr. Right.

On the day the frozen papa arrived in his nitrogen tank, we tested my ovulation and found a blue line. We decided to inseminate me that night.

Suzy took charge, donning long sleeves, long pants, leather gloves and safety goggles to open the tank. When she finally got it open, she looked like the Terminator at a dry-ice-filled junior-high dance. Definitely unsexy. Then she warmed the sperm and prepared to knock me up. I stared at the excruciatingly long catheter she was holding.

"This isn't going to work," I said. "I can't do this."

But I did; we did.

Within a week I was nauseated. I had a strange metallic taste in my mouth. I was woozy and tired all the time. I couldn't finish a full hike. When my period didn't come, we were certain I was pregnant. Suzy began to treat me gently, taking on extra chores and insisting I rest. Friends, too, were convinced I was pregnant. We thanked God for making this miracle happen—we'd never heard of artificial insemination working on the first try. Two weeks later, I began to bleed.

I cried for two days, trying not to tell everyone I encountered what an unfortunate and barren woman I was. We pulled out the fertility books again and discovered that nearly half of all pregnancies end in early miscarriage, usually in the form of a late period. It's nature's way, the experts agreed, of working out genetic defects.

Suzy and I were crestfallen. But she was loving and doting and sat me down for another long talk to make sure I remembered that we agreed that if it's meant to be, it will be, and if we're not meant to have children, we're happy with the family we do have. "I never imagined I could love someone like this," she told me. "Kids are just icing on the cake—if we don't have them, I won't be any less happy to spend my life with you."

And so, after the first effort, we decided to march on. We took new precautions. In addition to the ovulation tests, we began to chart my basal body temperature and my cervical mucus. We got into a rhythm: At five o'clock every morning, Suzy wakes up, rolls over and shoves the thermometer in my mouth. I grunt and fall back to sleep. She falls back to sleep. Five minutes later, she wakes up and takes it out, reads it, records it on our daily chart (which looks like a stock-market report in a bad year) and falls back to sleep. By then, I've woken up, wondered if I'm barren and fallen back to sleep.

For round two, we decided to switch donors in case the last one had anything to do with the (possible) miscarriage. This time we chose an Apache-Mexican donor. He sounded strong, athletic. I rationalized: The Apaches were hunter-raiders, so his offspring will be warriors. I could tell our child that her father was from a strong warrior family (instead of having to say he's a pharmacist and his family is from Tucson). But the sperm-bank order processor said that only one unit was available for frozen papa number two so on a whim Suzy ordered one unit of him and one unit of our backup. Within thirty-six hours, I would have two men's sperm inside me.

Suzy teased me and feigned arousal at my slutty reproductive behavior. I panicked about what we'd tell the child if we did indeed get pregnant. "Uh, your father is either a Mexican-born Apache soccer player or a German-Irish poet." I decided this would be the time. My pee sticks were dark blue, my days were perfect and what better motivation than potential for ridicule from my family (i.e., not even knowing which donor was the baby's father) to make me get pregnant?

This time we hedged our bets by having sex. The books are torn on whether having an orgasm is good for reproduction. It changes the pH of your vagina, but no one knows for sure whether that's good or not. Some experts say yes. My friend Angelina argues that it's not necessary (with generations of nonorgasmic women as proof). So we had sex one time, and didn't the next. Each time I lay on the couch, butt up, for several hours. The second time I fell off the couch.

Two weeks later, while we were waiting for the results (am I? am I not?), I fell in the street—tripping over a bump—and hit my head. I sat crying as people milled about, staring but not offering help. I wondered what the hell I was doing bringing a kid into this world.

The next day, I got my period.

We were down fifteen hundred dollars with all the thermometers, fertility aids, ovulation sticks, pregnancy kits, books and sperm. And still, no pregnancy. We both panicked. Maybe I was too fat. Maybe I was infertile. Maybe I wasn't ovulating. We looked at the charts; we read more books. We decided I was fine, that it just takes time.

Because of financial concerns, at some early point we decided to take breaks from our conception efforts, but each time I finish my period we both start getting antsy. On those off months we try to focus on how this is a lifetime process, so that a month here or there where we have to pay bills and not focus on my womb won't make such a big difference. If this insemination thing has given me anything, it's a sense of patience, which will be a great thing when and if we actually do have a child. Suzy's much better about keeping things in perspective.

Our core relationship has not really changed much; we were strong as partners before embarking on the trip to parenthood, and we waited as long as we did before trying because we knew that children could be a lot of pressure on a relationship. But it's changed how other people treat us. I think the men at Suzy's work—the other rangers—treat her like one of the guys now (they all have kids, wives). These other families seem really supportive of us, as though trying to have children is a universal bond we can all understand. It's strange to get validation and almost heterosexual privilege from something we *want* to do;

usually reactions are the opposite.

Just those three tries have been stressful, and a year of inseminating has seemed inconceivable. But a recent death in the family reminded us of how lucky we are, how happy we are. The next day we discovered my ovulation date would fall on my wife's birthday. It seemed too coincidental to ignore. The whole cycle of life thing sounds like crap when you aren't trying to conceive and like a miracle when you are. So, we're trying again. This time with one donor: a tall, blond Norwegian guy with ten siblings. At least he sounds fertile.

The Crossing of Arms:

A Pagan Handfasting

Denise Brennan Watson

Tonight under a full moon, we invoke the wisdom and beauty of the Old Religion of our ancestors to celebrate the joining together of the energies of the Moon and the Sun. Please bear witness as Denise and Jay are handfasted in Pagan tradition.

I never imagined that at age thirty, I would find myself living at a convent in Minnesota, studying feminist activism in a graduate program and planning a goddess-based union to a man living in Cincinnati, Ohio.

Jay and I spent our engagement apart, each using the time to prepare for our life together and to research rituals for the ceremony that would set us on our way. We wanted our wedding to be true to our lives and our values, while recognizing the role of the feminine in spirituality and commitment. After having been engaged for three months, we began planning the wedding, which would take place two years later in September 1996.

Having lived as a Catholic most of my life, I had grown beyond the hindrances of my family's religion, yet was uncomfortable dispensing with all of its associations. While a graduate student, I lived at the Good Counsel Convent, founded by the School Sisters of

Notre Dame, in Mankato, Minnesota—an alternative housing arrangement that offered me ample space, peace and quiet, community gardening, security and natural beauty. Though I no longer identified as a Catholic, living there allowed me to reflect on the role my religious background would play as my spirituality developed. Jay did not come from a traditional religious background, but had always regarded the earth and the feminine as sacred and spiritual. We discovered that our beliefs came together in nature spirituality, and planned a celebration within this framework.

Many couples who plan nature-spirituality weddings choose to have both a handfasting and a civil ceremony for legal purposes if an ordained Pagan celebrant is not available. During our engagement, Jay and I met Joan Marie Kelly, a Wiccan spiritual leader, and Rachel Olson, a ceremonialist from Duluth, who combined their gifts to create for us a rite of passage that spanned two days. The two walked with us through our engagement, civil ceremony, baptism by fire and water and the handfasting itself.

The private civil ceremony took place on September 26, 1996, under an eclipsing full moon in the woods of Joan's backyard, and was followed by a nuptial baptism, feast and fire ritual. The handfasting took place the following evening in a wooded grove at the convent.

While living at Good Counsel, I met many nuns who were curious, disturbed, flustered or even delighted about the feminist and Pagan foundations of my engagement and wedding. I gladly discussed with them the similarities between Catholicism and Pagan ways of being and introduced them to feminist perspectives on marital home life, name-sharing and identity. Some actively helped to plan our ceremony, and when a twist of circumstance prevented our getting married at the original chosen location in Cincinnati, the nuns helped relocate the wedding to the convent grounds.

Jay and I sought out wedding literature from popular presses and Pagan ministries, crafted our wedding raiment and invitations and prepared the menu of our wedding feast. We researched the historical foundations of current customs and of goddess-based unions that honor both marital partners. We learned that there is such a thing as a priestess and discovered handfasting, the ancient Pagan joining of hands that in the British Isles was the preferred method of nonecclesiastical marriage up to the middle of the nineteenth century. The rite remained legal in Scotland until 1939.*

The handfasting is a double handshake between matrimonial partners, a crossing of arms in which the bride and groom form a figure eight. The left-handed handshake is a symbol of agreement; the right-handed handshake has survived in western culture as the ultimate gesture of agreement in social settings. The following is an excerpt from my wedding ritual:

The handfasting

With incense, Joan marked a large figure eight in the air. Then she spoke:

The dual circle of the figure eight grew from the world's oldest wedding custom, the ceremonial joining of hands so the couple's arms formed the double circle. In Celtic tradition, this ceremony became known as handfasting. Tonight we revive that ancient ceremony, whereby this bride and groom may be united in the tradition of the oldest deity known to human beings. Denise and Jay, Heaven and Earth, Moon and Sun, please form the figure eight.

Facing each other, we clasped hands, left over right.

Jay and I had much freedom to shape our ceremony, name ourselves and decide the texture and number of ceremonies we would have. We used this leeway to transform spiritual differences into a bridge connecting Christian and Pagan paths. Each drew from and honored the other.

As part of this planning, Jay and I meditated on the ways our identities would evolve through marriage. The names by which we would be known as husband and wife were most important, having become a source of strength for us as we explored name-sharing alternatives; we wanted to preserve our individual identities while honoring our commitment and union. Our own last names were a part of our identities we were not willing to demote or cast away, so we chose to retain our

---

* *Barbara G. Walker,* The Woman's Dictionary of Symbols and Sacred Objects. *San Francisco: Harper & Row, 1988.*

fathers' last names. We wanted only three names, ones that flowed well together; hyphenating our names was not an attractive option. He had been born Jay William Pattison, and I was born Andrea Denise Watson. After much research, we decided that we would share a middle name to honor our union and that it would be "Brennan." Its sound seemed to complement our names. We also found that it derives from the Irish word for "dewdrops" (*broonón*), which appealed to us by representing a natural element.

Our unconventional name-sharing has put out of play "Mr. and Mrs. So-and-So," which irritates those who believe I should have adopted Jay's last name. Relatives, acquaintances and even people we've never met have cited confusion, personal inconvenience and eccentricity as reasons for their disapproval. Many nonsupporters complained we would deprive our children of their father's last name, asking how far we would go with these feminist revisions of marriage and naming. They, of course, assumed that we would be having children.

More people are more disturbed by the fact that our marriage will not involve procreation than by our adopting a feminism-inspired marital name. One nun at Good Counsel told me that I would be depriving my husband of heirs by not having children. When I asked her what sense it made to say that I was denying him something he did not wish to have, a gateway conversation began, opening the way for discussion about morality, forced matrimony and maternity, double standards, religious mandates and individual rights. Jay and I continue to encounter people who do not approve of child-free marriage. We explain to them that we are respectful of their style of living, as they should be of ours.

At the ceremony, after taking our vows, we symbolically washed our hands of the opinions of those eager to criticize our views on marriage and family. This ritual preceded the exchange of rings, serving as a kind of baptism prior to the joining of our hands. The handwashers came forth with a basin of rose-petal water as Joan recited, "The handwashing is symbolic of a casting off of outside expectations and judgments and a relinquishing of societal conventions to their originators. The ceremonial handwashing symbolizes the beginning of a common journey free of the weight of outside voices, opinions and values."

The basin of water was not unlike that which had cupped holy water at my childhood church in Corpus Christi, Texas. It was circular, with no beginning or end, offering those whose hands touched the water the power to self-anoint and cast away sentiments that are spiritually unserving.

Before crossing our left and right arms, Jay and I exchanged two rings each. A matching set of silver rings with inlaid stars and moons symbolized a marital pact between the right hands, and unique rings for the left symbolized our individuality. Before the exchange, we carried those rings in deerskin pouches of grain worn around our necks. Deblyn, a ceremonial artist, had hand-sewed these for us and filled them with kernels harvested by Minnesota farmer and ritualist Corn Woman, her partner in art. The aromatic pouches hung from leather cords, serving as a delicate part of our raiment.

In honor of Jay's Irish ancestry, I placed on his left ring finger a gold band handmade for him by a jeweler in Dublin. The traditional Celtic knotwork pattern in the gold symbolized the circle of life connecting current-day folks with those who came before. We completed the circle of commitment as Jay offered me a ring composed of three antique-style bands, garnet hearts and circles of diamonds. "Please take this ring as a symbol of the completeness of my commitment and as a seal of my vow," he said as he placed the ring on my left hand.

By carrying our own rings, Jay and I broke with western ring-bearing tradition in which the "best man" guards the ring intended for the bride. The origin of the role is Gothic, when a man and a sidekick would steal a young woman, force her into marriage and stand ready to fend off angry relatives who might try to steal the woman back. We chose to rename what would have been the best man in a mainstream wedding; we called him the "man of honor," which honors the male attendant while not dishonoring any other person.

Tying the knot and jumping the broom

In Pagan tradition, when precious metals were too expensive or un-available, lovers' hands were bound together in the infinity symbol and then they were separated ritually to symbolize one bonding of two separate individuals.

The man of honor facilitated our bonding by blessing the rope used during the handfasting (the ritual "tying of the knot" having been the pivotal moment of the union). The bonding of our wrists was followed by our jumping the wedding broom, a symbol of our commitment to take up housekeeping together. Jay and I were delighted that we were united further still centuries back by this rite practiced by my African ancestors in the U.S. and Jay's ancestors in Celtic Europe. In some weddings of African-American slaves, an elder woman would sweep the air around the couple with a broom in order to chase away harmful spirits. Then she'd place the broom at the feet of the couple, who jumped together from single life into married life.

Similarly, in Celtic times, a matron used a besom broom to sweep away evil spirits from the home the couple intended to share. This broom was then placed onto the ground during the ceremony to symbolize domestic union. The hand-locked pair jumped over the broom, into a new life.

Our African and Celtic ancestors saw the wedding broom as a symbol of a sweeping of a new path and as a threshold of a new kinship. Following their tradition, Denise and Jay will now jump the broom to consecrate their handfasting.

In addition to the broom-jumping custom, the scrolled invitations we'd designed honored our ancestries. Traditional African motifs of birds and fish, together with a Celtic knotwork pattern, flanked the full length of the wording. My husband, a visual artist, hand-drew the motifs to complement the text I had written.

We had harp accompaniment in the tradition of the sixteenth- and seventeenth-century Gaels. One day while at the convent I'd heard sounds of beautiful (recorded) Celtic harp music coming from the nuns' living room. We were delighted to learn that the musicians, a husband and wife duo called Clariseach (Gaelic for "harp"), were based in the area. As it is customary for Celtic musicians who perform at weddings to write one piece especially for the bride and groom, Ann and Charlie wrote a piece for us—tailored to the ideas and symbols used in our ceremony.

Our rite was constructed in a conscious effort to exclude customs and language we find offensive. We didn't throw flowers or garters. There was no veil for the bride. Rather than accentuating the opposition of male and female with traditional black and white attire, Jay and I were decked in forest green and violet crushed velvet. His garb was a medieval-style tunic, pants and cape, and mine a full-length dress decorated with violet beads and sequins that I had worked into figure-eight designs. Around my head I wore bands of corn harvested and transformed into a simple headpiece. Corn spirals encircled my left wrist and right ankle, together symbolizing the fertility of the earth. As grain had become a ritual aspect of our daily life, Jay and I included a corn blessing in our ceremony.

Corn blessing

The nuptial grain was given to us by Mother Earth, and tonight we shall return the fruit of the kernel to her as Jay and Denise are encircled by the bountiful powers radiating from the gift of the grain. The Grainkeepers and Corn Maiden will now bless Jay and Denise with the ritual pouring forth of the food of the soul and of the earth.

Drumming accompanied the reading of the blessing, and the jingle of tambourine disks resembled altar chimes during a Catholic Mass. As Corn Woman and her young daughter (the Corn Maiden) blessed Jay and me with grain, Deblyn (Dancing Fox) recited a chant that included the following:

Mother Earth
Mother Corn
Let the grain
Of your body
Rain softly
On our tables
Tonight

Let the gift
Of your kernel

Rain above us
Below us
Behind us
Before us
Around us
Within us

Joan brought the blessing to a close, asking Mother Corn to "hold hunger at bay" as Jay and I entered matrimony. The spiral dance, a customary closing to Pagan rites of passage, took place on the convent grounds in celebration of how the nuns helped usher me into a new chapter of my life. Though I had been concerned that sisters of the cloth would take offense at the Pagan and earth-based nature of my wedding, a nest of supportive nuns at the convent greeted me with warmth and admiration.

We were pleased that in our ceremony, differences were not simply tolerated, but embraced with song and solemnity. All persons who took part in the wedding rite set into motion the change we had celebrated in the wooded grove of the convent. The Celtic harpist, with her clicking of bones, and the reeds and bellows at the fingertips of her husband, filled the atmosphere with jigs for dancing as well as joy for the circle of supporters who had come forth to usher two people into a rite of passage that honored heaven and earth, Christians and Pagans, Africans and the Irish, man and woman.

The circle is open, but unbroken. So Mote It Be!

One Size Does Not Fit All

(or, My Brief Career as a Political Action Figure)

Leigh Cotnoir

"If you really want to make God laugh, tell him all about your plans."

The uttering of these words by a friend goes down on my list of crucial and ephemeral life moments, because in that instant I found the perfect lyrics to the background music of my life. What the words said about control over one's life—or lack thereof—made the proverbial light bulb go on over my head. It reminded me of the time a grade-school teacher demonstrated how one could sing any Emily Dickinson poem to the tune of "The Yellow Rose of Texas" (true and uncanny); I thought I'd never again witness such an amazing phenomenon. But lying there on that Southern California beach, I found my own multipurpose poetics, my perfect soundtrack. And it was there, right after the breakup of my eight-year marriage, that my illusions washed away with the waves.

But the first of my best-laid-plan debacles is one I had earlier in life, and it's one that contributed to other profound misconceptions I have had about my ability to rule my destiny with an iron fist. My idea went something like this: When I grew up I would marry a man, have children, have a decent job and live a life like my conservative Texas parents'. Doesn't sound too hard. Nevertheless, it was slated as Doomed Plan Number One. Raised Catholic with an enormous emphasis on the Protestant work ethic, I thought self-control was not an ideal but a part of my DNA. I was predestined for a certain kind of straight and monogamous existence, and I made plans accordingly. Like many gays and lesbians, I put an undeterminable amount of effort into trying to live a straight life until I finally became a stranger to myself and to my family.

I ended up coming out around the same time k.d. lang hovered over Cindy Crawford on the cover of *Vanity Fair*. Fortunately and unfortunately for me, it was a time of inspired gay political agendas: gay military troops, gay ministers of God, successful gay family adoptions, gay celebrities, domestic partnerships and the issue of gay marriage in the courts. It's the last one that really got me.

Assimilation is a very alluring prospect for a Catholic girl raised in a Republican household in the Bible belt. My parents have now been married for more than forty years, my older sister has been married for twenty-five years, another sister has been married for about twenty years and countless aunts and uncles have done the like. The family principle has always guided my existence, and my queerness for a while made me desperate to emulate what was familiar. While my first attempt at assimilation had failed, insofar as I never wanted to be with a man, I assumed that the idea of marriage had seemed awkward in the context of my life only because I had learned that girls marry only boys. But in the environment of gay revolution and "we are the same" and "you, too, can have this life" rhetoric, it seemed perfectly reasonable to assume I could swap the variables of the marriage equation and still have the outcome of "normal" marital bliss. After all, I was very much in love and had been with my lover for three years . . . how could things go wrong?

Being a furniture designer, I sometimes approach problem-solving in purely mechanical terms: What is the piece's function going to be? What kind of exposure to use will it have? In what environment will it be placed? You don't make a ten-foot-tall cabinet for a room with eight-foot ceilings, nor a blue, neon, ambient wall lamp for a traditional Victorian home.

So it is, too, with individual styles of living.

I met Heather in college, and we made a commitment to each other with the acknowledgement that there might be other people with whom we'd each fall in love in the future. After all, we were in our twenties and, barring disaster, we expected to live long enough to meet other amazing people for whom we would feel affection. In our brief romantic careers, we already had. Yet our original understanding was just that—an understanding and not an agreement. Although we nodded about and checklisted these distant and theoretical paramours, we never laid out a plan to manage them. Nor did we ever talk about it again. It was all out there, far away—bridges to be crossed when and if we happened by them, but nothing like the one we found ourselves on. Forever was now.

Before we moved to New York for Heather's post-graduate work, she and I lived incredibly visible lives as political and social gay people in Louisiana. This was a time when a former KKK grand wizard, David Duke, lost the governorship by only a tiny percent of the vote. We had a lot of support from our families and straight friends and, as a result, somehow ended up as the outspoken poster children for ideal lesbian couplehood. It seemed only right that we get married in front of our southern community before leaving Louisiana. At the time, we felt like we *were* the gay revolution.

Although I was with my lover happily for three years before having that ceremony and "legitimizing" our commitment to each other, she'd still been Heather and I'd still been Leigh. After getting married in front of family and friends, though, I noticed people started treating us as an inseparable package, even making the common, funny slip-up of calling us "Leather and He." We became Gilbert and Sullivan, Rodgers and Hammerstein, Fred and Ethel, Ozzie and Harriet.

When we moved to New York, Heather started veterinary school at Cornell and I started a job. She had an immediate social circle, and I did not. Heather was hardly ever home because of school, and I started spending my off hours immersed in her professional world just to spend time with her. I ended up helping her on weekends and at night in the avian clinic; I hung out with her while she studied at school; I went to all of her school social events. And what becomes habit eventually becomes expected. I became a prosthetic attachment to Heather's life. I had no community—living as Ward and June Gay Cleaver isolated me.

Heather's academic program wasn't any different from any other professional schools like law or human medicine; oftentimes the married students are supported by their spouses (usually by wives), and somehow I fell into that role by default. I was seen as the saint supporting Heather, expected to cook and clean (and work) and manage our lives and our multitude of pets while she was in school. I liked operations to run smoothly, and she was fine with relinquishing the details; there was precious little discussion as it all fell gradually and automatically into place. Vet-school friends—even gay ones—joked that everyone needed a housewife like me (calling me that despite the fact that I also worked sixty hours a week; this joke, of course, never would have been made to a straight couple, because it would come off as blatantly insulting or hit too close to home). Heather was The Husband—and much to my amazement, she seemed to find a cozy place in that comfort zone. I, too, allowed myself to fall into self-fulfilling prophesy by playing the martyred wife. I internalized the world's expectations for us, and "I" became "we."

Since high school, I'd done quite a bit of painting and drawing. I graduated with distinction in English literature from college. And then I'd packed up my canvas, brushes and diploma to come be an accountant in the frozen tundra of upstate New York. I was the constant companion to a dog, a cat, a giant iguana, land and sea turtles and a guinea pig. I scrubbed the bathtub, served up nourishing vegetarian meals and scraped ice off the car as my guitar collected dust in the corner.

After finally recognizing my misery, I hit bottom with the realization that the gay-revolution cruise ship had left port without me. Queer marriage often is thought to be free of the pitfalls of heterosexual unions, the solemn and solid weight of which brings with it eons of social baggage. So two women together equals tabula rasa, right? Beyond the obvious issue of legal (in)validation, gay unions are thought to exist in a state of entirely bearable lightness of being—take the parts you like of marriage, and leave the rest. For most, no obvious parental imprinting on your gender roles, right? Can you even still "turn into your mother"— if your mother not only wed your dad prior to women's lib but was straight as well? But supposed freedom from role models also means an absence of them. In a world with no Hallmark greeting cards for your gray aunties' fiftieth wedding anniversary, the breakup of the latest blond Hollywood-dyke power couple is a blow.

So when I would go to my gay or straight friends to discuss my problems with Heather, they would retreat. I became accustomed to hearing a certain mantra every time I tried to confide in someone about my marital discontent: "Oh, you and Heather are the best couple I've ever seen. You'll work it out." End of conversation. It is not in the best interest of progressives to hear that their favorite queer couple is not the picture of perfection they had assumed. It might mean that they would have to think of us as real people with normal problems instead of the political action figures we had become to them.

I am aware that this "1 + 1 = 1" problem does not plague just same-sex relationships. I am also aware that surrendering an identity is something women are more conditioned to do than men are. So, what a mess it can turn out to be when two women come together in a social institution that never was intended for them in the first place.

And so it was that, as a lesbian and working professional and new young thing of the 1990s, I found myself in a "traditional" marriage. We of the collegiate activism, of the big southern gay wedding and of the clean-slate discussions of romantic openness, had become the furthest thing from my and our imaginations. The effect this had on me was that I lost much of my drive and ambition, much of my own voice and independence. In short, it suffocated me.

Once I realized that the more I contributed to the "betterment" of my marriage the more I lost my selfhood, I started playing sports to build up my own circle of friends. While there was some overlap with Heather's vet-school world, I had found a niche. As soon as I found a place to be myself outside of Heather's planet, however, we started fighting about time and chores. Who would take care of the pets? Who would make dinner tonight? Who would vacuum? Amazingly, these kinds of questions never surfaced until I tried freeing up some of my life. These were not just Heather's expectations, but those of her fellow students as well. More than once she'd compared us to other married vet-school couples and asked, "Why can't we just be like that?"

On my rugby team, I met the woman with whom I would fall

completely in love, a woman who did not see me as a doctor's wife or Heather's partner, but instead as a good friend named Leigh. It was then that I was reminded of who I was—myself and myself alone, rather than a component of an institution. And it wasn't until I fell in love with her that I revived myself both personally and professionally.

I imagine that most people feel the way I do: that one's love life is like a *Star Wars* saga that goes on and on and on. The films your memory plays are all out of sequence, and the symbolism is hell to decode. I do, however, have some very specific recollections: letting myself get close to a friend who challenged me as an individual. Falling in love with her and having an affair, not realizing that I was having an affair since it wasn't sexual. And Heather giving me the ultimatum that I cease my other relationship or leave forever after eight years together. All the while, I still loved Heather deeply. I specifically recall intense depression and terrible guilt—for not following the rules and for hurting someone who had grown comfortable with an arrangement in which I should not have participated. I did not understand it then, but it was the beginning of my serious reservations about monogamy as a one-size-fits-all bargain.

I left.

The problem I had in my marriage, aside from not knowing myself as well as I thought, is that we did not have an explicit agreement on how we would lead our lives together. Sure, we skimmed over the hypothetical idea of seeing other people in the distant future and proceeded to make seemingly contradictory commitment declarations in front of a hundred people in a Unitarian church, but what I never said to my partner is that I need plurality in relationships—even in sexually exclusive ones. The all-important follow-up questions would have been: "Do you understand what that means? Do you have problems with that? Do you at all feel those same needs?" And so on.

Since I hope that the rest of my life spans a good amount of time, I cringe at the idea of again and again replicating the unpleasant mistakes I have made thus far. It would be like experiencing death over and over in the same video game because I hadn't learned the nuances of the joystick. Ridiculously, we can find lessons everywhere. I did, and decided I would no longer be a willing casualty of the "happily-ever-after" attempts to legitimize gay presence.

I loved my wife and I loved my friend, romantically. Not in the same capacity and not one to the exclusion of the other. Some of it's about falling in and out of love, and some of it's about finding your heart easily reaching out to two (or more) with no strain on itself. And because there really are no models for this either—this possibility of open adoration of a partner *and* a lover, or two lovers—you stumble, you grope.

Since my divorce, I've dated nonexclusively—not only because of being a little gun-shy about commitment, but also because I wanted to reorganize my priorities and focus on myself instead of on a primary relationship. In maintaining casual relationships, it sounds like I am only talking about sex, doesn't it? The language of "casual" is too easy, too flippant. Because I consider romantic love the sole determinant of what I define as intimacy, I consider myself a polyamorous person, whether I am at the time sleeping with one person or more than one. Granted, it's an unorthodox view of relationships, but where existing rules no longer seem to make sense, we must construct ones that do.

It takes a lot of energy to keep up with many people you love deeply. Perhaps one day I will not have that energy. But I do know that for a certain and important period of my life I *do* have it, and refuse to choose between sharing many intimate friendships and having only one lover who requires complete and total devotion. Complete and total devotion drains my battery faster than I can spit. And despite what we see in so many art films, love is not supposed to be about entropy. It's about how we can make one another's lives worthwhile, and my life has been and continues to be enriched by each person I let into it.

Someone once told me that my differently colored attitude is probably due to the fact I haven't met the "right person" yet. But if I have learned anything so far in life, it's that there is no single person in the world perfect for only one other person in the world. It defeats the laws of probability, not to mention common sense. Perhaps, instead, the reason why I feel the way I do is that I *have* met the right person. Again and again and again.

The Why of the Y

Leslie Miller

Who coude telle but he hadde wedded be
The joye, the ese, and the prosperitee
That is bitwixe an housbonde and his wif?
—*Geoffrey Chaucer's* Canterbury Tales

I am now forced to admit to some semblance of strategic essentialism, to some sort of solidarity with those goddess-loving, herstory-talking, herb-quaffing multitudes who embrace the term "womyn." I have been brought to understand the why of the *y*, the satisfaction of a semiotic gesture that (may I say) reeks of the misjudged efficacy of politically irrelevant yet deliciously discernible protestations.

But my alliance here is tenuous, my questions many. "Burn the bra!" Don't you need it when you go running? "Eliminate the 'men' (if only orthographically)!" I was raised by men—three brothers and a father and countless friends who inspired me, supported me, whose spectrum of male energy helped to inform my ever-shifting, multiplicitous feminine self. Are they necessarily eighty-sixed once I decide to commune with the womyn? Yikes. We were born in the seventies, weren't we? Did any of this a feminist make?

Maybe. Partially.

For perhaps it has less to do with global politics and more to do with personal comfort. Which is to say that a womyn's a woman no matter how you slice it, dice it or spell it, and just maybe that *y* helps some grown-up grrls to slip into a term that otherwise just doesn't seem to fit: It pinches, it binds, it bunches a little in the crotch. I believe this now, because though still a woman, I am also a wyfe.

There, see? The spellchecker just tried to change it for me, cheeky bugger—so difficult to be a wyfe in a world of wives. But I don't look like a wife (how does a wife look?), I don't act like a wife (or do I?), I never intended to be one (this part's true). But the great state of Nevada tells me that it's so, there's a checkbook that suggests a joint account and even the Social Security Administration's on the case: They sent me a letter suggesting I change my name. There's also a husband—a dear, loving life partner—who appears in my house in the evening (perhaps the most convincing piece of evidence yet). And where there's a husband then surely a wife will follow.

Did I say follow?

So now I must tell the story, because I always tell "the story," partly because it charms and pleases, and partly because the how explains the why of the wyfe. We met, we fell in love, we "dated" on the weekends for six weeks. Ex-punk tech geek with a steady job meets anti-boy grad student with a year left on her master's in English literature. Each of us was barely one foot out of our last long-term, cohabiting relationship. I was sort of in town for the summer: staying with my parents in the small town where I grew up, swinging in on weekends to scrounge some big-city crumbs in Seattle. He was a friend of a friend, we met in a bar . . . and the clichés stop there. After the first night, I was hooked. I stalked him the next and then we were both lost to this insane relationship in which two weeks felt like a year and our most intimate secrets were out by the third. Funny, that: The intense emotional purging was what connected us. Those "you never told me that!" sort of secrets were our chipper date-story fodder, but only yesterday I found out he doesn't really like pineapple.

The tesseract summer came to a close and reality set in: The job was in one state, school in another. As he drove with my beagle and me down to Los Angeles, we joked as we sped past the turnoff to Reno. The idea of marriage itself was laughable, and for two recent acquaintances about to be separated indefinitely by twelve hundred miles of sagebrush and beer bottles along I-5, it was a riot. The joke got better: There's I-10 to Barstow, Vegas just three hours away. Drive-up chapels, Elvis ministers—the Vegas quickie wedding was just kitschy enough to earn a hipster approval rating. Like Scotch and Dean Martin, it was back in style. Nevertheless, we kept driving south. We were, after all, fairly rational individuals not prone to following a fad for fad's sake (read: scared witless).

It took only three days to drive down and settle the pup and me into my little California bungalow. At the end of that week—the longest consecutive time we had spent in each other's company thus far—we named our options for Friday night: go to the beach with friends, go out to a bar, stay in and have more sex or go to Vegas and get married. There was no bended knee, gentle readers; neither of us asked—though he made me answer first. In the end we agreed that we wanted to be with each other forevermore. True, we had just met six weeks before, and yes, we lived in different states—but the fact was that we couldn't spend another moment sitting, staring at the other, attempting to articulate through some woefully inadequate, incredibly hackneyed, Hallmark-inspired dialogue how much we loved, respected and adored each other. And so I translated. "I guess that means I'd like to be your wife." I guessed. That's all I could do. Because the fact of the matter is that five hours later, as we sat in an overdone Vegas theme-restaurant in front of barely touched antipasto trading the pearlized white wedding license back and forth, we could only guess as to what that meant—to be married, to each other. Because we had been certain that we knew what it meant up to that point, and we knew that we didn't want what we thought we knew. At that point, as we were whispering back and forth like insults, "You're my husband," and "You're my wife," tasting the words through a patina of oil and vinegar, Matt stopped, and, like a kid, he took it back: "No, you're not a *wife*," he said. He took it back in order to be kind—"wife" sounded demeaning somehow, I felt it too. But what did that leave me with? If I wasn't a wife, then what was I?

And so the wyfe was born.

I must digress, briefly, to explain my personal etymology of the wyfe as I see it—the Miller Revision. And it begins with the Wife of Bath.[*] For those of you who don't routinely pick up fourteenth-century texts for a quick pleasure read (I include myself here), the Wife of Bath is a character in Chaucer's *Canterbury Tales:* Headstrong, lusty and clever, she talks circles around the largely dimwitted misogynist rabble also making a pilgrimage to the shrine of Thomas à Becket, Archbishop of Canterbury.

As the pilgrims make their way, they tell stories—those titular tales— through which Chaucer treats several hot topics of medieval Europe, including marriage and women's rights (we've come far). Indeed, many would name the Wife of Bath the first famous feminist; she's described as gap-toothed and full-figured, wearing scarlet stockings and spurs (who doesn't already like her?). In the face of learned men who spout textual examples to support their misogyny, she offers clear reason and personal experience in order to argue not just on behalf of marriage in general, but for remarriage, and, more important, for her right to marry again. She liked the institution so well, in fact, that she married no fewer than five times and was set for another go, claiming it was Venus who bestowed her with lust, and Mars who made her hearty enough to bear it out. Take that, John Gray.

But I admire the Wife of Bath's tale even more than her character, as both parable and gospel. In her story, a knight from King Arthur's court goes riding and, seized by lust and power, rapes a young woman. The knight is captured and sentenced to death; however, the queen makes him an offer. She gives him one year in which to scour the land and find the answer to the question: What is it that women desire most? If he succeeds, she will commute his sentence. If he fails, he dies. Never before or since

---

[*] *An explanation is warranted for the orthographical differences between "wyfe" (my locution) and "wif" (Chaucer's). Since I have given the wif as the source of the wyfe, why the y and not the i (and where did I get that e)? Entirely a lapse in memory, I'm afraid. More than a few years were wedged between the last time I read the* Canterbury Tales *and the only time that I got married, and "wyfe" looked medieval enough to me. (After all, I studied feminist theory, not Beowulf). Though a medieval scholar friend assures me that both "wyf" and "wif" could have been used, I still offer: mea culpa.*

has any man had such an incentive to tease out this enigma. Maybe *Cosmo* should suggest it: "Make Him Find Your G Spot or Die."

Not surprisingly, each person the knight asks responds differently. The knight, as he already proved, is not an innately good judge of what women want and has difficulty sorting through the responses. He's beginning to feel the sword on his neck when he runs into an old woman sitting by the side of the road. She promises to provide him with the answer he needs, if in return he does the next thing she asks of him.

They go to court, which is packed with not only the queen but also a multitude of wives, maidens and wise widows—all anxious to hear what the knight has to say, which is thus:

'My lige lady, generally,' quod he,
'Wommen desire to have sovereinetee
As wel over hir housbonde as hir love,
And for to been in maistrye him above.'

Not a woman in the room disagrees, and why should she? For no matter how egalitarian or fair-minded the woman (or man), who doesn't want the freedom to do as she pleases, to have dominion over her husband and over the deployment of her love? (And certainly the idea of "maistrye" over men hasn't ceased to titillate, either, not even for some womyn.) And that old woman, the one with it all figured out? After he answers correctly, she asks him to marry her.

I don't wish to be understood as bolstering the stereotype of the shrewish wife and the "yes, dear" husband; allow me to clarify that I mean anything but. Later in the *Canterbury Tales,* a character pronounces that women generally desire liberty, and not to be bound like slaves—*as do men.* The protagonist of this, the Franklin's story, of his free will swears to never take liberties with his wife against her wishes, or be jealous, but to obey and do her bidding, "As any lovere to his lady shal." And in return she promises to be humble and true, so taken with his promise is she. See what making nice gets you? It seems so reasonable that it sounds obvious, but I believe that many of us have trouble winnowing the chaff of power dynamics in order to find those small kernels of balance. Indeed, the first man who matched my will won my heart and hand, but the battles rage on, and, among the housbonde and the wyfe and the hounds, it is hard to say who is most willful.

Which is to say I think I actually was celebrating my independence when I got hitched. After all, it was as a recently married woman that I lived alone for the first time in my life. For one agonizing year . . . hold on a minute, it wasn't agonizing at all, was it? Now, as I write this in the quiet and the solitude I require (and don't get often enough), I remember that I did a bit more writing perhaps when I didn't just have a room of my own, but the whole damn house. I smile when I think of graduate school nights spent in fitful, fully clothed sleep after a midnight dinner and a long chat with the beagle. Vacuuming at two in the morning, because I was hopped up on caffeine and nicotine and couldn't bear to grade another paper. Sipping gin on my porch, smelling lemon blossoms and feeling not lonely, but alone, and self-sufficient, and pleased. And married.

And I have to admit that being married made a difference. It turned a six-week fling into a life commitment that would have to weather those twelve hundred miles—there wasn't a choice. For a girl prone to bolting at the first sign that she might have to not only compromise but even concede, it helped keep me there when I was so tired of processing that I wanted to throw up my hands and go back to relationships where I was in complete control. I don't like to admit that: I don't know how, or if, things would have turned out differently if we had attempted simply to maintain a monogamous commitment across two states, a commitment that had only six weeks to incubate. Part of my former argument against marriage (which I trotted out often) was that the marital bond was constructed for the weak-willed—a real woman in love could make a relationship work no matter the odds. But I needed it, we needed it, I now believe, because even with that false marital glue it was still hard as hell. The rub is that while getting married helped us—to express how much the other meant, to define the nature of our commitment—it also helps other people make incorrect assumptions about our choices: It helps my parents face the people at church; it encourages strangers to ask me about having children.

The "You, too, can be married to the love of your life in only six weeks and still be the same person you were before!" thing has been a hard sell; even though it's perfect infomercial material, no one wants to believe that marriage can be a large part of your life without it being everything, the everything that either saved or ruined you. Because they coincided, no one wanted to believe that my husband didn't have a thing to do with my returning to school thirty pounds lighter—far too light—than I had been six weeks before. He didn't. I didn't lose weight to get a husband, and I *certainly* didn't get a husband because I lost weight. The truth is that all that weight dropped away so quickly because I was sick: the sickness an oh-so-common demonstration of a self-loathing I acted out on my body. The truth is that although my eating disorder nearly ruined our early relationship (because I was in a relationship with "E.d." that left little room for hubby-to-be), without his support and tears and encouragement and anger—not at me, but at my self-loathing—I would have ended up in the hospital instead of a wedding chapel. It was then that I first let him—first let anyone—support me instead of just sucking it up. I discovered what true partnership meant.

Similarly, when I decided to not continue directly into my PhD, no one believed I really wanted to gain some perspective—write, work and live outside of academia—before continuing on in the program that had accepted me. This, too, was a timing issue: It so happened that I finished my master's as our one-year we've-never-lived-together wedding anniversary rolled around, which surely meant I was quitting to follow my husband, conceding to his lucrative, Seattle-based tech career instead of pursuing my own in academia. Matt did encourage me to follow my gut instead of being "safe" and "reasonable," that's true. He also sweated blood hoping that in a few years I wouldn't resent the hell out of him because I took my master's and ran, straight to him. The truth is I ran straight into writing, and editing and reading and creating—a side of myself I'd put on hold in graduate school, and a side I needed back, desperately. The difficulty we had negotiating my choice to leave—and it was mitigated by wanting to be together—helped point me in the direction of what I really wanted to do. Did I want to live with my husband? Of course. Would I trade vacuuming at two in the morning for one night with him? Not a chance. Besides, he does most of the vacuuming.

In short, it is others who impose servitude on me in my marriage, not my husband. And it was this overriding imperative to prove them wrong that prompted the wyfe. The first year was the easiest, because no one believed I was married: I lived alone, I was in graduate school and I wore thrift-store clothes and the highest, biggest shoes I could find. My hair was dyed and my bright tattoo flashed frequently from my belly. I was twenty-seven but looked remarkably more like the freshmen who filled my composition courses. I had a slim silver band with no hint of a diamond on that meaningful finger. I studied feminist theory; I was loud. I laughed a lot and I drank a lot of beer with the boys. I introduced myself as Leslie Miller. No one believed it, and so I delighted in the truth for its shock value, like a punk rocker who says she's been born again: It didn't fit, and so I didn't mind. And so I told "the story" not only as proof that true love exists, but that it doesn't always wear a white dress, and it doesn't always wait for propriety, and as proof that *I* didn't wear a white dress, and *I* didn't wait for propriety.

But I would wonder, what happens when no one wants to hear the story anymore? What happens after five or ten years, when people ask how long you've been married and then just nod, or don't even ask because you look like you've been married for a while (which I used to believe looked like a lack of passion and now think looks a bit like flannel pajamas or a wool hat)? I have a friend who shared a book with me, some little New Age guide on Buddhist coping mechanisms for love and trauma (and the inevitable intersection of the two). One exercise is on managing catastrophizing, or what to do when the very worst you can imagine is the wolf at your door. The example given is of being rejected by a lover: Now what? I'd cry. And then? I'd scream and yell and feel hurt and angry and cry more. And then? I'd probably get tired and go to bed.

And so I imagined the worst possible outcome of not being allowed to tell the story, a story that stood in for my lover during the year we were apart: Someone might think that I have a traditional marriage. Someone might say I'm not a "real" feminist. What else? Someone might think I quit school for a boy. Someone might think I had a big wedding and forced other decent women to wear mauve against their will. And then? Then I'd probably get tired (of them) and go to bed (with my husband!). I hoped that after one or five or ten years it would no longer matter whether or not someone wanted to hear the story, because, after all, wasn't it just for the two of us? Wouldn't we both be too wrapped up in real lives—together, independently—to care about the what or the how or the when or if anyone else gives a fuck that I ran off to Vegas, or that he makes more money and that still sticks in my craw, or that I didn't trade a PhD for an Mrs. or that envelopes addressed to Mrs. Hendel make me think of his grandmother?

I don't tell the story very much these days (thanks for giving it one last hurrah). There is nothing unusual-seeming about our marriage. We live in the same state (okay, the same house); we appear regularly together at functions. We've known each other for two years now and been married nearly that long, though we seem so comfortable with each other that no one does the math. I don't choke over "husband" anymore, because, what's the point? I could say "partner" (I'm not a cowboy); I could just say his name and make people guess (with dogs named Pete and Henri, they might guess wrong). It's semantics. I think word games are useful when one feels threatened, or when there's a statement to be made. Though it's not my choice, I understand the why behind womyn. But I've met the wolf at my door, and he turned out to be a beagle.

What happens when no one wants to hear the story anymore? You save it for the grandchildren or some stranger at a bar, or you write an essay about it. You don't care so much about the how or the when or the what, because the why hasn't changed. But I think maybe there is one *y* that needs an adjustment.

I am a woman, and I am also a wife.

Sex Scenes

Noelle Howey

Three turns of a key, two thumping footsteps, a door clicks closed. Five more footsteps, cupboard creaks. A crystal tumbler rattles on the Formica countertop. Freezer door opens, twelve ice cubes crash into the ice bin. Two in the glass. Clink, clink. A splash of vodka, then up to the top with OJ. One quick stir. The spoon hits the counter. Dad's home.

Parcheesi is boring, and I always lose. Monopoly takes forever. I don't even know what Banana Tree is, but the side of the box suggests players should be ages three to seven. I'm eight. It's raining. Mindy doesn't want to play Barbies, I don't want to play Matchbox cars. The only things on TV are *Donahue*, an afterschool special I already saw and *The Edge of Night*, which isn't half as good as *General Hospital*, so why bother. Mindy is slouched in the corner, chewing on her braid because her mother's not here to tell her to take her hair out of her mouth. After a few minutes, she suddenly perks up. I thought of a new game, she says. Love Boat. I stop fiddling with the snap on Ken's pants. This sounds promising. My dress-up box isn't quite up to the task, so we pull stray items out of my mom and dad's closet: rayon blouse with a satin tie, corduroy blazer, wool skirt and fringy brown suede boots. Anything adult-seeming. Two hours later, Mindy, as Phil, and I, as Myrna, meet on the bow of the ship just outside the second-floor bathroom. It's love at first sight. Did you have fun at the shuffleboard contest? Positively. Shall we take a stroll around Puerto Vallarta tomorrow? Oh, but how wonderful. As Eddie Rabbitt's "I Love a Rainy Night" swells on the radio, Phil moves in for the kiss. Myrna is blushing; she's never done this before. But as soon as she feels Phil's moist lips pressing sweetly, nervously against hers, she closes her eyes. She feels like she's caught a sudden chill. A moment later, Phil pulls back and shoves a braid into his mouth. His eyes dart around the room, looking anywhere but at Myrna. I want to play Banana Tree, he says.

In my parents' bedroom, a poem called "Fitzgerald Says" hung just above the laundry hamper. My mother told me it was a love poem that my father had written to her just after they got engaged, in the voice of Fitzgerald, their stuffed red-plaid dog. I didn't quite understand it—it had references to sharing burgers and pickles and making fun of Richard Nixon and all sorts of things that sounded not romantic in the least. My mom's eyes, watery blue behind fake tortoiseshell frames, looked distant and slightly hurt when I asked why they liked each other, so I eventually dropped the subject and assumed that I would understand their attraction better once I got older. I told myself that, too, when my father would eye my mother like she was retail merchandise and scoff at her taste in clothes or the way they fell over the curves of her round belly and bottom. I burned inside when he withheld a compliment before they went out to a formal gathering, or when he didn't hear her quiet, plaintive request that he come to bed. When I couldn't take it anymore, I would creep into the bedroom where my mother was paging through Silhouette romances, biding time until my father stumbled upstairs to bed in a tipsy haze. I would curl close to her voluminous breast, and she would stroke my hair, reassuring me that yes, honey, Dad loved us both. I nodded silently, but inwardly promised: Not me. This would never be me.

I got tired of Love Boat. I stopped liking it after I realized that Julie and Gopher weren't going to get married after all. Mindy and I changed the rules. Now we didn't bother with donning grown-up clothes, much less a plotline. We locked my bedroom door, stripped naked and climbed under my Holly Hobbie sheet, rolling over and touching and kissing and giggling. After one or two rounds, Mindy was tired of playing the boy, so I did it. I started with hearts and flowers. My Phil brought her Myrna flowers in a pot from the downstairs porch, Oreos from the pantry, poems clipped from old Valentine's Day cards. But Myrna seemed unimpressed. She would get into a giggle fit, which would lead to the hiccups, and then there'd be no kissing at all. So Phil, feeling that he obviously needed to be a tad more manly in his pursuit, got serious. He started pinning Myrna's soft, pink arms to the pillow until she begged for a kiss. That got her attention. He would tell her she was nothing. He used his black ballet tights to tie her hands together and make her whimper. It all seemed very dramatic, very *Gone With the Wind,* so much so that the area between Phil's legs would be damp by the time Myrna was ready to go home for supper.

When Phil perched atop Myrna's small body like a flag on undeclared land, his scalp felt alive with electricity. His whole body felt lit from within: tingly and goosepimply and wonderful. Phil was through with Barbies. That's for sure.

In ninth grade, I met Todd Louis Milton: six feet, blond hair, blue eyes, nothing but Gap clothing, bedroom with posters of Princess Leia and Yoda, never been kissed. Todd yelled "scud" (never "shit") if he stubbed his toe, drank Coke even at his cousin's wedding and all in all was a perfect template for the First Real Boyfriend. He was afraid to kiss me. I had to plant the first one on his cheek in a stealth move. He seemed vaguely pleased, and somewhat afraid. Which only egged me on. Within a few months, I practically forced him to feel me up by shoving the dead weight of his hand against my padded training bra. Horrified, he drew his hand back and ran into the bathroom, choking back tears. I followed behind him, ashamed. Pounding on the bathroom door, I wept to Todd that I was really, really sorry. I didn't know what on earth was wrong with me.

Boys always moved faster than girls, and here I was, moving a teenage boy to tears by making him touch my flat chest. But he was so cute, and so lovable, and it just felt so good when I got him to touch me in the places I asked him to. Still, I was painfully aware that if anyone was supposed to recoil from bases one through three and end up hiding in a bathroom snuffling into a roll of toilet paper, it was me. I was mortified that my sexual urges were so strong, so blatantly bad girl. I promised myself I would try to "let things happen" rather than force them. I would let him make the moves. And if nothing happened, so be it. Better that than be labeled one of those hateful, frightening words scribbled in toilet stalls about girls who pushed and pushed until they got what they wanted: Bitch. Cunt. Nympho. Slut. I tried to slow down. I even wrote a letter to *Seventeen* asking what to do when girls wanted it worse than boys. I got a form letter back that advised me to speak with my guidance counselor. I didn't think Mrs. "There's nothing pre- about the PSAT" Tillson was up to the challenge, so I tried talking to my mother while she was grilling hamburgers outside for a family barbecue. A bit aghast, she told me to respect Todd's wishes and to be patient. She burned two patties.

Soon enough, slowing down wasn't an option. Somehow, over a period of six months or so, Todd decided he could be a good boy and get some nooky on the side. When I sent him notes copied from the Forum section of my parents' *Penthouse*s, he started responding with gusto. Once I got the green light, I began to study how I could make him want me even more: flashing a bra strap between classes, showing up on my dad's basement pool table in nothing but undergarments, growing my blond hair long and wavy and wearing Cinderella ball gowns to prom because he got into that whole Disney heroine thing. As my crowning achievement, I learned how to choreograph a seduction: this one like Kelly McGillis in *Top Gun*, that one like Rebecca DeMornay in *Risky Business*. I had come to realize that, without actually pushing Todd's hand down my shorts or up my tank top, I could quietly make sex happen. I could drop hints and mimic sexy scenarios, and once we actually did it I could let both of us believe it was all his idea. This seemed completely normal to me. I stopped worrying about being a slut; I was just a healthy girl in love letting her boyfriend have a little jog around the sexual baseball diamond. When I strutted in front of him in a teddy with a boom box playing "Hungry Eyes" in the background, I was simply showing my devotion to his needs. That "ha, ha . . . now I've got you" feeling that swelled in my stomach? True love, pure and simple.

When Todd and I lost our virginity on New Year's Eve, 1988, I screamed with glee. Sex itself felt a little strange, a general rubbing sensation no more inherently exciting than getting VapoRub smeared on my chest when I had a cold. But what it meant felt incredible. It meant he loved me. Best of all, he wanted me more than he wanted to be good. When we lay there after sex, he whispered, You're mine, and I smiled, curling ever closer to him. Yes, I am, I murmured sweetly into his ear. I had never felt so confident in my powers of persuasion.

Looking back, I see how I convinced myself that playing the femme fatale was an act of submission (not domination), that I was simply looking for love (not power): Thirsting for love was comfortable, even expected of me—but there was nothing romantic whatsoever about a girl desperate for control.

Mindy moved to Chicago at the end of seventh grade, but we had stopped playing together long before then.

She didn't like our games anymore. It's not like I want to play the boy, she said, but I don't get why you have to be such a meanie when you do it. She said our parents were going to figure out what we were doing, anyway, and then we'd really get in trouble. How many seventh graders say they're going to take naps together in a locked bedroom once a week? she asked. Don't they think that's weird?

I guess so, I nodded blankly. I had become addicted to our playtime, the lazy hours spent rolling over her body, leaving mine sticky-warm and smelling of her mom's cocoa butter lotion; the way her green eyes widened in slight surprise every time I told her to do something; the secret, slightly superior glances we stole when someone asked us what we were doing for so long upstairs.

Before I leave, Mindy said hesitantly, you need to do something. Promise you'll never tell anyone what we did. It will ruin your career if you ever become famous, she said. You know, the *National Enquirer*.

I hadn't even thought about that. My heart started to pound. I had never considered the possibility of anyone except my parents finding out about Mindy and me, but now I realized that having this get out would be even worse than when Monique Kimball and Marcy Johnson smeared Chap Stick on each other's boobs in order to make them grow faster and Jeremy Goldberg told everyone. You're right, I assured Mindy, with a sudden, visceral desire to see her gone forever. No one will ever know.

When Dad left, he took his clothes, computer, a set of steak knives and the recliner that sat in the southwest corner of the den. He left the vodka. I assumed it was an oversight. When Dad left, he kissed me good-bye and was closer to crying than I had ever seen him. I'm going to see you this Saturday, he said through clenched teeth, with a fierceness he usually only showed when scolding. What's the rush? I asked. It's not like we normally saw each other for days in a row—at least not in a meaningful sense. No rush, Dad said. We've got time.

Once he was gone, I spent a half-hour on my hands and knees combing my fingers through the two-inch-thick grooves in the carpet where his recliner once was.

When Mom got home from work late that evening, she crumpled into a heap. Half the evening she wept, alternating shots of Grand Marnier with lazy forkfuls of a plain iceberg lettuce salad.

Your father loved me, I guess, but never knew how to show it, she muttered to me. I nodded, looking down at my lap. Well, I have had enough of that, Mom said, and turned on her side to sleep. In the morning, just before I headed off to school, I was surprised to find her still there, curled on the couch, sleeping like a baby.

In college I dumped Todd for Nat, a short, dimpled math major who promised that he could never love me.

Four years of being with Todd had grown tiresome. His niceness and accompanying malleability had lost their appeal. I began to confuse his essentially sweet nature with shallowness. Plus, I had grown tired of our seduction game. It was way, way too easy and predictable. Flash a boob: He gets an erection. Slowly lift the hem of a skirt: He gets an erection. Read a book . . . and so on.

I desperately missed the early jolts of seratonin when Todd's eyes first started to glide over my body, pausing at the curvy particulars, my surge of quick, breathless, completely self-absorbed thoughts like oh-yes-Noelle-see-you-are-sexy-see-he-wants-you-you-are-hot-and-beautiful-and-desirable-and-babelicious. I wanted to feel that power again—the unmistakable feeling of victory that came from being watched, and wanted—and I figured the payoff would be even bigger if the boy was more unattainable.

So I was looking for a challenge: a dreamboat of emotional inaccessibility, as congenitally unable to show me kindness as any Marlboro man. Unfortunately, there weren't many rugged cowboys at my hippie college in Ohio. So I settled for imagining myself with an Artist, preferably one with trendy wire-rimmed glasses, who would carry around a worn copy of Nietzsche and drink Scotch straight up, and with whom I would always come second—after his poetry, painting or organic gardening. Nat was passably close to this well-drawn stereotype. He wasn't a total intellectual, and didn't drink, but he sighed knowingly during jazz concerts and deified obscure science fiction writers.

Moreover, he had the core quality of aloofness I was going for. He didn't really seem like he needed me. The ultimate turn-on was the moment, on an early date, when he took me aside and bluntly informed me that his best friend was the closest female in his life and that no matter what I did or who I proved to be, he could never love me as much as her. Nor did he expect to try. He made this speech, coldly, holding my elbow firmly, as we stood in a stairwell just a few steps shy of two highly amused sophomores smoking a bong. I ran away to my bedroom and cried, and swore I would never speak to that conceited creep again. That cinched it: I wanted him bad.

As I dove into women's studies courses, carting home feminist tutorials like *I Know Why the Caged Bird Sings* and *This Bridge Called My Back*, I nonetheless made myself completely available for Nat, meeting him after computer lab, surprising him with candles and dinner in his monastic dorm room and, most of all, fashioning myself into a submissive sex fanatic so that he would never contemplate breaking up with me. It seemed to work. After a few months of my undivided attention, he swore he was in love with me. I was thrilled, and felt like I'd bagged the big prize.

Unfortunately, I told myself that getting what I wanted meant I had to keep up my all-sex-all-the-time routine, whether I liked it or not. (Sometimes I did; yet more and more often I found myself yearning just for a good book or a slice of pizza.) I looked for inspiration to keep me primed for sex. I studied the small cache of soft-porn mags a friend kept hidden in his sock drawer and learned the models' positions, the way they craned their backs and spread their legs. I didn't know what Nat's fantasies were, specifically, but I figured if I just did enough, and often, I'd happen upon one or two or ten of them in due time.

I wanted Nat's approval, to be sure, but only when mixed with disdain. And just as my father's moments of softness—amidst his general mood of sarcasm and displeasure—used to appease my mother for days at a time, so too did I find new thrills by pleasing Nat momentarily. When I could coax his sullenness into tenderness, it gave me a bigger charge than if he had been gentle all the time. Finding ways to trigger Nat's mood change became a pleasure almost as heady as sex. It means he likes you, my mother always said of the mean elementary-school boy who pulled my pigtails and launched spitballs into my hair (and finally, sheepishly, sent me a mushy valentine). Years later, like girls the world over who fetishize boys who berate them while ignoring the sweet, shy ones, I sought out someone with a mean streak. What greater power could there be than winning such reluctant approval?

Of course, intellectually, I told myself I wanted reciprocity. At night, after making love in variation number 62-A, Nat would fall asleep spooned behind me, his breath making moist Os between my shoulder blades. I would stare out the window into the student common, and if I happened to see a star, every time I would wish that we would be together forever, that Nat would love me as much as I loved him. I should have been careful what I wished for.

More than a year into our relationship, when I was thoroughly convinced that I would always love him more than he did me, Nat seemed newly infatuated. Out of nowhere, he began sending me a love note every day. He scrawled poems, promised me home-cooked meals and generally treated me with a gentle admiration. And I grew progressively less interested in him. I left the last three notes sealed in their envelopes. I realized for the first time, with trepidation, that my love for Nat wasn't unconditional after all: It only flourished when unrequited.

And I was disgusted. Forget Phyllis Schlafly, I thought. I was the ultimate antifeminist. After all, I was seeking male rejection and finding solace in being a martyr to it at the very same time I was chirpily marching for choice and silk-screening girl-power T-shirts. I felt really, really bad. But nothing changed.

On my summer vacation between sophomore and junior years, my mother introduced me to Mike, her new beau. We had zilch in common. Mike, an older gent, liked Ross Perot and duck hunting; I was absorbed by feminist theory and vegetarianism. But my mother adored him, with the giddiness of the proverbial schoolgirl. I espied them gazing at each other on the patio, sneaking out in the middle of the night to take a skinny dip in the hot tub. He brought her gifts; she cooked him dinner. It was shocking to see my mother with a man, laughing and kissing as though she had always known what constituted a normal romance. Oddly, I felt betrayed. I told myself that she *must* miss my father's sarcasm and coldness. It might have gotten a little ugly at times, but hell, my parents had had something deep—deep enough that I couldn't understand their love poems! Deep enough that I had to suffer through living with him for fourteen years. Certainly that couldn't have been for nothing.

The straightforward happiness my mother shared with Mike seemed suspicious for another reason, too. It looked too easy—a whole lot easier, in fact, than the mental calisthenics I was performing in my ever-rocky relationship with Nat. When Mom and Mike fell into an embrace, it looked disturbingly uncomplicated. Sometimes, she initiated; other times, he did. Either way, they simply looked happy.

Nothing was that simple when Nat and I kissed. I felt the same ennui with Nat's newly sensitive self as I had when Todd became easy prey. Nat was all lovey-dovey now, devising elaborate romantic settings and christening "our song" from his Ella Fitzgerald collection. I tried to kiss him back, but it was too sweet, too balanced. Plainly, I needed the high that came from the power struggle. A light bulb went on in my head. Aha! I thought. What about S/M?

Now, lest Susie Bright get all perturbed with me, let me say that I understand fully (feminist sex-manual consumer that I am) that S/M can be playful, enjoyable, innocent fun that uses power dynamics in healthy ways. Let me also say that when I first gingerly suggested to Nat that he tie me to my dorm dresser, such fun is not what I had in mind.

I decided that if Nat couldn't be snarly to me in the cafeteria or the common, I could coax him into being like that in private, whether he wanted to or not. So after getting him to relent and play along, I would plead for Nat's attention and attempt to fulfill his wishes as long as he would dominate me and tell me I was a dirty little girl. I insisted on his "abuse," for him to call me his slave or write swear words on my back in lipstick. In fact, I usually told him exactly what to say. Eventually, I couldn't make love unless I was being play-humiliated. And when I would return to my dorm room, burning between my legs and both nauseated and titillated, I would read my women's studies homework.

When my mother sensed my ambivalence about her new relationship—a fact not lightly cloaked by my rolling eyes and tendency to sneer in Mike's direction—she confronted me about it. I said that her relationship was obviously shallow and unfulfilling, not like her connection with Dad—or mine with Nat. I simply couldn't believe that love could exist without a concomitant power struggle. Wouldn't the relationship be hopelessly dull? Who would make the decisions? How would you know who was winning?

Dad was living in a nearby apartment complex with a bucolic name like Pleasant Meadows or Deer Valley, and had familiarized himself with all the conveniences of a modern home he had managed to neglect for twenty years.

I first dropped by during my freshman year in college. It had taken me several years to get up the gumption to see him without someone else there to keep the conversation going. In the past, our anemic exchanges had rarely gone deeper than a discussion of the three inches of snow we got last night and were punctuated with long, painful stretches of silence. Nervously, I rang the doorbell. Dad answered, balancing a basket of just-dried laundry against his hip and waving me in. Hey, he said, cheerfully. Pizza's almost ready. You like green peppers and onions, right? No pepperoni?

Two hours later, I was pleased to discover my father was willing to talk about subjects more scintillating than the lake effect. Even more exciting, as we dissed Dan Quayle and mocked people who didn't like *The Simpsons,* I realized—with some shock and trepidation—that I actually liked speaking to my father. Still reeling from having an unexpectedly good time, I excused myself to the bathroom. There, just above the toilet, was a small stack of reading material. Most of it was the usual: *Newsweek, National Geographic,* a funny movie quote book. But flipping through the pile, I found something I hadn't expected: Diane Ackerman's *A Natural History of Love.* Such a reading choice surprised me. It seemed so earnest, so sincere—like something my dad would make fun of, not absorb himself in.

I came out of the bathroom, still paging through it. My dad was sipping his Coke. Anything good in there? he asked. Yeah, I said. You never know what you're going to find.

It was 12:45 A.M., October 15, 1994. Nat and I had just finished making love. He rolled over, staring at the crack in the wood paneling next to my futon. True, it wasn't the best sex ever; I felt a little stressed and tired from going to temp job interviews all day where they acted like I was a Mensa pledge for knowing how to do long division. But I had moved all the way from the Midwest to Silicon Valley just to be with Nat, and I was determined to make it work.

I rubbed the small of his back and nuzzled his neck. Nat, I asked, as usual, do you think I'm pretty? Do you think I'm beautiful? For the three years I had been with Nat, I had asked these painfully insecure questions every time we made love.

C'mon, I begged, my voice crescendoing, please say it. Please? This exchange, like our sexual dirty talk and dominant/submissive games, was scripted. Nat knew to expect the questions; he knew what answers to give. And then I would lean back, newly relaxed, as mellow as if I had just smoked the clichéd postcoital cigarette. After his compliments, fished for and planned out as they were, I would feel comfortable in my body— at least for a day or two.

But tonight Nat was mute. He rolled back over to look at me, his eyes as hard and unflinching as marble. No, he answered. Frankly, Noelle, he said, wearily resting his head on his hands, I think you've gained too much weight. Your thighs look so fat, he said, that they repulse me. I can't bear to look between your legs. It's disgusting.

I drew a sheet over my bare body. Without warning, we were off the script. I had always dictated the insults Nat would hurl at me during sex. I called that being submissive. I suddenly realized, with a shudder, that real abuse was an altogether different story. I always picked out insults I could handle, ones that, in a weird way, were backhanded compliments, like "slut," or "bitch." "Fat" didn't make the cut. "Disgusting" and "repulsive" didn't either.

I leapt from the bed and threw on the first sweats I could find. I layered myself twice on top and bottom. Still, I was shivering violently. It wasn't like being cold; it was like being emptied out.

Nat, I swallowed, I'm 108 pounds. That's skinny.

Look, he said sternly and slowly, like a nineteenth-century schoolmaster, if you didn't want to know, you shouldn't have asked me.

But I was just kidding, I said, still shaking.

Nat softened, slightly. Well, we're a little old to be playing these bullshit games, aren't we?

Thanks to the so-called healing power of time, one year later I had gotten over Nat and started to date other, equally charming fellows in my new home, New York. I had learned my lesson. Date abusive guys, but keep the relationships short. That way you can get your sexual kicks, but not have a strong emotional attachment that might come back to bite you. This seemed like a very sensible plan. (Of course, I was also on Prozac.)

I trysted with Jason, who had a girlfriend and wasn't about to leave her; Lucas, who mocked the poor sops who didn't own cashmere; Philip, who thought compliments were bourgeois; and Michael, who simply kept forgetting he was dating me.

Like all my other friends, I bitched about dating Scummy, Jerky Guys, but I eschewed all contact with anyone who might not fit into that cohort of young urban males. After a while, I resigned myself to the fact that I was a Doomed Modern Woman, one of those unfortunate women's magazine demographics incapable of being attracted to a nice guy. This fate irritated me immensely. I didn't understand why I persisted in seeking out brusqueness, why I still wanted sex to be a dance of competing interests, more about cementing who was on top than expressing love or intimacy. After all, even my mother had moved on; why couldn't I?

Then, after two years in the city, I met Christopher. Christopher was assigned to be my partner in an acting class I was taking just to meet boys who were nothing like him. He was deeply considerate from the first, if a bit shy, and almost childlike in his guilelessness. He was hopelessly unfashionable, wearing white sneakers and Dockers with nondescript T-shirts and a backpack correctly worn on both shoulders for maximum chiropractic benefit. He worked as a data entry clerk, and didn't drink or smoke or have any other noticeable vices. He went to a no-name college. He blushed, and he used Binaca before rehearsal. He wanted to be an actor. He seemed so sweet that I was certain he was either gay or dumb.

Once I saw his apartment (during a platonic rehearsal), I knew for sure he wasn't gay. He had a poster of Gillian Anderson in his bedroom. But eek! I thought. I date guys with Picasso prints—framed—not slackers who still drool over movie stars. I was further discouraged by his bookshelves. He apparently subscribed to *TV Guide*, not the *New Yorker*, and played more Nintendo than I thought socially acceptable. Worst of all, when I asked him in passing what his favorite book was, he didn't know. Oh boy, I thought. At most, I'll fool around with this guy, but that's it. End of story.

That was the plan. And for a few hours, I stuck to it. As we were making out, on our first nonrehearsal date, he was shaking as though he hadn't touched a girl in years. (He hadn't.) It took him five tries to unsnap my bra, and he accidentally bit my lip. I was not touched by his boyish fumblings. Callously, I thought it was a little annoying in a one-night stand. But I stayed there all night; as we lay in a sweaty heap on his foldout sofa bed, I stared at his face, framed by long angelic eyelashes and high cheekbones, and thought, gently, how beautiful he looked when he slept.

The next afternoon, Christopher called me from a picnic. I had a great time, he told me. I didn't want to wait to tell you. I found myself smiling and rolling back on my bed to chat, with a bashfulness I no longer thought I had. By the end of the phone call I was infatuated. Unlike my usual choice of man, he hadn't waited the requisite three days to call and act like he didn't like me.

As the weeks progressed, we spent nearly every night together, mostly talking and getting him to relax into lovemaking. And entirely unexpectedly, we fell in love.

End of fairy tale? Well, no. I was still horrified by the cheesy paperbacks Christopher consumed with relish, and nervous that he didn't have enough intellectual acumen to keep me engaged. When we went out to dinner, I would pontificate. He would nod. Please say something smart, I would inwardly plead. He would ask for the check.

The sex was unnervingly reciprocal, without any weird mind games. I think I had been worn down by enough real neglect, abuse and generally inconsiderate behavior by guys that I no longer fetishized cruelty. Plus, I finally had a few years' experience of casual dating life, long enough to understand that having a man in the room did not equal companionship and that an evening at home with a book was vastly preferable to sex with a creep. Nonetheless, things progressed slowly with Christopher, largely because he didn't tell me what he thought. He never knew more than I did, or if he did, he was too passive to say so. And after a quarter-lifetime of desiring dominant men, his sensitive, quiet ways really upset me.

So I called him on it. Remarkably, he didn't flinch at criticism (though I later learned he was conditioned for it by years of withstanding his father's insults) and over the next few months began to proffer opinions, arguments, insights. He regaled me with anecdotes of how he performed an Aristophanes comedy in Greek at the Temple of Aphrodite. He talked to me about Bosnia. He pilloried Cybill Shepherd. And he told me that he had been threatened and mocked growing up, rendered mute by parents who used epithets like weapons. Who married at nineteen because he was on the way, never finished their educations and lived in poverty and resolute unhappiness. He told me he had been afraid to speak, and that our relationship had allowed him to come out—as a smart, well-spoken, breathtakingly gentle man without the urge to play power games.

I changed my mind about a lot of things because of Christopher. I had always seen myself married to a cuttingly sarcastic man with supernatural powers of aloofness, who subscribed to all the right magazines, could quote from esoteric authors and would probably irritate me with pretentious ramblings. A cardboard cutout of my father.

Christopher's kindness allowed me to be equally kind to myself. I also learned how vicious my own rigid stereotypes had been. I learned to see people more fluidly, more individually: not merely as dominant or submissive, winner or loser, man or woman. At night, when Christopher is curled next to me with his head nestled beside mine and his breath measured and calm, I feel blessed. He is nothing that I had ever been looking for, and yet he is everything I could have wanted.

Off the Map

Carrie Jones

My life is not turning out the way it was supposed to. The big choices I've made were not the ones I expected to make. Hell, most of them weren't even on the menu I envisioned when I was seventeen and Charting the Course of My Life. As a high-school senior, I was an honors-tracked slacker feminist with a flamethrower tongue. My yearbook is full of phrases like, "Be strong in your female power," and "I was so scared of you sophomore year."

This was the plan: I expected that by the age of twenty-five, I'd be well on my way to a PhD. I would have under my belt a small list of academic publications, a teaching job and several ill-fated affairs.

This is reality: At twenty-five, I'm a married homeowner with two cats and a mild addiction to digital cable. I'm a working writer and tutor who's about four semesters short of an undergraduate degree in English and government.

How the hell did this happen?

Here's how it started. Two months into my first year at college, I met Sean, the man I wanted to marry. Neither of us remembers exactly when we got engaged. It just became obvious that we were going to get married, and one day one of us said it.

After a year of banging my head against various walls, I realized that the first college I attended wasn't a good match for me. So when my honey, two years older than I, graduated, I left, too. His plan was graduate school in Pittsburgh. My plan was a good, cheap BA. Like any good Texan, I went home and transferred to the University of Texas at Austin. I got resident tuition there, which was a welcome change from my wacky little $20,000-a-year liberal arts college. I loved Austin: great bookstores, great live music, restaurants where you could get vegetarian crepes at four in the morning, tons of lefty weirdos. I loved being back with my friends—it seems like roughly every third person who graduates high school in the Lone Star State ends up at UT, and my friends were not exceptions. But I also loved my sweetie, who was roughly 1,424 miles away (but who was counting?). We talked all the time, sure; I shudder to think of my long-distance bills from those months. We sent letters and cards and packages. But I missed him so much I couldn't breathe sometimes. I missed cooking dinner with him, sleeping next to him, going to Ani DiFranco shows with him. I told myself to deal. Surely I didn't need a man to be happy. I was a good feminist. Those two concepts were obviously mutually exclusive. I struggled for a while. Talked to a trusted family friend.

"I'm miserable," I said.

"What would you change?" she asked. "No editing—tell me the first thing that comes to your mind."

I astonished myself by saying, "I want to go to Pittsburgh. I want to be with him."

Unbelievable.

I started planning to move to Pennsylvania for the following school year, continuing to anguish over why I was doing it. We got married in December. I finished out the spring semester in Austin, got myself accepted at a college in Pittsburgh and in August headed northeast in my car, with my mom driving a U-Haul behind me. For a little while after I arrived, everything seemed fine. Sean and I painted the bedroom in our new apartment. I made my first pot roast. I was happier—but I felt bad about it. Damn it, I'd read *The Feminine Mystique*. Feminist women had been fighting for the right to get out of the house for thirty years. So why was I taking so much pleasure in being in the house? Why wasn't I out there taking advantage of the rights they had won? I wasn't supposed to be getting my happiness through home and husband; it seemed against the rules for a sassy young feminist. I berated myself constantly for acting like a wife. Sometimes I didn't cook dinner when it was my turn to do so, just to prove to myself that I wasn't becoming Carol Brady.

In September, Sean thought he caught the flu. I fed him soup and vitamin C tablets and didn't think much of it. He started getting worse. We went to health services at his school. When they weighed him, Sean, normally a very skinny boy, was startled to discover he weighed forty pounds more than usual. The nurse practitioner said it was probably nothing but gastroenteritis (medico-speak for upset guts) and sent us home with a prescription for an antibiotic.

The next day, I found him in the bathroom on his knees in front of the toilet. I asked him what he'd had to eat. He said water and an antibiotic. I got scared. At that moment, our landlord knocked on the door. I opened it, and he came in, saying he was going to fix the back door. He saw Sean and said, "Good lord, boy, you look like a ghost." We spent that night in the emergency room.

And in the terror of the next week, I was glad I had moved to be with my lover. In that week, I almost lost him. Those forty extra pounds were water that Sean's body couldn't metabolize. There was water in his lungs. He was admitted for pneumonia. But something else was wrong. The doctors couldn't tell me what. They knew he had nephrotic syndrome, but it was thus far idiopathic. Translation: They knew his kidneys were screwed up, but couldn't pinpoint a cause. They asked him if he thought he was at risk for AIDS about every ten minutes, it seemed. They couldn't give us answers; they barely listened to me. All they could do was scare us with possibilities.

I called in the troops. Sean's whole family flew in on emergency medical fares: first his mom, Rose, and dad, Chuck; his brother, Charles, the next day; and his sister, Michelle, that weekend. My mom flew up. My brother and my dad spent hours on the Internet trying to find information for us. We came up with a list of possibilities. Every time I tried to talk to the doctors, they either patronized or ignored me. Rose told me that when Chuck had leukemia, the doctors treated her the same way. I remember the day I asked if the source might be focal segmented glomerular nephritis giving rise to the nephrotic syndrome. It was very satisfying to see a young intern's eyes nearly pop out of his skull with surprise that no matter how young or blond I was, I knew what I was talking about.

The days stretched on. We took turns staying at the hospital, going back to the apartment in shifts to shower or sleep. On the fifth day, I walked into Sean's hospital room to find his bed empty and Rose sitting alone by the window. She had bad news. They'd found a clot in the vessels between his heart and lungs. He was going down for surgery. I felt my knees buckle at the words "pulmonary embolism." He was going into the intensive care unit after the surgery.

Needless to say, those few hours he was in surgery are fuzzy in my mind. I was so afraid. I kept thinking, This is not how this was supposed to work. The sick spouse episode comes much later. This isn't supposed to happen until I'm older. Rose was in her mid-forties with two kids out of the house and one in high school when Chuck got sick. She had a whole life with him. I've had so little time. Please, please, let him be all right.

Three hours later, we met Sean in the ICU. He was drugged to the gills, but they'd gotten the clot. He was going to be okay. There was a tube running from the femoral artery in his thigh all the way up his torso to the pulmonary vessels, bombarding the clotted area with blood thinners. He would have to stay nearly motionless for a few days while the tube was in.

And so it was that at twenty-one, I helped my twenty-four-year-old husband turn on his side to urinate because he couldn't do it by himself. Drugged as he was, he looked at me with tears in his eyes and said, "Thank you. Thank you, my love, for staying with me through this." I would not allow myself to cry in front of him. I said, "Of course I'm staying, you goofball. I love you."

That moment will be with me for the rest of my life.

I stayed that night in the waiting room, with my mom, Rose and a stranger. The stranger was a woman whose husband was dying of liver cancer in a room across the ward from Sean. She was a nurse on another floor, she said, and was grateful to and impressed by the ICU nurses for their commitment and the quality of care they gave. The four of us chatted for hours. We talked about family, and she said she had a sister and brother-in-law in town. Rose said that if she needed to call them, we'd be happy to find her if the nurses called for her. She thanked us, but said matter-of-factly that she had spoken with her sister earlier, and she knew her sister couldn't take it. If support was what she wanted, she'd have to find it within herself; her sister was more likely to fall apart than to offer comfort. So she planned to stick out the night by herself and then call in the morning. In the morning, she said, her sister would feel stronger, more in control. She didn't want to shame her by asking for something she couldn't give.

She asked after my husband's condition, and we explained it. She said we shouldn't worry, that he had the best care he could get in Pittsburgh. We asked after her husband; she was quiet for a moment and then said, "He's tired. He's been fighting for a year. He's ready to go." I felt a small shock, knowing that someday, more than likely, I would be sitting in her place, waiting for my lover to die. And I felt intensely grateful that I wasn't there yet, that I had years of living with him and loving him ahead of me.

We spent six hours talking in the dim light of the waiting room— about men, hospital food, being there when you're needed, how to take stock of brutal situations and to find the strength to see them through, all the costly things women learn in staying through nights like these. I was having my first harsh lesson in powerlessness and vicarious pain. It was an initiation of sorts.

From that night on, I was counted among their numbers, women who have stayed through the darkest hours to help a child or sibling or lover, to be there at the bedside, to smile and be strong because your love compels you to do so.

My mom, Rose and the stranger made an odd trio. My Texas-born, upper-middle-class, Republican mom was running her own computer business. Rose, whose parents worked at the Hormel plant in Austin, Minnesota (home of Spam), worked part-time at a drugstore and spent her afternoons listening to her favorite leftist commentators on NPR. The stranger was a native Pittsburgher and a nurse. But these very different women, of a generation less ironic than my own, knew how to get through this horror, and they had much to talk about. They could speak of the prosaic, about dishwashers and laundry and menopause, and it was genuine. They had a kinship of laughter and pain. It was real, and it brought comfort. The cynical part of me dismissed all this as Erma Bombeck–style crap, and that part was almost strong enough to make me say something rude. I was glad that I didn't. My flame-thrower tongue couldn't help me in that place. That night taught me that what is common is not automatically banal. That night, what was common among us kept me alive and intact. These women, older than I, with stores of these memories to draw on for strength, had been through worse. They led me through my own first moments of tragedy as a wife. The grace of that act overwhelms me.

The next morning, I was feeding Sean his breakfast when an alarm came up on the monitor. (The alarms come up in every room, so that if a nurse happens to be with another patient, he or she knows which room to go to and exactly what's wrong.) The ICU alarms don't really sound very alarming anymore: They're simply repeated major chords, like the sounds that announce start-up on a Macintosh. They inform you calmly that, across the nurses' station from you, someone's heart has stopped beating.

The room number told me that it was the stranger's husband. I sent a prayer to a being I don't quite believe in that he would pass easily, that she would have family to hold her up and help her. I sent her a wish for peace, and went back to feeding my sweetie. Half an hour later, Sean needed more water with which to take his assortment of pills, and I went to the water fountain to get it. Coming back to his room, I passed her in the hall. She was crying softly. Her sister was holding her right hand, and her brother-in-law followed. They were walking slowly, all looking stricken and sad. I smiled at her as warmly and sadly as I could, and I think I said, "I'm so sorry." She smiled back sweetly, and she said through her tears, "Good luck, honey." And then she was gone.

From somewhere in the fresh shock of her grief, this woman offered me hope. She was no one you would look twice at on the street. Maybe if I knew the details of her life, my high-school self would've thought she was a sellout. But she had a strength that was queenly and epic. She gave me comfort and a kind of love that was beautiful in its simplicity. I decided that my version of feminism had to stretch to account for her.

She deserved it. Talk about woman power. In high school, my internal picture of feminism was unforgiving. Right was right, and wrong was wrong, and I never had any trouble deciding which was which. I knew who was On Our Side, and who wasn't. I don't know if that stranger identified as feminist. Hell, I don't even know her name. What I do know is that she knows how to stay through nightmares and help her sisters through them, too. At her worst moment, she offered me strength. There was no sarcasm, no ironic detachment, no judgment. Just a woman, reaching out to another woman. What could possibly be more feminist?

I don't need a man to be happy. Neither did she. That is to say, neither of us needed just any random man, needed that slot filled in our lives, in order to feel whole. We needed the men we'd chosen, the men we loved. As Erica Jong has written, "Hate generalizes; love is particular."* I need my particular man—the man who programs computers, plays piano and guitar, makes terrible puns, cooks a great keema masala, works hard at being a feminist and loves me. Sure, I could survive without him. I found that out in those long hours of waiting. But I want him in my life because he loves me, gives me support, challenges me, respects me. Any feminism that doesn't have room for that doesn't have room for humans. I'm glad now that I did the un-PC thing and moved to be with my man. He needed me when he was sick. I was there. When I had kidney stones, I needed him. When I had a horrible episode of the clinical depression that runs in my family, I needed him. Both times, and countless other times, he was there. We have taken good care of each other and I am deeply grateful for that. I'm glad, too, that I struggled and doubted and thought so much about it. I know that I did what I did for the right reasons.

Because the thing is, no matter how conventional my choices might have appeared, at every turning point, in every crucial decision I made, I followed my heart. My big, loving, rebellious, generous, feminist heart has led me to places I never thought I would go, and it's been a hell of a ride. I'm definitely not where I thought I would be, but the place I am in is good. I am a wiser person because of all my detours, and I believe I'm a better feminist as well.

---

* "The Truce Between the Sexes." Becoming Light: Poems New and Selected. New York: HarperPerennial, 1991.

I never thought, at eighteen, that at twenty-five I would be taking a break from school and tutoring in a transitional home for foster kids. But in spending time with my students, including teen mothers-to-be and others whose life challenges I couldn't have dreamed of at their age, I am learning more about what feminism needs to accomplish than I ever would have as the sheltered academic I thought I would grow up to be. I still have plans and dreams, but I'm smart enough now to accept that, to a great extent, I don't know what will happen in my life—and that that's for the better. I know I will always write. I will always teach. I will always write outraged letters to Congress. And I will always be a feminist.

Most of the other stuff is up for grabs. I am living my life off the map, and sketching the scenery as I go.

Bitter Pill

A.E. Berkowitz

I am a smart, practical, mature, long-time feminist. I've always been outspoken about what I want from men (and as for those who don't like it, I am happy to see them go). I am scrupulous about paying my bills on time, compulsively punctual when meeting my friends for drinks or dinner and extremely skilled at keeping track of appointments and umbrellas. I record my periods with little red marks in my datebook. I have never lost my wallet.

I married a strong-woman-loving man, a poster boy for feminist mates. Max embraces my politics, champions my hell-raising and took my name. He developed a crush on me through my work as a writer. He's more than happy to let me be the ambitious one, the moneymaking one, the one in the spotlight. He's attentive and sensitive and as proud of my accomplishments as I could wish. He is as independent as I am, content to spend the evening with his guitar, a book or a friend when I'm not around (and sometimes when I am). He cooks a mean chicken curry, straight from his mother's recipe.

Max's organic take on feminism makes him the perfect match for me—he doesn't go all insincerely analytical at the drop of a hat, like those guys I knew in college who just loved to take women's studies classes so they could dominate discussions with irrelevant personal comments about how being raised by a single mom made them oh so sensitive to feminist issues. Instead, he simply feels freed by the notion of not having to be some stereotypical manly man, and is quietly respectful of women and their opinions. He knows how to take care of himself and expects that I can do the same—but recognizes the pleasure that we can both take in caring for each other. He never expects anything from me that he wouldn't be willing to give himself. Instead of flowers he brings me the latest kick-ass female PI paperbacks and underground women's magazines, and he's always ready to share my outrage at the latest vodka ad that implicitly condones drunken date rape.

And from the time we started dating until almost a year and a half after we were married, my husband and I used birth control exactly once: an under-duress and fairly uncomfortable fifteen minutes of condom usage during which neither of us, I think, felt much pleasure.

You can forget any finger-wagging; it's not necessary. What with my extensive sex education in the many methods of contraception and STD prevention, I've already scolded myself plenty. You see, until I started seeing Max, I'd had condomless sex with exactly one person, my high-school sweetheart, who lost his virginity to me; I had been on the Pill a full two months before we did the deed. My previous possible pregnancy- or disease-causing experience had consisted of one nervous, painful, sweaty and fully latex-protected encounter with a boy I had known (and had been fooling around with on and off) for several years. For the first nine years of my sexually active life, I prided myself on being a safer-sex queen, daring to perform oral sex without condoms only until the dreaded pre-ejaculate began to make an appearance, at which point I would switch to my hand. (Not exactly foolproof, I grant, but I don't care how many hip sex educators tell you that mint-flavored condoms are perfect for oral sex—latex tastes like chemicals, and mint-flavored chemicals are still disgusting.) In alternating semesters of college I dutifully availed my conscientious ass of the free, anonymous HIV testing offered by campus health services. My first post-collegiate apartment was located conveniently around the corner from a Planned Parenthood clinic, where I continued my ruthless STD screenings as regularly as my (often sparse) sexual schedule demanded.

Somehow, when I met Max, I allowed all that careful attention to the details of sexual health to fall by the wayside. It was one of the situations that all those sex educators warned us about: I really liked him, trusted him for no real reason other than pure instinct, knew that he'd had only a handful of previous partners. He hadn't been tested for anything. I had no birth-control method aside from condoms, which he didn't much care for, and by the time we got around to actual intercourse, I wanted nothing more than to feel his skin inside me. I don't remember the conversation we had right before the first time I let him enter me totally naked. There must have been one—I just don't know what we said, which bothers me almost as much as the fact that that night marked the permanent end of my painstakingly safe sexual career.

Because once we'd started, of course, it was impossible to stop. The sex was incredible: the heat of him in me like nothing else, that unmistakable feeling of flesh on flesh. I kept telling myself that next time I'd whip out the condoms and my lapse would be repaired, but I could never bring myself to actually do it. I had become spoiled by the sensations, and I was surprisingly unwilling to give them up. By then we were falling in love, too, so the sheer power of being as close, physically, as it is possible to be to another person was too heady to abandon. I calmed my worries with all the usual clichéd rationalizations: He'd had so few partners, there surely could be no viral or bacterial surprises lurking inside him (and I'd been tested yet again for everything under the sun in the weeks before our sexual involvement); I felt safe with him, so he must be safe. While I knew I was making error after ecstatic error, I made no move to change it. I didn't want to (who relishes the thought of foisting medical tests on a partner in the blush of new love?), and I didn't think I needed to (for the same reasons I allowed us to have unprotected sex in the first place).

Meanwhile, our relationship continued to develop. I spent more and more time with him, allowed him emotional access I'd never before granted anyone, came to depend on seeing him. Soon enough, perhaps lulled by the rhythm of our deepening involvement, I stopped worrying about disease and focused on the more mundane risk of pregnancy.

See, we were using the tried-and-untrue withdrawal "method," decried by doctors, nurses and pregnant teenagers everywhere, combined with an approximation of the rhythm method, knowing when I was ovulating and concocting alternative activities for those nights.

Sure, I worried about what would happen if one errant sperm happened to wend its way up the garden path of my fallopian tube, but I was protected by a tidy bit of magical thinking. While (like any heterosexual woman who's been sexually active for a dozen years) I've had a number of pregnancy scares, I've never actually been pregnant, leading me to suspect it's just not that easy to knock me up. With one boyfriend in particular I broke many a condom, and although we were scrupulous with the nonoxynol-9, I thought there was something more going on. It could have been that the sheer volume of pot he smoked eliminated all viable swimmers, but I preferred, then and now, to believe that it was something about me, that my body—in one lovely, stunning gift amidst a host of pedestrian betrayals—had its own private and secret form of birth control.

Nonetheless I knew that I could not trip blithely through my sex life indefinitely, mating with Max like a bunny, without any organized form of birth control. Though neither Max nor I would have any second thoughts about terminating a pregnancy, I don't even have time to go to the dentist, much less have an abortion. Nor do I have any affection for anesthesia and painful medical procedures. Hence the night of the condom.

"We really need to get a birth-control method," I said to him.

Blank look.

"We can't go on like this," I continued, feeling like a southern soap opera heroine.

"Why not?" he asked.

"Well," I began, trying not to show my utter shock at his cluelessness, "it's not exactly reliable."

"It's been fine so far," he replied. "And I'm perfectly satisfied with the way things are."

Sure you are, I thought meanly, 'cause not only do you get to have the cool porno come-shot moment all the time, but you're not the one who's going to have to get her insides vacuumed out when it stops being fine.

I knew I was being unfair, since I had never given Max any clue that my thoughts about our (lack of) birth control were any less casual than his. At the same time, I had assumed that he knew as well as I did that some sort of drug or device was looming large on our mutual to-do list.

"It's not a long-term solution," I said stiffly, trying not to cry from the notion that I had married someone who could be so unmindful not only of biology but of politics—and my feelings. How could my sensitive sweetie be presenting this ignorant, uncaring attitude? Plus, I'd never confronted this problem before: All the men I'd slept with before Max—even the ones who wouldn't dream of using "gender" and "politics" in the same sentence—had accepted latex as a simple fact of life. And, with few exceptions, I'd always been happy to have that barrier between us.

"Well, I think I have some condoms around here someplace," he said, rummaging through the nightstand.

The sex, predictably, was terrible. I was still upset and pissed off about our conversation, and in the intervening years since I'd last used a condom I'd forgotten just how unpleasant they are. We pumped away for a while and then gave up.

"See, I don't want to keep doing that," I said. "We need something better." I reeled off the options and their drawbacks: a diaphragm would bring back my chronic urinary tract infections (plus I would always be worried that it wasn't in right); ditto the cervical cap; I'm suspicious of Depo-Provera and Norplant, which aside from being creepy are, in my mind, a long way from being proven safe; the Pill I believe to have been a major contributor to my high-school depression; IUDs sound compelling but have pretty unpleasant side effects, plus that nasty risk of uterine perforation.

"I just assumed that eventually I'd have a vasectomy," said Max. (We'd long ago had the I-don't-want-kids discussion.) "Until then, I thought we could just do what we've been doing. I had no idea that you were so worried about it."

Well, I was just as surprised that he'd been so blasé. How anyone with even a rudimentary sex education could actually believe that withdrawal was a perfectly fine method of birth control was just beyond me. But then again, I had been aiding and most assuredly abetting that belief for (gulp) long enough to birth a set of Irish twins.

It was then that I came to the dreaded realization that as feminist as my relationship is, I'm on my own when it comes to birth control. Any fantasies I'd been harboring of my partner reading aloud from *Our Bodies, Ourselves* as we pondered the pros and cons of modern pregnancy prevention were history. He simply did not—could not—share my understanding of the gravity of this decision. He wasn't the one who was going to be swallowing, injecting or shoving some foreign object inside himself. For all my grand ideas about shared responsibilities, here was one area where biology was going to have to be destiny.

I could have forced the issue, I suppose. I could have withheld sex and held forth at the dinner table about equal responsibility. But even the thought of trying to give Max a quickie Politics of Fertility 101 exhausted me; I was obsessing over these issues all the time myself, and now I was supposed to talk about them ad nauseum as well? No, thanks. And what if I tried my little heart out and he still didn't get it? If I did all I could to convince him to shoulder the burden and he still resisted, it would puncture my image of him as feminist helpmeet extraordinaire. Was I ready for that possibility?

It's Max's fault, and my own, and no one's at all: He didn't see birth control as a big concern; I was unable, for the reasons enumerated above, to call him on it. And once I allowed him to duck the obligation—both psychologically and physically—I found I could not go back. It was just easier to take care of it myself than to do the difficult emotional work of making Max see why our current situation was not okay and why he should be as exercised about it as I was. I decided to take this easy way out, and in doing so I became, for once in my life, the typical, mythical girl my mother raised me never to be: accommodating, self-sacrificing, spineless. I made myself sick.

I also came to another dreaded realization: There's no way that Max could be all that involved even if he wanted to. There exists no male-controlled, nonpermanent method of contraception other than the condom. And using a method that neither of us would ever be satisfied with wasn't going to make me feel better. (While a vasectomy is still a likely eventual outcome, Max and I decided that it would be unwise to make such an irrevocable decision while still hovering around age thirty. Plus, with his fear of doctors, I knew that even if we planned to do it "now" it could be years before the actual snipping occurred.) If I had convinced him to take on the responsibility, what could he have done about it? A big fat nothing.

Max and I are both, in some ways, supremely practical people. Nothing would have left us more frustrated than having a huge discussion about fertility, partnership and responsibility if afterward there were no possible action items. In every other disagreement we've had, there's been a goal: I was taking on too much household responsibility? I asked him to be conscious of the division of labor and do more. He did. We disagreed about the right time to start looking for a house? We compromised and made a timeline. If a problem's not fixable, in our eyes, better to just accept it and move on.

So my cowardice-laced pragmatism conspired with sexist contraceptive-industry reality to create a situation in which pregnancy prevention was my burden, and mine alone. Compounding my inner turmoil was the fact I already knew the eventual outcome of my careful contraception cogitation. For all my opposition to ingesting artificial hormones, for all my fears about the breast cancer that killed both of my grandmothers, for all my determination not to be at the mercy of a health-care system that would rather see women gobbling pill after pill than do some real research into, say, the effect of ultrasound waves on sperm production, I knew that I would end up swallowing those pills as well. Why? Because it's the easy way out. Because I'm lazy. Because I knew I'd have one hell of a time convincing a gynecologist to put an IUD in my under-thirty, nulliparous uterus. Because there simply isn't anything better.

I made an appointment at the local women's health facility and came home, my breasts palpated and my Pap smeared—and, of course, having been STD tested for what I dearly hope is the last time—toting a supply of plastic rectangles with their estradiol-laden pellets sealed neatly inside. The funny thing is, taking the Pill has been incredibly easy. Thanks to the nice doctor who heard my tale of woe and put me on the lowest-dose Pill in existence, there's been no muss, no fuss and no unpleasant side effects like the nausea, blackheads, gangbusters breast growth and depression that characterized my last foray into the realm of oral contraceptives. I feel like my old responsible self again—no stupid risks for me, no ma'am. I barely even notice it, except to take it every morning. My alarm sounds; I sit up and poke the white disc from its foil. As I place it on my tongue and carry it in my mouth to the sink for water, I taste failure. Then I swallow it right down.

Something to Believe In

Jennifer M. Collins

Tonight is the last night of Hanukkah. Due to Anna's work schedule and a conference that I desperately wanted to attend, we were unable to spend all eight days of Hanukkah together this year. For the first several nights, Anna lit the candles on our menorah alone. When I returned home from my conference, I lit the candles alone for the next few nights while we were on the phone together—I could imagine her hand underneath my own. But now her work week is done. Anna and I are crouched down tonight in front of the menorah together, each of us with a hand curled around the *shabes* candle, the one used to light each of the eight others. We stop periodically to take pictures of each other—this is the first Hanukkah in our new home, and we want to remember. As I sit and pose for her photo, holding up my first attempt at challah, shiny brown and covered with sesame seeds, I am crying. The tears come from deep inside, with no warning, and run down my cheeks while she snaps the cheap, disposable camera with fingers crossed in the hopes that at least one picture comes out.

The Hanukkah ritual became a part of my life only when Anna and I began dating. Hanukkah is a time for retelling stories, that

212

they may never be forgotten. The word "Hanukkah" means "dedication," in remembrance of the great Hebrew temple desecrated by the Assyrians. It is a festival of lights and a celebration of the triumph of freedom, and has resonated with me as an abuse survivor and as a queer woman. At Hanukkah, one tells the old stories so that each generation will remember the horrors of the past and the continued survival of the Jewish people.

We're not religious, Anna and I; her upbringing was culturally Jewish, and mine, culturally Anglo-Saxon Catholic/Protestant. Neither of us is especially spiritual, either—although I am a Pisces and half of myself is always up in the clouds looking for answers to questions I cannot articulate. Our religious traditions would deny us our full womanhood and our union. Neither of us believes in a deity who would strike us down for stepping out from under the thumb of a man, or for reaching out for each other, for other sisters. But how else to define that part of our connection that is of the spirit, the breath, the part that rose up and above everything that tried to get in its way: the closet, my abusive stepfather, others with whom we made intimate relationships? We did not choose this. Love chose us.

I have never been as certain as Anna is about marriage and family. When I was old enough to know what marriage meant, I was watching my parents quietly destroy each other in a divorce. Anna's parents knew they would marry within a week of meeting each other, forty years ago, and are still intensely in love. Anna always wanted marriage for herself, and that desire didn't waver when she came out as a dyke—she shifted the mate she envisioned from a man to a woman, and that was that.

One Valentine's Day, shortly after Anna and I began dating, she came to sit with me at a cafe in New Hampshire where I spent hours journaling. I picked through a bag of candy message-hearts and selected one for her that read Marry Me. I smiled, handing it to her, and she returned the smile, more sly, and said, "Yes!" I could see that under her flirting she was quite serious. She wanted to get married and wanted to have that connection with me. I wish I could remember more about that day. Did she ask me right then to set a date, only to have me demur? Did we talk about how, if we got married, we'd dress or behave, who would be there, and so on?

I don't think so. I was not so serious with that candy heart, and it took some returning to the matter for her to convince me that she was. I wondered why a ceremony was necessary for her. Wasn't it enough that we loved each other and were sharing our lives? But the ceremony Anna wanted was about more than bringing our lives together. It would be a rite of passage for us, and in the eyes of our families and friends. The recognition itself was what was so important.

I was terrified. How would we come together around this celebration when one of us was likely to run off as soon as the procession began? I had not wanted to get married or make any kind of serious commitment until I felt more fully healed from the abuse I had suffered. I thought I was broken and needed to be fixed. I had trouble believing Anna when she said, "I don't think you need fixing. And I want to share my life with you as you are now." She wants to get married in a year, I'd think. So I need to get serious in therapy! Let's work out all these demons! Needless to say, those sorts of demands don't work too well. I am old enough now to know that nothing meaningful in life comes with a guarantee of constancy. Slowly, I realized that coming together in this way could deepen the commitment on both our parts to work on our relationship. I would need to trust Anna to be there as I continued my healing. And I did not have to be "fixed" in order to come fully into marriage.

At the end of 1997, Anna and I set a date for the ceremony: September 1998. We wanted to tell our families while we were with them for the winter holidays. I did not know what reaction to expect and prepared myself for their confusion and questions. (Let me say that Anna's family welcomed me into its folds from the first. Any holding back has been on my part, out of an idea that families are "supposed" to treat their child's same-sex partner with skepticism, if not overt hostility.) Her family greeted the announcement with shouts of "Mazel tov!" and joyful hugs. Each member of my family welcomed our news as well, although their excitement was tempered by memories and concerns about my well-being. In the end we had the blessing of everyone we loved and the assurance that all would be present on the day of our union.

We planned and planned the structure of the ceremony, spending more time deciding what the day would mean for us than arranging more mundane details (e.g., booking a caterer, a DJ, a florist—these details were left until two weeks before the event. This is what happens when procrastinators couple). Not a piece of the ceremony went unexamined. In the end we wove into the cloth of our ceremony cultural elements from Jewish and Christian wedding ceremonies, along with expressions of ourselves and our queerness, our history and our families. Our rite of passage displayed who we are and who we wish to be—from our *chuppah* canopy, carried by four close friends, upon which was painted a bright and bold rainbow Pride flag, to the breaking of the glass (both of us in heels, mind you), which took three attempts before it shattered under Anna's foot. Everyone gathered released cheers of relief and celebration.

We brought ourselves fully into our union with each word spoken and read, each action performed and note sung. All could see the nature of our relationship as we walked under our chuppah among those we love. There on a misty seaside, a subtle yet enormous shift took place, rather like bedrock easing into a more solid placement, as I stood before my chosen family and articulated my love and commitment to this woman. Our love had, and still has, a tangible quality, and I do not mean simply the gold rings that each placed on the other's left hand that day.

I don't know how to define spirituality, but I know it when I feel it. I have felt spiritual at the Atlantic coast, when the rocks are breaking incoming waves with thundering constancy; have felt it early in the morning as the sun rises and the chickadees and robins outside my windows begin to sing; and have felt it on the dance floor, surrounded by a hundred other people, when the music has been perfect for an hour. I feel spiritual when my heart is full, when I can let down my guard to the joy in life for even a moment. When I chose Anna, I chose this joy. I understood spirituality most clearly on a September afternoon on the Maine seaside, when I vowed to love and be honest with and cherish this woman and our relationship. I felt our vows caught in the web of the universe, held there by an awareness greater than the sum of all gathered to witness. It was an intense and powerful experience, and I carry it with me still. The breath of Anna's spirit, and the spirit of our love, is always with me.

We have been together five years and married two, and we celebrate two anniversaries: the day we took the risk to step onto a path together and begin dating, and the day we leapt into this indescribable shadowland of marriage as two women together. I am still often terrified, but I know I have someone at my back, holding my hand. If not physically able to catch me when I fall, she will be able to help me dust off and listen to my story and laugh with me. Has marriage strengthened our coupling? There's a quiet difference in how we relate to each other, a new strength. It took courage to stand up, as two women, before friends and family, the earth, wind and sea, and proclaim our intentions. That courage and our togetherness were affirmed by all who witnessed. Affirmation is a powerful force in a society filled with the consistent violence of "no."

Ours is a partnership that my mother (indirectly) and my stepfather (explicitly) taught me not to expect for myself. But it is exactly the sort of togetherness I need and for which I was searching.

I did not fall into our marriage. I reaffirm my love, my relationship and my vows daily. I choose Anna's smile and eyes, arms and legs, hair and teeth, every day. We choose each other. When we are honest about attractions to others, we choose each other once again. When we struggle through conflict, rather than denying it, we choose each other again. We choose joy each time we reach for each other in a world that often utterly denies our right to be together, to be ourselves. We will be just as deliberate about children.

The challah has been torn and shared, the nine candles on the menorah are burning low, and we are sitting together in an overstuffed chair, crying over very different things—she is remembering her grandmother, how she was before senility took her away, and I cry over something indefinable. We are together as individuals, neither lost in the other. Yet a third is here with us, the entity of our love and togetherness, which is fullest and most wholly present in our shared physical space. This manifestation is what I refer to as the shadowland of marriage—not some dark, lurking specter but a real and palpable sense of light that surrounds me wherever I am, with Anna or separated from her.

Our relationship is "yes" in a world consumed by "no," a ray of sun through a clouded sky, laughter before sleep, hope in an often hopeless world. Our love tells the truth. Its breath gives me greater life. Our love is the spirituality I can believe in.

Reluctant Bride and Groom

Juhu Thukral

My wedding two years ago was one of the most chaotic and stressful endeavors in which I have ever engaged. I don't know that I'll ever feel as conflicted about a decision again. Jeff and I got married as a result of intense emotional blackmail and guilt; my wedding day was the culmination of years of gender and culture obligations that had hovered over me all my life. I compromised my principles and begged/forced Jeff into having a wedding that neither of us wanted but that I ultimately felt was necessary for our peace of mind and long-term success as a couple, even though it created a strain that still exists between us. Ironically, it was all about creating harmony between my mate and my family of origin, whose commitment to thousands of years of tradition was never going to change. My goal was to compromise and then get on with our lives.

For most of my life—until I hit law school and my early twenties—I wanted to get married. Not right away, of course, but it was something I assumed I would do. A part of it came from being saturated with generic images of blushing brides, Cinderella stories and all the happily-ever-afters that young American girls are fed. (It didn't help that I grew up in Texas, where people are still expected to get married and start raising families in their early twenties.) However, my biggest influences were my family and heritage. As part of a first-generation immigrant Indian family, my siblings and I, and others like us, grew up tiptoeing back and forth across the line that defined us as either Indian or American—and entering into a suitable marriage is, after all, the essence of being an Indian girl.

My parents always held with an iron grip to the notion that we would be raised as Indians in America—and with this came all the arguments about control, independence, privacy and, naturally, boys. They'd informed me and my older sister that we would each meet an appropriate boy through them and have a modern arranged marriage (in which each family has checked out the potential partner's background and made the introductions, but you get to know each other before making the final decision). We both rejected this plan. Thus came the epic struggles over dating, male friends and leaving home for college, where our behavior would be much more difficult to supervise.

Although my parents are traditional about marriage customs, they are simultaneously very nontraditional about the way marriage itself works. Both have careers outside the home, and they share managing the household equitably. They make decisions together, and they present a united front. They raised us to expect that we would be successful in our professional lives and in overcoming the sexism and racism that we inevitably would face—and my sister and I certainly would not be economically dependent on our husbands. Unfortunately for my parents, their valuable lessons did not stay confined to the worlds of work, achievement and not letting some jerk take advantage of us. Due to their immense capacity for denial and their immigrant faith that native culture could survive unaltered, they simply did not think that their lessons would mutate as they did.

Looking back, it isn't surprising that I took so long to question the validity of the institution of marriage. My sister got married, to a white man, when she was twenty-one. She was the first Indian girl in our Houston community to marry a non-Indian. You can only imagine the pain and furor that this caused in my family. It had powerful repercussions: Although my parents accepted my brother-in-law once they realized there was nothing they could do, and have treated him with love and respect ever since, they intensified their efforts to ensure that I would not stray as well. After all, if I didn't find an Indian spouse, how would I ever stay connected to my heritage? I was so busy fighting with them over whom and how I would eventually marry—and so engaged in other battles over my autonomy and self-determination as a female in a first-generation Indian-American family—that I never stopped to think about whether I even wanted to get married at all.

After college, I moved from Houston to Austin and went to work at a women's rights advocacy group. Fissures began to open in my view of marriage and its necessity. For the first time in my life, I met single and divorced women in their thirties and forties who had created alternative families and support circles for themselves. I learned about infidelity in some of the supposedly monogamous marriages that I knew. I questioned why anyone would make a commitment that he or she wasn't capable of keeping, why anyone would choose to marry when it's no longer the official precursor to sex and why I should take part in an institution that excludes same-sex couples.

The First in a Series of Compromises
The kind of relationship I've wanted hasn't changed much over the years. I want to be seriously, profoundly in love; I want an equal partner who values me and treats me with respect, and whom I can respect. I've never cared how much money someone makes, or what kind of career he has, as long as he has dreams and does his best to pursue them. I want someone who pushes me to be a better person. And I sure as hell don't want to be with someone who wants me to take his name. I credit these standards to my parents' marriage and to the self-respect I've gained along with my feminist principles.

I have been blessed to find someone who fits this description. (We discussed the name-changing issue on date number two, since it was going so well.) Despite the conflicts that belong to any long-term relationship, we have the partnership we want and we negotiate it together, with both parties fully present. Neither of us feels like we have compromised ourselves in developing this relationship. Being together has changed us, but still we maintain separate identities—and we're pretty happy. The private side of our relationship is exactly how we intend it.

Our public relationship is an altogether different story. I never wanted to be trapped, forced to work through fights because of a contract we made with the state. It may sound naive, but I wanted our bond as soulmates to be the only reason we stayed together. Jeff, once he thought about it, felt the same way. However, because of our families, avoiding marriage was a fantasy we were not going to achieve in this lifetime.

My parents have dealt with a number of changes they never imagined when they moved to this country: My sister married a white guy; after college I moved away from home as an unmarried girl; I went to law school halfway across the country in San Francisco (again, unmarried); and then I too got involved with a non-Indian (Jeff is half Japanese and half Swedish). "What will people think?" and "How could you do this to us?" are part of the soundtrack to my life. I made each decision knowing that, despite all the drama, my parents would accept it eventually. But I also knew that the thought of me living with a man in eternal unsanctioned bliss would break their hearts. Period. Jeff and I never would have had any peace of mind. I simply did not want to look back on my life and think I made my parents more unhappy than I had to in order to live with some integrity. My husband's family, devout Christians who believe in the sanctity of marriage, also would have been devastated if we never got married, never understanding why we couldn't make a "proper" commitment.

Both of us are practical people, and the cost-benefit analysis weighed in favor of getting hitched. We could shut everybody up, achieve some calm and get on with our lives without alienating anyone important. We knew my parents would treat Jeff as a family member only if he were my husband, and he didn't want to be treated like an outsider forever. The legalities of property and health-care decision-making rights were a bonus.

A Seemingly Clever Solution to a Delicate Situation

Since Jeff and I both hate weddings—they're colossal wastes of money and generally turn rational people into psychos—we wanted to go the city hall route. Again, the strain of "What will people think?" played in my head, and we decided that we could at least avoid the traditional three-hundred-person Hindu wedding by having something in our current home city of San Francisco and doing it ourselves (compromise number two). When I got a job offer in New York, I came up with a brilliant solution. According to our families, we couldn't move across the country at the end of the summer without being married. We would have to do the deed beforehand. Since that was less than four months away, there wasn't time for a wedding. We would just have a civil ceremony and get it over with, and everyone would understand, considering the exigent circumstances. I prepped my sister and two brothers, and they agreed to back me up when my parents implored them to talk some sense into me.

Unfortunately, when you live away from your parents, you lose touch with reality and begin to think that they are rational people. I completely underestimated them.

I went home for a visit I had planned before this drama transpired. I explained that we were overwhelmed with trying to apartment-hunt from the opposite coast, and we had all sorts of things to do before we made such a momentous move (neither one of us had ever been to New York, even on a visit). None of it mattered—they told me I was being selfish by trying to elope, that our marriage would be doomed and, by the way, what had they done to deserve this? My parents offered to plan the wedding for me—I wouldn't have to do anything. I made my final offer: They could throw us a reception in Houston once we were settled in New York. None of their friends would have to know that we had gotten married and moved to New York before their reception. Then their argument became about God—they didn't care about what other people thought. If we weren't married in a Hindu wedding, then we may as well not be married: "Just go ahead and destroy us."

I held on to my resolve. On the way to the airport, I told them that I wasn't trying to hurt them, and that they were going to have to accept our decision. They laughed and said that they guessed I could do what I want, like I always do, and they would have to deal with it. I honestly thought they would come to some understanding and acceptance. I was foolish not to recognize that weekend for what it was: Round One.

A miracle happened on the flight home. I sat next to a woman from a conservative Mormon family who told me that she and her husband had eloped about a month before, and that even though their families were initially upset, they were getting over it. She asked me if I was married. Needing no further invitation, I blurted out the whole story. She seemed to read my mind. She nodded wisely and said, "They may say they'll never get over it, but they will. And they say this is because they love you, but they're manipulating you." God had sent me an angel with a powerful message: Stick to your guns, sister; it's all going to work out. I was elated when I got off the plane—I ran to Jeff and told him I knew now that we could make this work. He, of course, knew better: "Come talk to me in a couple of days, after your mother calls you, crying."

But it wasn't my mother who called—it was my sister. My mother had called her (crying), asking why I was so ashamed of them. My sister told me there was no reason why I shouldn't let them plan this wedding for me. As far as she was concerned, since we were younger, Jeff and I were more capable of compromise, regardless of what it might cost us. Our parents, on the other hand, would never change. A solid argument, except that already we were compromising a great deal (not that anyone noticed or cared), we were the principal actors in this whole mess and the timing was rotten. She argued that it was one day out of our lives and we were being selfish not to give it to my parents. The next day, I received an email from one of my brothers, telling me that he had reevaluated my position, and he thought it best that Jeff and I go through with an official wedding ceremony. The ranks were closing.

Once my siblings sided with my parents, it was over. At that point, I was willing to capitulate—the stress and the guilt were killing me—even if I resented the outcome and the methods they employed. I love my parents, and I understand the cultural imperative of a religious wedding in which they give me away.

But Jeff did not. My parents had snubbed him consistently (my mother pretended not to know we were dating the first time she met him), and he was reluctant to cave in to their pressure now. He didn't care that this treatment was simply what Indian parents do—that once we were married, everything would change. He didn't care that I have Indian friends whose parents snubbed even nice Indian boys until after the wedding. It was especially difficult for him because his family welcomed me from the first time we met. Even when they didn't agree with us, they treated me with respect.

My white friends made an excellent point—my loyalty was to my partner now, and while I'd had my whole life to get used to my parents and the crazy restraints of Indian culture, he hadn't. My Indian and Asian friends said I was insane to fight it—my parents would never recognize my autonomy unless I went through with their plan. An acquaintance summed it up best: "You can't run away from your culture."

But I couldn't capitulate without Jeff being on board, and he wasn't moving. I was trapped in the middle, at least until his mother decided that all this nonsense had to stop and told me we were "all going to Texas and having that wedding. And don't you worry about a thing—I'll talk to him." Finally, Jeff agreed; he didn't want to come between me and my family.

It was a miserable summer, filled with anger and resentment. My family kept involving Jeff and me in details in which we had zero interest, and it was all too clear that the wedding wasn't enough for them—there were blowouts over numerous ancillary issues. I felt sixteen again. It took me back to all my other struggles for independence, and it felt awful to fight for the same damn things at twenty-eight. My family had managed to morph me into one of those pathetic adults who still wear their mommy and daddy issues on their sleeve.

On top of that, now Jeff was mad at me. He still thought we were giving in to their pride and selfishness and that if we didn't go through with the wedding they would eventually get over it; if they didn't, they were horrible parents who didn't deserve me. I had to defend our decision to him constantly.

The Happy Day

Our wedding weekend was a whirlwind. We were scheduled to fly to Texas on Thursday evening, get married on Saturday and by early Monday morning be on our way to New York. We even had to have a civil ceremony in California after all because we weren't going to be in Texas long enough to get a marriage license.

The night we arrived, I had my *mehndi* done. Despite the promise that there would be no accompanying *sangeet* (a gathering similar to a bridal shower), all these female family friends showed up. This was when I finally understood that I had lost. From that moment on, I smiled on command and let all these women whose names I didn't even know grab my hands, touch my face and chatter about how nervous and excited I looked. Fortunately for everyone, I was so exhausted from packing that I was completely pliant.

The woman applying my mehndi also did my makeup on my wedding day. When I told her that I didn't wear much makeup, she looked at me sternly, said, "Your mother saw my photo album and hired me on the basis of those pictures," and went on with her business. Even Usha the makeup lady had more power than I did. By the time she was done with me, I looked like Sita.

It was a beautiful wedding, completely wasted on us. Hindu ceremonies are long and informal, and people walk around and talk the whole time. So Jeff and I amused ourselves by smiling at friends in the crowd, trying to figure out how much longer it would be before it was over and trying not to laugh at how ridiculous the whole thing was, especially since the *pujari* could not remember our names.

Living with the Consequences

Once it was over and we were in New York, I was relieved: Everyone was finally off our backs, and we no longer had to live under the stress of that all-consuming negotiation. Though some tension remained between me and my mother and sister for a few weeks (it hurt their feelings that I had been such a bitch to them all summer), most of it dissipated rather quickly. It took almost a year, however, for my underlying hostility and resentment to abate completely.

Jeff's bitterness has not quite gone away. He's getting over it as time passes—and we have visited my family as a married couple, which let him see that they are genuinely good, if uncompromising, people. It has also helped that my parents now treat him as a member of the family. However, he still sees their behavior as selfish.

Am I too attached to my family, and not loyal enough as a partner? Did I betray Jeff or our relationship by agreeing to the wedding? I don't believe so. He knew from day one what baggage came with me—that I was part of a first-generation immigrant family and that my family was important to me. His own parents are an interracial couple; they faced resistance from their families when they got married. He knew all this, and still he chose to love me and commit to me. I know going through with the ceremony was the right thing, because the Romeo and Juliet "my family hates you" model does not sustain relationships for long. It creates too much damn stress, and takes time from more important things in life. For me, his choice not to let go of anger toward my family is exactly that—he can choose to let it go, as he has, slowly, over the last two years, or cling to the remnants of anger and destroy us.

As so many people tried to tell me (and I foolishly failed to accept until the end), my role as an Indian daughter transcended any other facet of my identity until my family properly gave me away on that elaborate night. That was never going to change, no matter how fervently I held on to my principles. Ironically, submitting to my family's wishes freed me and Jeff to have more autonomy in our life together. Jeff and I are not entirely comfortable with the result—but we made the best decisions possible: I imagine that's all I could have expected from a spectacle in which I was the center of attention, but that ultimately had very little to do with me.

In Search of the Elusive Orgasm

Lori L. Tharps

Ask me why I never had an orgasm until I was a married woman of twenty-eight. I blame it on Harlequin. Publisher of romantic fantasies, mass-distributor of schoolgirl dreams. All that fiery passion, those heart-wrenching betrayals and predictable happily-ever-afters are addicting and dangerous, especially for a girl on the cusp of womanhood. While my classmates traded copies of Sweet Valley High novels, I was pilfering paperback Harlequins from my Auntie's attic collection. I am not proud of that time. And as I look back, I realize how much damage was done in those formative years.

Basically, it comes down to this: The Harlequin romance novel and all of its heftier bodice-ripping incarnations shaped the way I viewed sexuality. It's how I cobbled together my understanding of what really went on between a man and a woman, only to discover eighteen years later that I got it all wrong.

I could see pretty easily where the stories were psychologically mistaken. (All men aren't misunderstood brutes who need a virginal but passionate woman to unlock their tortured spirits.) But from a physical standpoint I was misguided, thinking a woman's role in sex was to lie back and prepare for cascading waves of pleasure to wash over her lithe and quivering form. I basically gathered that true love and good sex were synonymous. The only other options were rape and chastity. The virginal protagonist always turned out to be an excellent lover on her very first tumble with the man she loved. And she wasn't just good; she was always better than the buxom harlot the hero used to visit to satisfy his lusty loins. As long as the heroine was infused with true love for her roving stud, she would prove to be a treasure betwixt the sheets. And, more important, he would know instinctively how to make her squirm with orgiastic ecstasy. I was totally brainwashed.

This is my story of orgasmic recovery and Harlequin deprogramming.

It started innocently enough. My older sister, whom I worshipped and adored, had finished reading *Ashes in the Wind,* a Civil War romance novel, and couldn't stop raving about it. Although I was only eleven and the book was more than three hundred pages long, anything my infallible older sister recommended I would latch onto blindly. So I started reading about the young southern belle who disguised herself as a boy to escape to the North only to find herself in love with a Yankee surgeon. It was riveting. I read it in the car. I took it to school and read during recess. I even wedged it into my Bible so I could read during church. Somehow, that book was able to transport me out of my oh-so-regular life in the suburbs of Middle America to a world where love conquered everything, from paralysis to murderous pirates hell-bent on revenge. Once I finished *Ashes,* I was desperate for another story to give me that warm-all-over tingly rush. I was a junkie looking for another fix. Instead of a pharmacological high, though, I wanted something to fill in for the romance so lacking in my prepubescent seventh-grade world.

Since the only contemporary literature my parents owned was the kind that was supposed to be good for you, I turned to the public library. I would check out a single trashy novel (of the long-winded gothic variety), return it a week later and repeat. I wasn't satisfied with a beefcake, a deflowering and a happy ending, either. I needed good background details, quality writing and believable dialogue. When the library's collection ceased to excite me, I started looking for another supplier. It was quite by accident that I stumbled upon the hidden box of Harlequins in my Aunt Mary's attic one Thanksgiving. She must have belonged to a mail-order club, because there was no end to her supply. On discovering the contemporary Harlequin model, I entered the next phase of addiction—delusions of romantic grandeur.

It was really quite perfect to discover Harlequins at about the same time I started high school. Where historical romances had seemed an escape to another world, the Harlequins presented a real woman in modern times, and it wasn't too much of a stretch to imagine myself in the same situation. I could be a zoologist working in Wyoming or an antique collector looking for Mr. Right in a cozy hamlet in Vermont. Although the stories were maddeningly formulaic, I still could count on finding just the right one to heal my adolescent angst or provide comfort while I sat home on prom night without a date. Although I quit cold turkey when I went away to school (at my politically active, left-leaning women's college, my penchant for Cinderella fairy tales seemed akin to treason), those Harlequin notions of love and romance stayed with me.

Toward the end of my third year, spent studying in Spain, I met the man who would become my husband. I first saw Javier in German class. He walked into the room and I fell for him instantly. After months of trying to attract his attention away from the other women who followed his every move, he finally noticed me, and we started a good old-fashioned courtship. We walked home together from school and went out for coffee in the afternoons and tapas on the weekends. By the time I had to leave España, we were deliriously in love. But I returned to the United States thinking I'd simply had "an affair to remember." Little did I know I'd discovered "endless love." We spent the next two years pouring our hearts out in handwritten letters, spending gobs of money listening to each other breathe on transatlantic phone calls and traveling back and forth across the pond for visits on major holidays. When Javier finally moved to New York to be with me, I was ecstatic. Danielle Steel could not have penned a better ending. But that was only the beginning.

The intensity of learning to live with and love someone, especially someone from a completely different culture, took so much time and patience I almost considered trading my real-life romance for the comforting predictability of a literary one. Javier and I loved and fought, broke up and started all over again several times. By the time we decided to get married five years later, I thought I had wiped out all remaining vestiges of Harlequin happy endings.

But then came the wedding night, a night I had dubbed the "night o' passion." Even though we had moved in together a few months before the wedding, we made it a point not to have sex so the wedding night would be that much more exquisite. Every "first time" story from my Harlequin junkie past flooded my mind and enlivened my imagination. I just knew our night o' passion would be filled with effortless, ecstatic sexual release. We stayed in a charming bed and breakfast that just oozed rustic romance with a touch of convenient modernity. The stone fireplace burst into roaring flames with the flip of a bedside switch. The sunken Jacuzzi was surrounded by gilded mirrors. We took advantage of all the amenities, and the sex was sweet and passionate—but there was no big O for me. No cascading waves of pleasure. No joyous heights of ecstasy. I wasn't too discouraged, though. The way I saw it, we had the rest of our lives to compensate.

But one night turned into a series of nights, which turned into a year of pleasant but orgasmless sex for me. My husband tried every position, trick and technique he knew to help me have an orgasm. And it wasn't that I wasn't enjoying it—I just didn't experience that explosion that supposedly everyone else was experiencing. After a year of tenderness and patience, my husband began to get frustrated that he wasn't able to make me come. This wasn't his macho Spanish ego shining through—he felt like he was letting me down. He thought I didn't find him attractive enough. He began to doubt his own sexual prowess. I tried to assure him that I was still enjoying myself, but a man needs to see results. I'm sure he wanted to believe me and for a while he did, but in the back of his mind he was plagued with guilt. Since we were each other's first and only sex partners, neither of us had a basis for comparison, which didn't help put any of this into perspective.

The worst part of this entire experience was having no one to talk to. According to a survey in a popular women's magazine I read at the time, more than 85 percent of sexually active women achieve orgasm. Unfortunately, I didn't know where to find the other 15 percent. I listened to the women around me discuss their sexual activities, and it seemed as if they were all happily ensconced within that majority group. I couldn't figure out why I was different. I mean, I relished the idea of reaching soaring heights of pleasure with my husband just as much as the next woman. I yearned for that magical release I had been reading about for so many years. I wanted to feel like an empowered sex goddess at least once in my life. I just knew if someone could lead me down the road to orgasm, I'd be just like the passionate yet virginal heroines on the covers of my favorite books—"a nascent body leaping to life." I tried to ascertain exactly what my friends and co-workers were doing behind closed doors, but I just couldn't gather the courage to approach somebody and ask, "What are the precise steps—in order, please—of having an orgasm?" In fact, most people probably assumed I was happily orgasmic. I never actually said I had orgasms, but I also never said I didn't. Basically, I was faking it with everyone except my husband.

I finally decided something was either physically or emotionally wrong with me. I wondered if perhaps I was gay and this was my body's reaction to being in a heterosexual union. I stared at my clitoris until I was convinced it was deformed. I ran through every excuse in the book. Eventually, Javier's guilt coupled with my own frustrations caused me to dread having sex. Finally, when it looked like my husband had given up all hope, I decided to approach the problem head-on, just like I approached every other obstacle. I bought a penis-shaped vibrator and an instructional tome on becoming orgasmic and promised my husband I wouldn't give up until my loins were throbbing with pleasure.

It didn't happen. Even with my fancy equipment, the manual and the encouragement of a few good friends, I wasn't getting any closer to the big O. By then my husband was suggesting I seek professional help. He was convinced that my politically conservative mother had raised me to be afraid of my own sexuality, but I assured him that was not the case: I played spin-the-bottle in junior high. I French-kissed a stranger at a rock concert. I read *Delta of Venus* in the bathtub. He wasn't buying it. What he saw was a woman unable to experience sexual pleasure fully— reason being, we both concluded, that I didn't have the first clue how to get there.

This is where the side effects of romance novel addiction come in. The typical climactic love scene in a bodice ripper reads like this: "Marcus kissed Brandy hard; his hands tightened on her bottom, lifting her up, and he began to thrust wildly inside her. He raised her legs and wrapped them around his waist, bunching her green muslin gown, pounding into her again and again. All the while, she kissed him . . . in minutes she reached a crashing release and he followed." That's not so hard to comprehend. He's in, he's thrusting, she feels a crashing release. Sounds better with a green muslin gown, but essentially, the girl just has to stand there while the stud orchestrates her orgasm with a bit of pounding. That sounded a lot different from the self-help books, which said I'd have to mas-tur-bate before I'd ever be able to experience that crashing release with a partner. In my "I am woman, hear me roar" spirit, I could accept that. But I don't think my heart or my clitoris could shake the "in, thrust, release" example. The Harlequin model was indelible; no matter how much playtime I spent with my new battery-operated friend, I came no closer to my goal. I don't think I ever gave myself a chance. Masturbating just wasn't romantic. It felt like homework, like punishment for not being a heroine who was just naturally good at pleasing both her man and herself. She didn't have to work at it—why should I? I also believed that if an orgasm didn't come naturally at the hands of the man I loved, then it was never going to happen at all.

Having failed with the masturbation routine, I tried to convince myself that an orgasm was not the benchmark for a meaningful relationship. But every time my husband and I went in for the bedroom gymnastics, I would be consumed with jealousy (he was enjoying it more than I was), anger (why wasn't it happening?) and massive performance anxiety (would I get it right this time?). Not surprisingly, sex stopped being pleasurable in any way, so I tried to reason that sex was nothing more than animalistic behavior and lobbied for a sex-free, spiritually heavy relationship. My husband wasn't having it. He argued that sex was not just about physical release; it was a form of corporeal communication and another way for us to deepen our relationship. I tried to tell him that if he truly loved me for my mind and spirit, we technically didn't need to have sex. That just about sent Javier over the edge— which made me think he was just being horny and selfish. I felt like a failure as a woman, and Javier was frustrated and angry that after only one year of marriage our sex life was rapidly disintegrating. Suffice it to say, our entire relationship was suffering.

About six months shy of our second wedding anniversary, Javier and I started talking about having a child. Although the conversation was still in the abstract, it struck me that I might experience sex for procreation before I experienced it for pure physical pleasure—and that seemed fundamentally wrong. Or at least unfair. I grew up believing women had the right to be sexual. An orgasm was my due. My reward, if you will, for waiting for Mr. Right. Having let the pursuit of the big O lie dormant for a period, once again it reared its hooded head. This time I was more adamant about it than Javier, determined to experience an orgasm before the idea of motherhood dominated all the conversations about sex. Now the issue was more about me than us. Around this time, my husband left to visit his family in Spain for an entire month. I dedicated that very same month to becoming orgasmic. I dusted off the books, videos and vibrator, lit candles every night and became obsessed with taking bubble baths. Although I got to know certain parts of my body better than ever before, I didn't find myself any closer to feeling that special thing (by the way, I didn't even know what to expect—just that I'd know it when I felt it).

One evening during Operation Orgasm, I had dinner with a friend (let's call her Simone). She wasn't a good friend yet, just a kindred spirit I had been meaning to get to know better. Our conversation touched on several topics and finally settled on sex and relationships. That's when Simone confessed to me that she was almost twenty-eight years old and she had never had an orgasm. I knew I could top that story. I was twenty-eight, *married* and had never had an orgasm. But I struggled with sharing this information. As many mixed signals as there are about female sexuality in western culture, in groups of women being orgasmic is a sign of achievement. More than a sign of sexual maturity, it's a status symbol of intrinsic sexuality. Outing myself as inorgasmic felt like admitting I still wet the bed.

For a moment I considered offering Simone only a sympathetic ear and not admitting I had the same problem, but I changed my mind. I figured maybe I'd find out what was wrong with me by spilling my guts to someone else. That night over Cambodian food in Brooklyn, we told each other everything that frustrated us about living an orgasm-free life. Then we tried to figure out what had gone wrong. She thought it was because her mother had raised her in a repressive environment where emotion and overt affection were restricted. As I sat there and listened, I wondered what that had to do with me. My family was loud and affectionate, and sex was talked about without shame. In fact, on the day after my wedding, I was forced to divulge all the intimate details from the night o' passion to my aunties, who were just dying to share with me their own wedding-night stories.

As Simone and I rehashed our childhood, adolescence and sexual experiences, I began to realize how much I romanticized sex. Even though I considered myself a strong, independent woman, I truly believed my man was supposed to take charge of my sexual pleasure. Masturbation did not work for me because deep down I didn't believe in it. I wanted the fairy tale. I wanted, "In a cascade, his essence, the life force of his manhood, coursed into her, flooding and filling and fulfilling every last fragment of her body. [Insert my name here] gasped with happiness, then convulsed again and again, then catapulted like a projectile into realms beyond reality." How could K-Y Jelly and a dildo compete with that?

The following day, still high off our night of divulgence, my new best friend and I went on a field trip to an elegant little sex shop in midtown Manhattan. We were determined that our time had come. After spending close to one hundred dollars, I came home with a state-of-the-art vibrating turtle (designed to nestle comfortably in the folds of the vagina), an erotic video and a lifetime supply of personal lubricant. I told myself I deserved these indulgences and felt euphoria and trepidation all mixed up together as I contemplated the evening ahead. After cooking myself an elaborate dinner, washing the dishes and taking a long, hot shower, I slipped into my one pair of silk pajamas and lay down on the couch. I placed my new toys around me and put the video in the VCR. This time, instead of thinking about masturbation, I just focused on feeling pleasure.

When my loins started quivering and my hips started thrusting of their own accord, I turned on my turtle and immediately started shivering with waves of pleasure. In less than five minutes, I felt it. Something like a dam bursting sent the most delicious waves of pleasure zinging through my body and ended in a roaring crescendo. I was laughing and crying at the same time. I finally got it. I understood. I knew. I wanted to call my husband immediately and let him share my exhilaration. I wanted to tell everyone I had ever lied to that now I knew the truth. I ended up calling my mom, unable to get any words out—just a continuous stream of giggles. (She thought I was on drugs.) Before I forgot what it felt like, I grabbed my journal and wrote this down: "Ain't I a woman."

For the rest of the week, I tried to make up for lost time. I'd wake up and turn on the turtle, run home from work to turtle myself and put myself to sleep with a little swish of my soft pink reptile. I felt like a naughty thirteen-year-old boy, yet deliciously indulgent. And the more often I made myself orgasm, the more I realized it didn't require male participation. While I looked forward to my hubby coming home and experiencing a new level of pleasure with him, I also felt possessive of my developing sexual relationship with myself.

When I called Javier in Spain and told him about my great new discovery, he was thrilled. His advice? "Keep practicing." He also wanted to know if he could play with the turtle when he came home. Luckily, unlike many men, he did not feel he'd been replaced by a battery-operated piece of rubber. He was just so happy that I'd finally felt the big O. When he did come home, intercourse still didn't mean an orgasm for me, but it felt like a tremendous burden was lifted. In addition, Javier respected how I had unlocked my sexual powers, and he finally believed I wasn't suffering from the effects of a repressive childhood. Now we use the turtle and incorporate all kinds of play into our sex. Sometimes I get to O, sometimes Javier does; we're working on the day when we come together . . . just like in the movies! (I'm kidding.)

Clearly, I can't condemn Harlequin romance novels for every woman's sexual dysfunction, but I can lay part of the blame on the powerful myth that they—and the rest of popular culture—continue to perpetuate. In movies, on television and in those ubiquitous love tomes, women enter the throes of ecstasy by having a man on top of them. Since my own personal orgasmic revelation, I can't keep my mouth shut. It is high time for women to examine their sexual expectations and stop buying into the pop culture paradigm of female pleasure coming only at the hands of a seasoned lover who looks like Fabio. The job can be well-served by a piece of machinery, one's own hand and a clear conscience. It wasn't until I decided I deserved to feel sexual pleasure for myself and by myself that I was able to experience results (although I still stumble over the word "masturbate"). Sure, our partners can be part of the equation, but all we really need in order to reach the pinnacles of earth-shattering desire are a vibrating turtle and a ban on bodice-ripper romances.

Answering Homer

Katie Hubert

When I left for a two-year stint in the Peace Corps that sent me to tiny Ryki, Poland, Adam and I made one promise to each other: Neither would get married or get (anyone) pregnant.

There were sub-points to our contract: I was to figure out the "girl-crush" thing; he would go to grad school.

We were twenty-two. I had met Adam in the dorm four years before. He was tall and handsome and smart, the kind of good-looking man in whose wake people turned to stare, the kind of smart that energized the blood. We swooped in on each other occasionally during college, circling and feinting, mostly, though clinching up now and again. Only when departure loomed did we admit we wanted more. Only when we couldn't have it.

Our friends nodded in sage agreement when we shared the details of our two-year separation. They accepted as a matter of course that we would be together eventually. But equally certain was that independence came first. None of the friends with whom we surrounded ourselves, male or female, believed in haste. To Adam, to me, to our whole crowd, the compact seemed the most commitment one unproven human being could expect from another.

I reveled in the inverted gender roles. He was Penelope to my

Odysseus. Better yet, he pointed out this reversal. The mythology of our romance swelled between us.

When I had fulfilled my Peace Corps responsibilities, I traveled for six months and then came back to the U.S. to resume the relationship. Adam was finishing a master's in English lit at a prestigious East Coast university, specializing in feminist theory. He had a semester remaining when I returned in January. The month before, he'd received notification that he had not been granted permission to proceed to the doctoral program. "Permission to succeed," he called it. Denied that, he longed to go to Alaska, to slime fish in a cannery, live in a tent and wallow in physicality, he said. No gatekeeping professors could keep him from that.

"Come along," he implored. "Forge our bond in primal fires beneath glacial walls."

(He really said things like that. We both did.)

As I was still itchy-footed, I agreed.

But there were four months of school for Adam to survive first. Plus the not-so-small matter of my acclimation to the wealthy western world.

Readjusting proved much harder than I had expected. Everything seemed excessive, including my reactions. Rainbow piles of produce reduced me to tears: tears of relief to be home and tears for the coalsmoke-colored root vegetables, and the people who eat them, that I'd left behind. Soft wool and thick cotton moved me to nausea: such plenty, such waste, such luxury—and all accepted as a matter of course! Americans were so swift: in speech, in emotional openness, in decisions. I, accustomed to Eastern European slow motion and glowers, endured migraines and uncontrolled (but silent) weeping in the face of such extremes. Adam was patient and loving, holding me in the car outside the grocery stores that appalled me, walking home with me from bars when drunken grad students crossed well within my psychological comfort zone.

But "home" offered no relief. We lived together in Adam's four-bedroom rental with three housemates, a communal coexistence that his letters had described in ecstatic detail: group meals, afternoons on campus waging fierce ultimate-frisbee wars, nighttime games of charades and hearts. A continent away, enduring Slavic winters, I had longed to join their starving student co-op, to spoon beans and rice into my belly, to argue politics and religion while the creek out back bubbled and cheap beer cooled my throat. But their intimacy had grown up without me, and while his new friends accepted me kindly, I knew I was only a friend by proxy. After carving my way through the trials of a small, isolated village, battling language acquisition and crafting friendships with people who had not welcomed the notion of an American English teacher, I wanted more than casual acceptance in my own land. I wanted passion.

Two years is a long time. Adam and I were both fond of companionship.

Pregnancy and marriage were the only forbidden activities. Surely Odysseus had his dalliances—and if Penelope did not, well, in our modern retelling, Penelope did.

Soon after our geographic separation began, we started dating other people. Other women, more precisely. (This was part of my assignment, remember. The girl-crush thing worried Adam. He wasn't sure he could compete with women, feminist-theory degree notwithstanding.)

Before this, I'd had a single spectacular one-night stand with a woman who'd been my best friend. The morning after, she freaked out and dumped me entirely from her life. (She got married the same weekend I left for the Peace Corps.) I didn't freak out; I was sort of relieved. I'd made love with a woman, and woke to find the world still spun. Admittedly, thirteen years of Catholic school ensured that I was more than a little uncomfortable with the implications, but I'd had years of growing certainty that my interest in women was more than platonic to prepare me.

In Poland, far from my conservative home (anti-choice, Catholic and right-wing), I found the freedom to explore sexually, and I found a British woman willing to share the journey. Fiona didn't relish the idea of a man waiting for me in America, but she rose to the challenge. This was going to be a fling, after all, both of us far from home, neither looking for happily-ever-after. Perfect world. Adam found someone, too: Xhosa, a child of Peace Corps volunteers who hadn't returned to the U.S. Xhosa grew up in Africa and was in America for college. She had an exotic name, spoke three languages in addition to English and was athletic to boot. I worried a bit, I confess. But Adam and I assured each other that our deal still stood. And somehow, the four of us put up with the bizarre limitations that two of us had imposed.

Fiona and I traveled together for six months. I saw her safely home to England and then returned to Adam, who had ended his relationship with Xhosa.

It turned out that Adam hadn't been entirely honest with me. Xhosa had lived with Adam for several months (though paying rent elsewhere). The three empty drawers I'd thought he was so sweet to clear out for me actually had been filled with her clothes until a week before my arrival. That seemed benign compared to what remained: in his bedside table, an open box of condoms; in the bathroom medicine chest, Tampax.

"Did it ever cross your mind to throw this shit away?" I whisper-hissed (his housemates were home) in our first flare-up, two days into cohabitation.

He shrugged slowly. "Seemed like a waste of money."

"But they're Tampax," I gritted out. "I don't *use* Tampax."

As if brand names were the point.

But I valiantly carried on, explaining that o.b.'s were the only choice for me: no landfill threat, and the intimacy of finger insertion. (Had the recent lover's tampons been free of applicators and designed by a female gynecologist, some part of me believed I would not have minded so much.)

Adam felt compelled to remind me that he had racked up forty thousand dollars of debt. Condoms were expensive. My sensibilities, he announced, were unaffordable. In an earlier decade, he would have called me bourgeois.

We'd reached our first impasse.

Adam had taken every feminist theory class offered, often spending the first week of seminar discussions defending his right to be there. On one occasion, the professor challenged him as well. Somehow, I never doubted his sincerity. It seemed perfectly natural that the man I was living with wanted to read Kristeva and Dworkin. In retrospect, what seems natural is that Adam was the kind of man I would sleep with. His interest in the politics of gender made him unique among the men I knew, especially as he shared my unwillingness to accept assumptions about sexuality, relationships or biological function. We so often felt like differently gendered versions of the same person. This twinship was the cornerstone of the mythology we spun around ourselves.

During the first days of my return, I accompanied him to classes, listening to the circuitous references to Derrida, Cixous and Barthes. The scholarship seemed airy and unreal compared to the lurching, crowded trains, handkerchiefed babushkas and hoar-frosted winters that dominated my imagination. I envied him the graduate school experience but didn't want it for myself. Instead I took a minimum-wage job baking croissants, muffins and baguettes at a bakery Adam had described romantically in letters.

What he had never once described was the only woman among his housemates. She was a gorgeous green-eyed woman, complete with a butch and feisty lover who took one look at me and asked what the hell I was doing with a man. Because "swooning over your girlfriend" seemed a dangerous reply, I could only shrug. Eventually I trotted out stories of ex-girlfriends. With perhaps some embellishment.

To complicate an almost unbearably complex scene, Adam's gorgeous green-eyed housemate's feisty butch lover was the ex-girlfriend of the woman whose Tampax Adam had neglected to discard. In other words, Adam's ex, Xhosa, was also Butch's ex, Xhosa. Xhosa started coming over for supper once the hullabaloo of my arrival died down. What a perfect little family we were turning out to be, gathered around our communal dinner table, eyeing one another, swilling beer and stepping out back to smoke.

On weekends, we played football. Tackle. A couple of male professors in Adam's program organized the games. Butch and Green had played once or twice, and so all three of us began to accompany Adam to the Sunday morning games. I quarterbacked eventually, earning surprised approbation from the beer-bellied professors. Butch always seemed to be on the opposing team, body-slamming me to the ground. I carefully avoided thinking about the implications. After the games, Adam would sling his arm around my shoulder. We'd limp from the field, grass-stained and smelling of earth. I'd be torn: to lean into him, or to stride on untangled by relationship. Once or twice, sore from one too many tackles, I yielded, breathing his boy-sweat. Green and Butch, walking home behind us, kept a careful distance between them. I would hope they weren't getting along.

During the week, my baking job required me to wake at three, bike two miles in the motionless dark of predawn and measure, mix, knead and bake 'til eleven. Alone in the shop for three hours every morning, I'd crank Melissa Etheridge, the Indigo Girls and k.d. lang, singing at the top of my lungs. Contemplative above the rich yeast of the dough I was shaping, I'd consider Adam and me.

Living with Adam was far more difficult than dating him in college had been. Back then, his slobby housekeeping had seemed vaguely charming to my sitcomesque mentality, and as sitcom couples (Joanie and Chachi, Shirley and Carmine, Diane and Sam) had formed my expectations for boys my age, I was repulsed only in a laugh-track sort of way. The reality of a man who made my sink gunky and choked up our shower drain with long hippie hair was too much. When I sat down with him to express my uneasiness about becoming the cleaning lady, I could see him trying to be sensitive.

"I see how that would upset you," he said, rubbing his chin.

"But you think I'm nagging you," I suggested.

"I wouldn't say nagging," he answered. "But I will admit I don't notice any mess."

I didn't believe him at first. Not notice? The bathroom was so foul that even now, five years later, the memory disgusts me. So I said, facetiously, that I'd prompt him when cleaning needed to happen. He nodded, in all seriousness. And grateful for even that much, I decided to play along.

About a week later, I nudged him. "Bathroom time."

He looked at me blankly.

I returned the look, equally blank.

"Oh right," he said, moving toward the stairs. "That's my cue."

An hour later, I told myself I needed to use the bathroom. I definitely wasn't checking up on anybody. Once there, how could I help but notice that the shaving cream can still rusted its circle on the sink?

The toilet was untouched. Bathtub? Unaltered. Floor? Unwashed.

I found him lying in bed, a skinny Willa Cather novel in his hands. "Are you going to do it, then?"

Another blank look.

I waited.

"Read?" he asked, helpfully lifting the book.

"Clean," I supplied.

Genuine pride suffused him. "I already did!"

I won't detail the subsequent conversation, but it ended with me frustrated and Adam bemused.

Another truth: I found myself strangely fascinated by the sweat-stained jockstrap he'd hang on our bedroom doorknob between basketball games. For all that I tried not to touch the thing, I looked at it a lot. On him and off him. I made witty dinnertime conversation with comments such as this: "As support appliances go, bras simply are not as strange as jocks." Butch would smirk at me; Xhosa would pat Adam's hand; Green just watched her plate. It didn't feel safe to admit that my intrigue with his jockstrap feuded passionately with disgust.

One more truth: Adam and I had extremely similar taste in women. Xhosa—a regular at the house for Sunday brunch, Wednesday night poker, Monday morning runs with Green and Butch—was a fierce athlete with a lovely smile. Drunk one night, she and I sat on the curb out front wondering how the threesome of me, her and Adam would have been configured had the chronology of meeting been altered. We toasted to the idea of Adam never entering the loop. He pouted when we reeled inside giggling to share this image with him. Xhosa and I were best of friends that night.

A corollary: Adam dated only bisexual women.

However, my inclusion on this list complicated matters, since "bisexual" was a term I was not happy applying to myself. It sounded so ineffectual. So afraid to commit.

The maddening reality was that bisexual most accurately described the in-between place I was living, but as I didn't like where I found myself, I rejected claiming the title. I refused to hold hands with Adam at the grocery store because it bespoke heterosexual privilege, yet I grew increasingly irritated with Butch for accusing me of taking the easy out.

"You can't have it both ways," she told me one night.

"Apparently, I can," I snapped. But a real feminist, it seemed to me, was either a Birkenstock-wearing straight woman with baby in a hemp backpack and a hippie husband, or a hairy-legged earth mama lesbian with a lambda sticker on her Subaru Loyale. Clichés, to be sure, but they described whole and unreserved lives. They allowed no room for the self-doubt I felt; I yearned for that one-dimensional clarity.

And in the mornings, kneading yeasty dough, wailing along with Ani DiFranco, I worried.

Nothing was resolved before Adam's program ran out. We stuffed our meager belongings into backpacks, and eleven pioneers, Adam, Xhosa, Green and I among them, boarded a psychedelic school bus headed for Alaska. (Butch saw us off, kissing Green a permanent good-bye, intent on some new local conquest.) Our crew spent a month on board, chugging slowly through America, from Washington, D.C., to the Kenai Peninsula. Adam, Xhosa, Green and I. And Lord, if that dinner table had seemed cramped, this rebuilt school bus was a steaming petri dish.

Here I have to interrupt my story, because when I tell it to new friends, this is where everyone interrupts. As they react, I can see them, behind their smiles of confusion, reevaluating the woman before them. There has been head-shaking throughout this story: the no pregnancy/no marriage deal, the girls on the side, the open boxes of tampons and condoms, Xhosa at dinner and so on. But this . . .

"I thought you were so . . . " they sometimes begin.

I wait for the adjectives.

"Together," one friend said.

"Evolved," said another.

The rest say nothing, but their eyes narrow slightly. For them, I provide words—perhaps to avoid hearing those they might choose.

"Crazy, huh?" I say, trying to pretend this all happened fifty years ago to some girl who only resembles my current self.

"Something like that," the more polite will say.

I am of two minds. Our willingness to travel together seems sensible. We were in our mid-twenties, finished with school, unwilling to leap immediately into real jobs and curious about the world. How rare to find one person who shares even a fraction of like-mindedness, and here we were with a busload. To ignore this opportunity because of squeamishness about sleeping arrangements seems—well, like throwing away perfectly good tampons. At the time, we congratulated ourselves on our ability to coexist: Xhosa eyeing Adam, Green and I edging around each other, Adam watching all three of us and the rest of the crew pumping Grateful Dead bootlegs through the bus's tinny speakers and singing along.

But I cannot believe that I abetted Adam's continuing infatuation with Xhosa or that I worked to snare Green into our romantic morass. (Well, into mine, anyway. I ached for her.) Xhosa took every possible opportunity to be with Adam, and as they were late-nighters and I an early-to-bedder, she found many moments alone with him. I could not protest, as their nighttime conversations allowed me time in the mornings with Green. Somehow, as that heavy old bus chugged across America, we all managed to be not only civil but also cordial, affectionate even. But the selfishness! Green, Xhosa and I would in any other situation have been lifelong friends, or lovers, or at least affable companions. Instead, we were competitors.

Reader, I broke up with him.

In the aftermath, I was shocked to watch him withdraw completely, in anger and in pain. I thought he'd seen the moment coming as clearly as I had. I thought we'd both understood that sooner or later one or both of us would find a woman who made us whole. I thought he could not be hurt if I chose a woman over him—how could he possibly be hurt by someone with whom he could not compete? I thought he knew that our mythology was what we wanted to be true, not what would finally become truth.

Green and I shacked up.

I finally came out to myself and to my family. (This moment was not particularly significant to my friends. They to a person replied, "*Finally!*")

Three months later, Green and I split.

Adam traveled to Asia with a woman from Alaska he would marry and with whom he'd raise a child. I went to the Midwest for graduate school, found a great therapist and met Kimberly, the woman I would marry. Adam, his partner, my partner and I all live on the West Coast—though in different cities. We went to their wedding. They came to our housewarming. We run into one another every year or so: at the Lilith Fair, say, or coffee shops. Everyone is cordial.

On those occasions, Adam and I avoid long eye contact. One too-long pause, and we curtail the conversation. Emails are infrequent, informative and brief. Phone conversations consist of exchanges of email addresses for mutual acquaintances, English teaching tips (he, community college; I, high school), requests for recipes. We seem afraid, wary, nervous. I have little experience in making friends of ex-lovers. Frankly, I don't know what to do with Adam and his wife and child. Who are we going to be to one another? The future is unclear. For now, we keep our distance.

We've become, I suppose, realism's answer to Homer: Penelope and Odysseus, safely returned, making lives apart.

My feelings for Adam were always complicated, and they remain that way. I was with him longer than anyone aside from my current partner. We met our first year of college; the bus trip took place eight years later. We were not a couple for much of that time, but we were close friends throughout.

I have to admit, I loved the way he mythologized our relationship. We would lie in our tent, mummy bags zipped together, and watch the wind play across the nylon walls while Adam would describe our lives. We would raise children together, androgynous like us, who would go out into the world and make it better. This was his favorite dream, to make a Telemachus of our own.

Perhaps we chose the wrong myth. Odysseus comes home suspicious, after all, wearing a disguise to gain an unfiltered impression of his kingdom in his absence. He finds his castle filled with suitors, whom Penelope valiantly outwits; but even after he disposes of his competition Penelope is not willing to recognize him. She's been too long alone, it seems, to take her man back into her bed readily. (In the end, however, she knows him, and the goddess Athena makes everything all right.)

Perhaps our undoing was expectations. I expected so little from him, really. For example, the bathroom. I played a game with Adam rather than dealing straight on. Because he was a man, I assumed he would not clean, or at least not clean well. Today, I say to my wife, "Honey, the bathroom needs to be cleaned, and I've done it the past four times." And she says, "Look. You have a thing about the bathroom. If it looks dirty to you, clean it. Because frankly, you leave the kitchen in a permanent state, and I clean that without complaint." And so I clean the bathroom. Not because she's a woman, or not a man, or because I am and am not. But because she's right.

I was afraid to make demands on Adam. I felt lucky to be with him, in an unpleasantly unhealthy way. He was the consummate man; even strangers stopped to tell me so. And yet, when I imagined our future, I felt certain that each of us would have affairs with women over the years—and because I felt that necessity for myself, I granted begrudging (but unspoken) permission to Adam to do the same. All of this was unspoken. I assumed—based on our time apart, I suppose—that we both accepted its inevitability. Adam's reaction to our breakup was my first clue that I had underestimated his commitment. My low expectations for him were low expectations of and for myself.

Because I learned from my experiences with Adam, because I am kinder to myself these days and because I was not programmed to behave one way with a woman, I find myself with few preconceived expectations about my current partner and our relationship. There was no *Lesbos Know Best* or *The Lady Bunch* to form my core beliefs. No Lesbian Charm School at the mall to teach me proper baby-dyke decorum. I didn't grow up watching my two moms repair plumbing or take turns cooking dinner. So when Kimberly speaks or acts, I—unencumbered by myth—understand that she as an individual has acted or spoken. Chloe may very well love Olivia, but there were no Lilian Faderman texts at my local childhood bookshop. I believe, and this belief feels far less idealized than it may sound, that these conditions of semi-purity make me more honest. I love and am loved not as a gender representative, but as a discrete entity. In a lovely, simple way, despite the lack of an accompanying myth, that love renews my trust in happily-ever-after.

Outside Expectations

Lilace Mellin Guignard

But theory precedes exploration . . . we are, actually, pioneers trying to find a new path through the maze of tradition, convention and dogma.
—*Anne Morrow Lindbergh,* Gift from the Sea

Right after we got married, Jimmy and I moved from North Carolina to Nevada, a state so remote, so rarely mentioned, that many of our friends still do not believe it exists. Officially, we're here for him to get his PhD and for me to write. The unofficial reasons are the opportunities to rock climb, kayak, mountain bike, backpack and ski in the different ecosystems surrounding Reno. Like pioneers, we packed up our southern drawls and headed west. What would happen to our relationship once we left the physical and emotional landscape of home? We couldn't be sure, but intended to take advantage of the new geography and christen our life together with some serious play.

I'm an independent woman—still—and the fact that I married a southern man continues to amuse me. Fate's a funny broad. But Jimmy doesn't have a stereotypical view of women, and I credit his strong and gracious mother for that fact. He got his gift for play from his father (who used to ride motocross); both have the same spark of mischief in their eyes. When Jimmy and I are outdoors, all "shoulds" and "shouldn'ts" blow away with the wind. In a very real sense, play is a form of my feminist practice. On the rock or river, I make my own choices about what risks I will or won't take. And Jimmy honors those choices. I evaluate my body for its strength and grace, rather than waist and breast size. And I get constant reminders from Jimmy that this is the woman, the body, he loves—dirt, sweat, big smile and size Bs.

Our marriage might be described best as ecological: an organic system in which each person fills a niche, a connection that assumes change is constant and all life moves in cycles. These cycles include shifts in power—who knows more or is more capable in a given situation—rather than a stable state of equality. Like in the larger natural sphere, adaptability is our ultimate survival skill. Laughter and praise are survival skills, too, and playing provides ample occasions for both. "For humans, play is a refuge from ordinary life, a sanctuary of the mind," writes Diane Ackerman in *Deep Play*, "where one is exempt from life's customs, methods, and decrees." It's also a sanctuary of the body, at least for me. I am accosted by daily messages dictating what I should look like, how I should act, how to cross my legs and what tasks are the wife's responsibility. These imposed expectations are part of the "civilizing" aspects of our culture. Luckily, Jimmy doesn't believe these messages any more than I do, but we're both susceptible to cultural pressures even when we don't buy into them. When life gets hectic, I start worrying about what to have for dinner and get mad that it's my responsibility. Then Jimmy reminds me he has no such expectations. And if I stop obsessing, I find it's true—he fends for himself fine. At times like this I know I've been inside too long.

When climbing, we slow down and fit ourselves to the geologic pace of mountains, focusing on one move at a time. Through paddling we find ways to pause in the current, eddies where we can stop and recoup. Rivers require us to react, to refine our reflexes in tense moments. We need these survival skills in everyday life, too. Getting outdoors alone together is our marriage-maintenance plan. And out there—among the High Sierra conifers, in the cold Appalachian rivers and on the scalding sandstone cliffs—Jimmy and I can concentrate on who we *want* to be for each other, not who we *should* be.

I'd known Jimmy about three weeks before we went climbing at Looking Glass Rock in western North Carolina. What I knew of him was from phone conversations about our common interests in education, literature and the environment, and from looking into his oceanic eyes. Staring up at that broad face framed by brown surfer-length hair, I'd try to keep my head above water as his laughter and sincere care for others drew me like the tide. We'd share stories about outdoor excursions, turning moderate adventures into epics. But this was our first day sharing one of those activities.

We were with his friends, preparing to ascend Sun Dial and the Nose, classic 5.8 friction routes. Jimmy started uncoiling the rope and one of his buddies got ready to lead the first pitch. "Want to belay?" Jimmy asked me. I buckled my harness and clipped it to the pink and blue lifeline. My job was to monitor the amount of slack the lead climber had and catch him if he fell. Jimmy watched as I got in position. If this was a test, it was a necessary one. I had climbed most recently a year before, and then only twice. I felt better being double-checked. The fall sky was clear and the granite warm; my cheeks were flushed. As his buddy moved up the rock, placing gear, Jimmy yelled support. He never corrected my methods or refined my style. "Nice belay," he said when his friend on top had clipped to a bolt. "Want to go next?"

What the hell. Tying in, I felt put on the spot, like when a high-school boy picks up his date and the girl's father is waiting to give him the once-over. No way around it. All those stereotypical female concerns—like if my butt looked big with the harness hugging my black lycra shorts—competed with concerns about getting up the rock face. But fresh air and dirt grounded me. As much as I liked Jimmy, if he judged me by my butt size or climbing ability, he could go jump off a cliff. There were plenty handy.

Rock climbing focuses me like nothing else. Even that day. I let the belayer above know I was ready, brushed off the rubber soles of my climbing shoes and flattened my palms against rough granite in greeting. It was just us now, the rock and me. Up a few steps, I searched under what climbers call eyebrows, looking for enough space to hook my fingers, palm up. These underclings are a Looking Glass trademark. Limber from yoga, I steadily rose above the male eyes below me. I felt my back muscles absorb the warm sun. Once safely on the ledge, I turned to face the autumn-spangled hills and valley. And to wait for Jimmy.

After that great day of climbing, you could say we both fell.

As we got to know each other, I found that Jimmy could offer suggestions about my climbing without being condescending. By leading routes with me belaying him, we grew experienced in interdependence: He needed me to make sure he didn't hit the deck if he fell, and I needed him—with his experience and skill—to climb the rock first. Of course we talked, too—on quartzite ledges far above the everyday world, during hand-holding hikes through spring wildflowers and camp-outs on windy Appalachian balds.

We spent our first night together under the stars a week after our first climb. I was in a nervous frenzy over sleeping arrangements. Solitude was the issue, not sex. We lived more than an hour apart and had decided he'd stay the weekend. So comfortable with him so soon, I worried he would too quickly become a familiar presence. Worried that, without him, my house would soon seem empty. I knew if this happened I'd end up resenting him and myself for not maintaining some space. In a flash of brilliance, I decided we'd sleep on Black Balsam nearby. After dinner, we hefted our small packs—filled with only sleeping bags, pads and a tarp—and followed my dog up a steep trail to the rocky bald. We used flashlights at first through the pine and spruce, but once in the open we walked slowly in the dark. No moon. Stars flecked the sky like serviceberry blossoms awakening the Blue Ridge in early spring, their promise somehow the same.

That night, in sleeping bags with the dog between us, I talked more candidly and less fearfully than I ever had with a man. Maybe it was Jimmy, maybe the example of starlight's faith as it careened through space toward an unknown future. But both of us, in that place, starting the second month of our lives together, cleared so much air that I expected to wake and see all the smog from Ohio Valley factories gone, and wave upon blue mountain wave cresting before us.

Aside from the future, we discussed why I enjoy backpacking and car camping alone. In a gently curious way, Jimmy asked about trips I'd taken and if I ever got scared. Earlier in the night there'd been a couple of drunk fellas walking around, unaware of us flattened against the dark bald. Or were they? At some point, after it'd grown quiet, Jimmy called my attention to two silhouettes a hundred yards away. "Is that those guys?" he whispered.

I squinted but couldn't tell. "I reckon."

Throughout the night, we checked periodically and they were still there, though quiet. "Would you sleep out here alone?" Jimmy asked.

"Probably. And I might worry all night, too."

"Take me," he said, pleading rather than commanding. "I might not be able to do anything, but I'd like to be there."

I rolled on my side to look at him. He actually seemed vulnerable. "I like to go by myself," I said lightly. "But not always, and not everywhere."

I wonder how long it would have taken to discuss my need for solitude if we hadn't mistaken a couple of spruce trees for drunks. As it was, that conversation freed me from worrying as we spent more time together. Even now, three years later, I occasionally take off alone for a weekend backpacking. And Jimmy handles with grace the questions from folks assuming he should be out there protecting me, who imply that he's not much of a man for "letting" me go solo.

One particularly memorable evening, Jimmy burst into his one-room apartment after a late class discussing Milton's portrayal of Adam and Eve. "I figured out what it is I love about you so much, about *us*," the words were flung as the door slammed closed. He strode like a purposeful animal to where I sat curled up reading, wearing one of his large T-shirts. He stressed each word: "Neither of us dominates the other." As if released, he rocked back on his heels. "I've never had that happen before," he added before kissing me with eyes open wide.

For my part, the weekend I met his folks I knew with stunning certainty this was the man I wanted to marry. We'd waited up with his mother for his father, who drove trucks for a hardware chain and was due home from a three-day trip. Each of us took catnaps as the other two talked. When Sam arrived at one o'clock in the morning, a big grin ran across his tired face at the sight of us flopped out on the couches.

After introductions and a short conversation, Jimmy and his dad kissed good night, both saying "I love you." And not only that night, but every night we were there. Oh yes, here was the father of *my* children. The men in his family are as affectionate and expressive as the women. How nice to share this with my husband: We both get scared, triumphant, embarrassed, cocky, gleeful, protective and stern.

A stretch of growth in our relationship followed when we routinely experienced being insecure in each other's company. During this phase, every time I tried an activity that scared me, or chose not to do something for the same reason, I wondered if I was risking our relationship. Would he think I was a sissy for being frightened? Would he get tired of climbing with me if I didn't always want to do the routes he did? These were important fears to settle, and each activity pushed us in unique ways: Traditional climbing offers different challenges to individuals depending on ability, but biking and kayaking are much more interpersonally demanding.

Jimmy had mountain biked for years, even raced some. He was a mud machine. I liked mud fine, but steering around rocks and roots, hopping logs and "catching air" were not my skills. What's more, I wasn't sure I wanted to acquire them. As much as we tried to be clear about what type of ride we were going on, each turned out more full of obstacles than I was ready for, scarier than he realized. Insidious trees (remember *The Wizard of Oz?*) would hook my handlebars with their branches, dry leaves cackling hysterically. I did have the pleasure of giving Jimmy a heart attack once ("He cares!") when I launched over my front wheel into the mud. And so it went, with me gritting my teeth on grit for an afternoon because he loved this sport and I was afraid to disappoint him. To make matters worse, we were usually with his buddies, and I couldn't shake my anxiety about holding everyone up. In the aftermath of that hell, I can state calmly that a man new at mountain biking would ride slower too, but as the only woman I felt pressured to represent my gender well. And wouldn't you know, these rides happened at the same time every month, at the time when I'm more emotional and my body channels its energy inward. I don't have as much to spare for physical activities and judge myself more harshly. Try explaining that to your boyfriend's buddies the first time you meet. "Hi, I'm Lilace. I'm on the rag."

Meanwhile, Jimmy began whitewater kayaking, something I'd done for years. As he learned more and we began going down easy rivers together, our roles reversed. I confess, I reveled in his terrified expression as he entered small rapids. The way he held his breath, cheeks bulging Louis Armstrong–style, afraid he'd flip. And when he once did, and cut his brow slightly, I washed and bandaged it ("She loves me!"). Reading the river, surfing a wave and paddling straight on flatwater all came relatively easy to me, while the thrill and fright of being in the water's grip intimidated Jimmy at first. Then one day I checked the knots after Jimmy had loaded the boats. There was more slack than I liked, so I retied them. I must have made some snippy comment, because he retorted, "Don't talk to me as if I'm one of your students!" I got my first taste of his anger and a real lesson in leadership. As much as I hate condescension, I had done exactly that to Jimmy. I promised to work on it.

Over the next six months of climbing, mountain biking and kayaking, we took turns leading. Jimmy learned to recognize when he was pushing me without meaning to and got comfortable letting me call the shots sometimes. I learned to quiet the critical voices in my head that nibbled at my confidence, and to handle being the most knowledgeable one without going on a power trip. We adapted to shifting roles, riding the currents of our relationship better and trusting that direct communication would help us navigate any rough water ahead.

During this period, my parents died. Dad first, then Mom. If I hadn't known Jimmy was "on belay" for me, I would've felt even more untethered. Still, asking him to fly up to Mom's service with me was hard. We'd known each other barely three months. But if we were going to spend our lives together—and we'd begun talking that way—he needed to be there: not because I couldn't handle it alone, but because I wanted him to share one of the most significant events in my life.

Asking for help, asking for *anything*, makes me choke. If we hadn't already established a pattern of asking for more rope, less slack, a rest break or help in dumping a boat, I might not have gotten up the nerve. A hole would've been created that we couldn't go back and fill.

In most of my previous relationships, the getting-to-know-you part consisted of telling each other who we were. Going to the movies, sharing dinner and hanging out with friends are all great, but there's a trap. After a few months something would happen, something bizarre or seedy, that showed he was not the person he pretended to be. Sometimes it was news to him as well. After perfecting the "get lost" speech, I still wondered how to troubleshoot for self-deluders who talked like enlightened Romeos. Actions *do* speak louder than words. Hell, they holler. And after a couple of months with Jimmy, I didn't worry about unpleasant surprises. We'd spent too much time together in intense situations, reacting under pressure. We each knew the other didn't become verbally abusive, cast blame or turn into a useless, sniveling blob. I learned he'd forgive me for tossing his front bike-tire onto the pavement when unloading the truck; and he saw that once I realized it wasn't *my* tire, I was so horrified and distraught that I forgot to reattach my brakes before starting to ride. I loved how Jimmy used humor to lighten the mood when we were hungry or hurting and farther from the car than we wished. How a person acts when facing a little discomfort and a lot of dirt is extremely revealing.

So, after many long trails hiked and biked, many cliffs scaled and rapids run, Jimmy and I decided to get married. But what then? The only other long-term relationship I'd had, other than ones I was born into, was with the mountains of North Carolina. Everything I knew about appreciating the familiar—about how deepening contact means deepening understanding and leads to greater love, about staying put—I tried to transfer to our relationship. But climbing one 5.9 route or paddling one class-IV river doesn't prepare you for others. As a blunt, outspoken woman who didn't wait around hoping for a boyfriend, I lacked experience with all but the first and last stages of intimate relationships—as if I'd known bookends without the books.

Now we own a house and are thinking about kids. Finances need planning, small repairs need making and, since the puppy joined us, a lot of landscaping chores lurk outside the back door. But so do the snowy peaks of the easternmost range of the Sierra. In forty minutes we can be up there with dogs and snowshoes, laughing at our clumsy pratfalls, at the dogs disappearing in drifts, at the icicles on our nose hairs. In North

Carolina, Jimmy and I knew the terrain, access trails and what to expect from the weather. But we are learning more about each other in Nevada's desert climate, the Sierra's deep snow and fast rivers. We must cooperate, because the only familiar element is each other.

"Lilace, John wants to know if we'll paddle the American with him Saturday." Jimmy has been itching to get on a river since we moved here.

"That's in California, right? How far a drive is it? What level?" I'm extremely cautious about jumping on new rivers and like a lot of information.

"Class II to III mostly. There's one class IV but you can walk around it if you want. And it's less than two hours away."

I don't respond. He knows the nervous me is arguing with the eager me. I barely know John and wonder what kind of a boater he is. Still, the longer we wait, the more effort it'll take to return to paddling shape.

Hoping to tip the odds toward going, Jimmy says, "A friend of his is boating, too. A doctor at the university."

"Fine. At least there'll be someone to pick up our pieces who knows how to put them back together."

On Saturday we beach our kayaks and hike down for a view of Troublemaker, the class IV. What makes this more challenging than the big rapids upriver is a huge jumble of rocks on river left that force the current to narrow, speed up and turn hard right. After the turn, a large rock in the middle called Gunsight demands that you commit to one side or the other. We watch John run it. The key is to enter at a point that gives you time to anticipate the turning current before back waves from the left rocks catch you. Then it's a matter of not getting slammed into Gunsight. Dr. Dave looks at Jimmy and me.

"I'm going to walk it," Jimmy says.

"I'll run it," I say at nearly the same time. We exchange looks, each surprised by the other's answer.

Back at our boats, Dave and I wait so Jimmy can get in position to watch. I breathe deep. It's a wonderful sensation to be sure of my ability. This morning the current seemed pushy, and I wasn't making my moves with the precision needed in big rapids. I couldn't tell if it was my imagination or the unfamiliar dynamics of western rivers (which are wider, have higher water volume and generally contain series of large waves).

By midday, though, I was hitting all my moves, working with the river instead of against her, feeling the thrill of courting a force of nature. I know this rapid is within my ability.

From the calm spot where we sit I look downriver. The big drop means only a horizon line is visible, the rapid and all the landmarks hidden below. "You go first," I tell Dave, "and I'll watch where you enter."

With a big smile he digs his paddle in deep and noses down into the current. Bloop, he's gone. I memorize the little rooster tail wave to the left of which his boat disappeared. My paddle whirls almost of its own accord and my eyes never leave that wave. Then I'm close enough to see turbulence beyond. Dave's line is good. Waves shout in my ears. A sweep with the left blade, lifting that knee and hip to carve right, I aim down the chute left of Gunsight and eddy into the calm below. Jimmy and the others are grinning. "Way to go, babe," he slaps my purple life jacket. "I'm proud of you."

We're always revising what we know of each other. Now I'm climbing harder and Jimmy doesn't have a problem with me finishing routes he's backed off of—in fact, he brags about it to friends: "That's my wife!" But he *is* concerned over my apparent lack of fear. I, of course, remind him that when he first kayaked I was watching and seething over his gutsy approach. It helps that we each experience both sides. The moderate physical risks we take train us and build our confidence in each other, so when we hit the tricky bumps in our marriage we can draw on muscle memory to make the hard moves together. It's like divine marriage counseling. Our culture expects every relationship to have a stronger and weaker partner, one who loves more and one less. But nature has no such expectations.

So Yoro Ka Djan*
(Home Is Far Away)

Lauren Smith

My perennial garden is on the verge of its two best weeks, when
the largest number and widest variety of flowers are in bloom at
the same time. I say "my," but I inherited this garden with the
house I bought last year, and the garden is still a mystery to me.
Knowing the weeds from the desired perennials has been mostly a
matter of intuition, though I sometimes get advice from my neighbors. Mrs. Paxton, for example, who lives across the street, pointed
out one furry-leafed interloper grown so lush I had not suspected
it, and my friend Linda, who lives around the corner, indicated
several small elms that should not be allowed to get any larger.
"They get woody," she said, "and put down deep roots." But I
am reluctant to dig the elms out, and while I procrastinate the tree
roots make their slow, blind journey down.

My husband and I are not from here, not from the Midwest,
though we met here and are likely to stay through all the perpetuity
that is relevant to us. Without meaning to, we have accumulated
attachments: house, jobs, friends and a decade of personal history.
I am from the South—where people don't labor over perennial

---

* *Non-English words are either Diula, a West African dialect of Bambara, or French.*

gardens, where everything bursts into bloom each March of its own accord. Hassimi is from the orange plains of sub-Saharan Africa, where you brush your teeth over the tomato plants in order to conserve water and where flower gardens are a luxury reserved for the *toubabou mousso* (white woman).

I'd always imagined marriage as building a home with another person in a particular place—we'd plant things together, visit the neighbors, settle down. Our lives would be woven through those of our families and communities, and we would be an integral part of that larger tapestry. But neither my husband nor I feel entirely at home in these states whose names our families confuse (they can't tell Iowa, Illinois and Wisconsin from Ohio, Indiana and Minnesota). So we build our lives together not only across our own cultural differences, but also on foreign territory.

My discomforts in the Midwest have been subtle, but Hassimi's are sometimes more acute. West Africans may confuse Illinois and Indiana, but the people here have never even heard of Burkina Faso, his home country. Even the midwesterner Tom Brokaw, who once signed his autograph for us, smiled blankly when Hassimi named his homeland. "Burkina Faso," we say over and over again to the people we meet. "East of Mali," we say, "north of Ghana." We draw a picture of Africa on a napkin, arrange objects on a table. "Here is the Ivory Coast. Here is Niger." Nothing, it seems, brings that country into view over this wide, corn-green horizon.

At night, Hassimi often dreams of that invisible place while the dog chases squirrels in his sleep and rabbits eat the zinnias I planted in the backyard. He likes to pull the sheet up over his head—because of the lions, he says, and I like to imagine them leaping over the chainlink fences of my neighborhood. I know he carries images of his home around with him as if on an internal TV monitor. We go to endless garage sales, for example, where I buy old scarves and sweaters and Hassimi accumulates the detritus of American technology. He bargains for twenty-year-old stereos, five-year-old fax machines, old radios and answering machines—all of which he sees in terms of their usefulness in Burkina Faso. "It only costs four dollars," he says, and I take the purchase, whatever it is, down to the basement. Certain items he finds at garage sales and surplus stores will find their way to Burkina—like the sixty-some Mesozoic-era computers one university surplus store agreed to give the University of Ouagadougou. But much of it will be damaged by water and mildew in the basement or simply will prove impossible to transport.

When we head out to garage sales on a Saturday morning, our neighbor Gup is awake already, clipping a hedge or digging a hole. Sometimes the smell of burned oatmeal from nearby cereal factories comes to us in an incongruously cool breeze. Often, the retired couple across the street is standing on the front steps saying hello or good-bye to grandchildren. Not all of these neighbors felt comfortable with us immediately. While I was poking at the perennial garden one afternoon, Mrs. Paxton came over to warn me about a neighborhood family with particularly rowdy teenagers. "The mother," she said as if this explained everything, "ran off with a colored man." "Oh," I said, jarred out of my concerns about a mass of brown stems that I guessed were dead. The father of the difficult teenagers startled me in a similar way by asking, when Hassimi had been out of town for several weeks, where "the colored guy" had gone. Despite having seen us walking in the neighborhood and working in the yard, he was surprised when I said, "He's my husband; he lives here with me."

Recently, other intercultural families have moved into the neighborhood, but at first Hassimi and I were an anomaly. People watched us as we walked down the street. We were more interesting (and for some people, more troubling), than the other men and women heading out for shopping or breakfast on a Saturday morning.

Hassimi and I met in Iowa, mid-July, after the ducklings on the river had grown sleek and the apples in the orchard had turned into hard, sour knobs big enough to see from the road. I had a summer job and a good life, which I was not interested in changing, but Hassimi told me his life story, drove me around in his car and brought me plastic bags full of groceries from Aldi's or Econofoods—oranges, bananas, loaves of French bread. Sometimes we'd sit on the front porch of my house in the evening and watch the lights flickering on the surface of the river a block below.

On those nights we'd talk about our homes, our work, the things that had happened to us during the day. For every difficulty I brought to Hassimi, he had cheerful encouragement or a West African proverb, always delivered with sounds and gestures meant to make me laugh. "The fish is in the water," he would say if I complained about a recurring situation—meaning the problem was so predictable it needn't even be mentioned. Or "You play your drum and you dance" when he felt I'd gotten myself unnecessarily agitated. Mostly, he told me stories about his own life and the people he knew—his face deeply expressive, his large hands shaping the air in front of him into human forms and landscapes.

I was impressed by what I learned about him during these early talks, especially his determination. Hassimi's father had died when he was a year old, and his mother supported the family by selling crackers and small cakes at the market. When he arrived in the U.S. in 1985, he barely spoke English and had little more than two hundred dollars in his pocket. A cabby took the first eighty, and all but twenty of what remained went for a Greyhound bus ticket. He arrived in Iowa on a frigid January night—his winter clothes too small, ankles covered only by thin socks, wrists and neck entirely exposed. He borrowed enough money to rent a couch to sleep on, and he cut the tops of socks off to cover his wrists in the cold. But *a banban ra*, he survived, learned English, earned a degree in math and went on to do difficult and high-tech laser research as a doctoral student in the chemistry department.

I also admired Hassimi's self-possession, that he never seemed to doubt who he was, that he could stride through a world of seed-company caps and sweatshirts in his brightly colored shirts and ties or voluminous *grands boubous* (long cotton shirt and pants, often beautifully embroidered) without ever trying to be more American. He had an implacable confidence in himself and in the world around him, that everything would turn out all right in the end, and it was comforting to walk with him through the cricket-loud nights.

Finally, we drove together out to a place called Kent Park, the quintessential plot of midwestern public space, the grass mowed, the trees trimmed, a hundred rules and a hundred Department of Natural Resources employees in brown uniforms to enforce them. We sat on an old pinwheel quilt given to Hassimi by an Iowa family he had befriended.

The orange triangles at the center of the quilt were worn away, and I rubbed my fingers absently over the exposed cotton tufts. While I looked out at the smooth curves of the man-made pond, Hassimi silently dipped corn chips into a can of bean dip and held them, one by one, up to my mouth. I could not resist him then, his breath already brushing the side of my face, his full attention on this act of feeding me. I kissed him seriously for the first time on the carefully clipped grass of that hill, overlooking a pond where children swam in buoyed-off wedges of water.

It was a little like dating a celebrity. Hassimi, with his height (nearly six-feet-ten), long foreign stride and very dark skin, attracted midwestern eyes everywhere we went. Heads in coffee shops and grocery stores turned in synchrony. Men, slipping on dusty windbreakers, hats in hand, approached our tables while they pulled their wallets out to pay their bills (laughing slightly, embarrassed, thumbs poised on the seams of their wallets—suggesting they were just curious, didn't mean to bother us for long). Iowa farm-girl cashiers in blue smocks woke from their trances to watch what came out of the cart, looked up at Hassimi's face, looked at me.

Sometimes the attention was hostile. I've been called a whore, for example, and once some boys threw cigarette butts out a car window at Hassimi. Most of them landed in the grass, but one tapped him lightly on the shin and skidded onto the curb—a crumpled child's L. L for "lollipop"; L for "love." Another time, while Hassimi waited for me in the parking lot of an unlikely middle-of-the-fields hotel and lounge (his car had broken down on the highway), the same police car drove by him five times in twenty-five minutes—circling slowly into the lot, sketching a large teardrop shape in the gravel and then pulling out. When I picked him up, he was tense and exhausted; he'd heard too many stories about American cops not to be frightened.

Mostly, the attention was more benign, simply reflecting his foreignness—our foreignness as a mixed couple—back at us. One day, while we were still living in Iowa City, we went for a drive north, into the hilly country where a number of Amish families have their farms. It was late summer, and many of the fields were a dry yellow. Here and there were cracks in the earth into which I could slide my hand. We looked for the signs of Amish farms—well-fed brown horses in the field, neat outbuildings, no electric lines going in anywhere—and we looked for their buggies. We felt lucky. Many families were out in their angular black carts, horses flicking and twitching in the heat and plumes of dust flying up behind the buggies' thin wheels. In fact, for every several cars, there seemed to be one horse cart with a black-clad and bonneted family bouncing along inside.

Eventually we discovered their destination. Maybe forty buggies were parked in neat lines across a field—in the barn was an auction of old farm equipment. Against my protests, Hassimi pulled over to the shoulder, stopped the car and got out. I was uncomfortable, didn't want to gape (at least not outside the safety of the car), didn't want to be caught watching these strange and interesting people. But I didn't need to worry so much about making these Amish, these Iowans, into a spectacle. Smiling and nodding his head along the way, Hassimi made his way toward the center of the action, and a hundred heads swiveled in *our* direction. The auctioneer never stopped, but concentric arcs of silence rippled through the crowd as we progressed. Children laughed and hid. Women appeared in doorways. The flickering pale circle of a face appeared in the rippled glass of an old window.

Afterward, we stopped for a late lunch at a nondescript country restaurant. The waitress who seated us—young, with glossy hair and a wide, glittery smile—looked at Hassimi and me with candid surprise. At the end of our meal, one of our neighbors leaned back in his chair to ask the requisite questions. Several other tables listened for the answers, and our waitress paused, coffee pots in hand, to smile at us across the room. "How's the weather up there? You a basketball player? Where you from?"

Hassimi's answers vary. Sometimes he says he is from Mali, home of his ethnic group. Sometimes he says he is from Burkina Faso, where he grew up. Sometimes he says he is "just a poor boy from the bush" or simply that he is African. He never says, "I am from here."

We broke up twice during our first several years together, both times motivated by the same cluster of issues: We wanted different things, missed different things, worked so often at cross purposes. Our tastes clashed, sometimes our friends clashed, our expectations clashed. My limited spare time I spent in cafes and parks; he spent his on the Internet, on the telephone or listening to the radio, searching for news of his homeland. I wanted to find some of the wildness I left behind in North Carolina; he wanted his friends, his newspaper, his plates of rice. I wanted beauty, to watch films and go on adventures; he wanted utility, to work and eat and rest.

Also, and this was always the subject of our most difficult conversations, I often had the impression that my husband's eyes—his real eyes, his inner eyes—were turned away from me. As we were supposed to be having fun or making plans or in some other way attending to our life together, I would sense him focusing on something else. He would hurry through our picnic, drift away from an important conversation, or in some other way show a lack of engagement in what we were doing. Usually, he would say that he was thinking about work, but he was also, at the same time, thinking of home: that he should put a better roof on his mother's house, build a school in the village, struggle and struggle harder for that poor and tiny, faraway spot that is his home.

It is harder for me to pinpoint the reasons we got back together in those rocky early years. We just missed each other, I guess. I was his best friend, he would always tell me, and I never stopped loving his intelligent humor, the clarity of his convictions, the way gentleness and strength were matched in everything he did.

And we did build a life together in Iowa. At the time, I shared a house with three other graduate students—an Iowan, a Taiwanese and a Bulgarian. We played jokes on one another, talked about our families—the calligraphy of Kai-lin's father, the house Katy's sister built on the Black Sea, reunions where Debbie's family gathers on her mother's front lawn for Jell-O and macaroni and fried chicken, the markets where Hassimi's mother sold meat-filled cakes called *farnii*. Sometimes, we would assemble in the kitchen and eat Debbie's chicken, Katy's *bonitsa* (feta, eggs and filo dough) or the sushi rolls Kai-lin made from a Japanese-food cookbook, the recipes all written in neat lines of Chinese. Frequently, the things we ate together were an omnium-gatherum of whatever was at hand—reflecting our cultures, our interests and the Iowa growing season. When the corn was good and cheap, we boiled it up, like everybody else, in a big deep pot on the stove.

Other times, Hassimi and I had parties in his apartment, where I would be one of only two or three pink faces in a room full of Africans laughing and eating and trading issues of the African newsmagazine *Le Monde*. Hassimi and I are not especially good cooks, but it never seemed to matter. People would argue over their paper plates about pan-Africanism and the stupidity of American foreign policy, stabbing their forks toward fellow discussants for emphasis. Zairian music would replace reggae, which had replaced the strange, wailing rhythms of Mali, until eventually the last people were saying good-bye, making their last point in a night full of ditch grasses and hedgehogs nibbling their way through backyard gardens.

More of our courtship, though, was spent in the realm of the practical—going together to the lab, the library, the grocery store, home. Often we walked the distance between his apartment and my house, past a late-seventies apartment complex, over a hill and past a school and a small park planted with coneflowers, black-eyed Susans, fleabane. When the coneflower blooms waved dry and crispy on the top of stiff, fragile stems, we stopped, and I pulled a palmful of seeds out of their corollas. I thought I might plant them in the backyard of my rented house, but they have moved, taped up in a paper towel, from one drawer to another as I have moved from house to house, and now I do not think that they will germinate.

These days, we live in Illinois. I have a job near Champaign, and Hassimi commutes back and forth between Illinois and Wisconsin, where he teaches chemistry. The jobs and the house mean that we are no longer sojourners on our way to some other place. I wish I could say that we are happy about this, and sometimes I can—in the fall, for example, when the soybean fields turn a deep gold-orange and the birds sweep down from Wisconsin and Canada to settle into and rise out of the cornfields in kinetic waves. But often it seems that all the beauty of this land has been mowed down. Much of what I see as I drive is leached and uniform: rows and rows of cornstalks grown to feed rows of cattle somewhere else, tractors and large farm equipment in the distance.

Ironically, our travel away from the state—to Burkina Faso—has helped us make a life together in Illinois. Partly, our journey helped me understand Hassimi better. Ouagadougou, the capital city of Burkina Faso, is like no place else I've visited. The downtown is paved and features western-style buildings, but most of the city is woven together by a huge network of wide, unpaved streets—pitted, dusty and nameless. These orange roads are lined on either side with a kind of frenzied microcommerce that makes Chicago seem dull and slow-paced. Every spot reasonably secure from motor vehicles is made use of. Women on blankets sell fruits and vegetables, packages of snack crackers and gum. Men with small carts sell everything from sunglasses to sandals. And everywhere are makeshift *boissoneries* (drink shops) and restaurants. Many have nothing more than a few old vinyl chairs and a cooler full of drinks or a rotisserie with a couple of chickens, affectionately referred to as *poulet bicyclette* (bicycle chicken) because they are bicycled in early each morning from the countryside. Threading through this crowd are more women, selling plastic bags of refrigerated juice or dusty peanuts from baskets they carry on their heads.

In addition, bouncing through or swerving around the potholes in those orange streets are vehicles of every kind—cars, trucks and buses, but also ox-drawn carts and more bikes and mopeds than I knew had ever been manufactured. Just as every square foot of the street sides is made use of, every vehicle is employed to its maximum potential. Bikes are loaded down with firewood, which can be stacked as high as the bicyclist's shoulders. Mopeds can carry three grown people and a baby, as well as grocery sacks and other necessities. Vans are packed to the brim with people and loaded on top with trunks and boxes, suitcases, even live animals. All this movement and human enterprise make a spectacular sight—the hawked wares in all their different shapes and colors, bright head wraps and blankets, colorful *pagnes* (cloth wrapped into a skirt, belt or baby carrier).

Being part of this frenetic activity helped me make sense of Hassimi's extreme work ethic. People in Burkina do not take extra jobs or work extra hours because they want new leather jackets or fancy stereos in their cars. They work, sometimes frantically—even turning extra corners of their homes into telephone centers or hairstyling salons that can stay open late into the night—in order to put their children in school and buy medicine for their parents. Hassimi works with the same intensity as many of his countrymen and -women, and for the same reason—to buy medicine and pay tuition, buy shoes and pay for electric bills, when he can, for his nieces and nephews, siblings and cousins. And out of habit: This is what he's always done to make life better for the people he loves.

After visiting Burkina, I also better understood the utilitarian nature of my husband's tastes, why he might buy me blue jeans or a cotton shirt for our anniversary but never cut flowers or costume jewelry. I could see why he hoards every broken table and ancient electronic device that passes through our lives, his comfort with the stained and battered, as well as his great satisfaction with the new, no matter how flimsy or unappealing. For most Burkinabé people, life goes cheerfully and energetically forward without benefit of one single brand-new, undamaged and well-made piece of consumer goods. If you can sit on a chair, it is still valuable, even if it's made of cheap materials and the vinyl is torn, even if it's taped together with electrical tape and is the single ugliest thing your wife has seen in all her born days.

Sometimes now, when my husband seems to be thinking about something else, something distant, I can imagine what he might be seeing—maybe a skinny boy carrying a basket of fruit to the market or an old woman selling crackers from a torn and dusty blanket. Once Hassimi showed his homeland to me, that place became a more natural part of our conversations together, a more visible part of the world we shared. I decorated the house with masks and hats we'd bought at the market, sometimes wore the grands boubous and pagnes I'd been given as gifts. Hassimi saw his homeland in a new way, he told me, after we had explored it together. For example, the first time he saw elephants or wild pigs was on a photo safari with me; and he'd never thought much about how busy and colorful the streets of Ouagadougou are, or about the beauty of the old clay mosques that rise up from the villages around his home.

When we returned to Illinois we began to find reflections of Burkina in surprising places: in the face shapes of African-American people, in the sounds of old blues music and especially in the landscape. The grasses we saw in Burkina lay against the flat ground in waves, like some of those we have seen on the Illinois prairie, but the African grasses cover the ground more sparsely, leaving the bright red earth visible in every direction. As in Illinois, most Burkinabé land is inhabited by farmers. Where we were, in the center of Burkina Faso, we saw primarily Mossi people, who wear sturdy, tepee-shaped straw hats to protect themselves from the sun and live in clusters of round, straw huts with tepee-shaped roofs. Despite the obvious differences, those collections of huts reminded us, we decided later, of Illinois farmhouses surrounded by outbuildings—isolated, tiny and shivering in the distance, blurred by dust and heat and the warp of heavy air.

We also learned to appreciate the drama of harsh weather—drought, tearing winds, heavy storms, temperature extremes. Hassimi and I went to Burkina Faso just before the rainy season started. For the first week, we endured searing heat that kicked in full blast by nine in the morning, the sky unmarked blue all day long. In the second week the storms began, short at first, and every other day—longer and every day later on. The early ones, despite their relative brevity, were the most dramatic. They came rolling and powerful and dark, the wind an undertow tugging at the back of our knees and pulling orange dust into the wall of coming water. Or like tornado clouds in Illinois seen from the highway—a wave of black over a wave of green, field and roadside grit stinging the sides and windows of the car.

On pretty weekends, Hassimi and I sometimes stroll in the Illinois prairie together. There's not much of it left, but what there is helps us feel a connection to the land and to each other. The prairie embodies the wildness of the forests I played in as a child and rustles in the wind like the Sahel grasses of Burkina.

The particular small piece of prairie we visit most often is just south of town, separated from the road by a large meadow and a bank of trees. Its approach is long and usually just ours, a path passing through playground, meadow and borderland. I bought a book about prairie flowers and I take it along, looking for plants to identify while my husband watches the dog pace back and forth along the tall yellow wall of grasses and c flowers—cupflowers, coneflowers, compass flowers—through which we are not allowed to pass. Sometimes, the grass along the walking path is the wall of a yellow room we cannot enter. We are nothing more than tourists. We are visiting Lincoln's home, straining over the guard rope to see a beautiful old desk or dresser—excluded, foreign, hurried along by the guide.

But sometimes we feel deeply rewarded by these trips, like we are taking our place in the landscape, the three-pronged propeller of the big blue-stem grass swinging overhead, the coreopsis just out of reach, a goldfinch lifting out of a shuddering thistle, deep enough in its sanctuary of grasses to ignore us.

The first time we visited the prairie together, we were braving a front that we hoped might blow by just south of us or douse some town northeast; we had just reached the raucous waves of grass and flowers when curtains of water fell down around us. The second time, we were more fortunate and stood, quiet and admiring, in front of the rolling flora. Hassimi was particularly thoughtful. "When I was a kid, we used to chase each other through the grass, which was more than five feet high," he said. "You could only find your friend by looking for the grass waving over his head."

Love, Loner Style

Andi Zeisler

What if Prince Charming showed up on his white horse at the would-be princess's house only to find a note nailed to the door that read, "Spending time alone tonight. Movie tomorrow?" It's not supposed to be the way every little girl's fantasy goes, but for me it was a lot more apt than the glittery swirl of glass slippers and magic kisses and riding off into happily-ever-after, the classic formula of everlasting love peddled to wide-eyed tykes.

In my girlhood fantasy, the princess lived in a little house perched high on the dunes, the ocean murmuring outside the open windows. Inside, the house was cozy and stuffed with colorful warmth: big, shaded lamps throwing pools of light across the sleepy dogs and cats who lounge on the wooden floor and the unfinished canvases propped against the wall, awaiting completion. The princess sat happily at a desk, writing stories and illustrating them, stopping only to change the radio station, or to offer tea and cookies to one of the neighbors who came by to say hello. She went contentedly about her day, and only when the sunset began to purple the fantasy horizon would she gaze down at the ring that winked contentedly on her left hand.

Where's her Prince Charming, you wonder? Well, he's away.

He's an ornithologist, you see, and he's gone on a bird-watching trek in South America. Or maybe he's a dashing photojournalist on assignment in Zimbabwe. Regardless, he won't be back for a few days. It's just her, and she's perfectly happy with that.

"I wanna be by myself/I came in this world alone," sang Joan Armatrading, and to my ears that always sounded much more like truth than any of the saccharine sentiments offered up by the likes of the Carpenters. I've been a private person for as long as I can remember, in as many ways as there are. Simply put: I like to be alone. I don't relish talking about myself or being the center of attention. I truly enjoy the company of my friends, acquaintances and co-workers, but if I'm around people for too long I start getting a little jittery. I need solitude like other people need cigarettes or church—it's sometimes guilty and ambrosial, other times soothing and sustaining.

I had plenty of privacy when I was younger, and no one questioned it. My mother recalls that, as a child, I could entertain myself for hours with made-up games and invented companions. (An earnest veteran of the Parent Effectiveness Training courses of the seventies, she was all for this development of inner resources.) And adolescent girls are understood to require long bouts of time alone, lest they explode in a riot of hormones and Love's Baby Soft from the insecurities and expectations pressing in on them.

But the need for privacy in adulthood is something different. It can make other people feel uncomfortable and hurt their feelings, not to mention make them suspicious of you. As Erica Jong noted in *Fear of Flying*, "Solitude is un-American." In my case, a byproduct of this long-time comfort with my own company is that it often takes me a while to cement friendships and relationships. I've had more than a few people tell me, years after the fact, that I didn't make the friendliest first impression. (Or, more bluntly, "I thought you hated me.") Still, it hasn't rendered me friendless. Nor has it kept me from having a fairly swinging bachelor-girl lifestyle, with a boyfriend or two, a few intense flings and several long-term friends-plus arrangements notched on my lipstick case. But in almost every one of these boy-girl relationships my need for privacy raised red flags.

There was Nathan, a scientist who, after having me under his microscope for a mere month, announced that my inability to be outgoing was an affront to his deeply held belief that people should always put social graces above their own comfort and happiness. (Although I should add that this belief didn't extend to actually verbally informing me that we would no longer be seeing each other.)

Then there was Hank, a former long-time beau who, when he wasn't touring the country with his free-jazz band, lounged in my bed delivering motormouthed disquisitions on why I would be single forever. "You're too independent. You need your privacy. I think that's cool, but I don't really think other men are gonna be into that. Then again, you have good taste in music. Nah, you're always gonna be alone. You're a loner. You're like the female Jack Kerouac." (Admittedly, best to take his opinions with an econo-sized box of salt—though Hank is an excellent friend and an inspired musician, his logic is itself a little free-jazzy at times, and he would often end these character assessments with an exasperated and totally contradictory statement like, "Whatever. I'll move to Paris and you'll be married before you're thirty.")

But then there was David, the man who tried dauntlessly to change my solitude-lovin' ways and made me feel like a freak in the process. Our relationship was a two-and-a-half-year paradox: It seemed to me I never had enough privacy, but David felt I had entirely too much. My need for solitude was an endless source of peevishness to him, and the outward manifestations of my craving—the fact that I refused to spend more than two nights in a row with him; my tendency, whenever his friends inquired what I was doing or how work was going, to shrug an answer and quickly turn the topic back to them; my repeated insistence that, no, he wasn't allowed to read my journal; my interest in taking long walks by myself—grew, over time, to be the *bête noire* of our relationship. "Why do you have to keep yourself such a secret?" he demanded during one of our regular bouts of push-me-pull-you. I didn't have an answer.

I've always felt a kind of kinship with one of the characters in a favorite book, Laurie Colwin's *Happy All the Time*. Holly is an intensely private person, dense with quirks, not least of which is that she's always, in her husband Guido's eyes, running away. She retreats for weeks at a time, at crucial life moments—before getting married, for instance, or when she becomes pregnant—but also when she feels that her life and relationship have become too static, too smooth, too predictable. The sly humor that buttresses the exchanges between Holly and Guido serves to point out the crucial ways in which privacy is misunderstood: Holly's solo escapes are meant to help retain her personal selfhood, which by extension preserves the richness of her relationship with her husband; yet Guido insists that her need to be alone constitutes abandonment. Her petty treachery is compounded, as far as he's concerned, by the fact that he never knows what his wife is thinking as she makes these decisions. I thought of Holly and Guido often as my relationship with David deteriorated, and wished that our own differences could be settled with witty banter and tender, opposites-attract resolution, instead of frustrated outbursts (him) and frustrated silence (me).

It's not like I was making dramatic, Garbo-esque, hand-on-the-forehead pronouncements. I wasn't delivering speeches about solitude being necessary for my art. I just found ways to be alone. But I knew that my foundering relationships weren't just a matter of Nathan being intolerant, or Hank being goofy, or David being jealous and insecure. Throughout these arrangements, whatever their degrees of seriousness, I never felt . . . *coupled*. I may have been dining at an oyster bar with Nathan, or wrapped up in the sheets with Hank, or accompanying David on one of his monomaniacal comic-book shopping expeditions, but I always felt like an outsider, detachedly watching myself be this thing commonly known as a girlfriend. No matter how much I liked these men, or how much fun I was having, I didn't feel like part of a unit that included them. And always, in the back of my mind, I was waiting and plotting for the time when I could go home and be by myself for a little while.

Which led me to believe that maybe the source of my feeling of uncoupleability wasn't just these guys and their own issues. Maybe it was me. Maybe I was deeply, irreconcilably selfish. Maybe all this wanting to be alone was going to ensure that I *was* alone. Not *by myself*, like in those marriage fantasies of my youth—in which solitude is a temporary respite from the intensity of a passion-filled partnership—but alone. Permanently. The cruel finish, after the ellipsis of the be-careful-what-you-wish-for warning.

The loner is a figurehead of American culture, cutting a dashing, unforgettable path through our collective consciousness. This romantic personage has, however, pretty much always been male. The ingrained prejudices of our society ensure that if there has ever been a female Shane, a distaff Neal Cassady, a Siddhartha with tits, she's no doubt been dissed and dismissed as frumpy, insane, overly aggressive/opinionated, a closeted lesbian, or otherwise unmarryable—lack of marriageability being the only reason many of us can still see for a woman to be alone. Take Emily Dickinson. Take Jodie Foster. Take Janet Reno. Take, um . . . you get my point. These loner women are nothing to sneeze at, but it'd be nice to see more of our own kind in the public eye.

And while you'd think this attitude toward solitude—particularly in the context of love and relationships—would start to shift as women continue breaking gender molds in other areas, nothing seems to be changing. In recent years, an upswing in catch-a-man guides and marriage-obsessive movie plots has found women both buying and selling validation for the back-assward wisdom that says solitude is a hell to be avoided at any cost, that says it's better to be with the wrong man than with no man at all. These books and magazines, with their facile equations (couplehood = happiness! solitude = sad spinsterhood!), are the modern-day descendants of Victorian-era conduct literature, and their language has retained the same doomsaying timbre. From bestselling dating guide *The Rules* and movies like *Runaway Bride* and *My Best Friend's Wedding* to the recent rash of novels featuring single women who elevate marriage to godhead status, the world of relationships is framed as frighteningly binary (either you're married and thereby happy, or you die alone and your corpse is eventually eaten by your house pets—see *Bridget Jones's Diary* and *Otherwise Engaged* for more on this lovely notion). Being unpartnered by choice is looked on with raised eyebrows, pitying smiles and knowing smirks, and privacy seen as something that lonely, deluded women convince themselves is as pleasurable and life-enhancing as any hot date.

Our pop culture pays lip service to quality time with oneself, of course, but in ways that suggest it's only meant as a sweet little side dish to the entree of couplehood. *The Rules,* for instance, suggests cultivating and enriching private time not for its own rewards but for the intrigue it provides for your man-catching schemes. And some women's magazines have started featuring sections devoted to spending the afternoon alone, but they never fail to make clear that enjoying moments of solitude is, like all the beauty and fashion and exercise and sex tips they offer, part of the long march of self-improvement that, if all goes well, ends with you on the arm of some guy in a tux.

It's probably fair to say that few (if any) of us relish the thought of dying with no partner or long-time friend around to care, much less the gruesome vision of being snacked on by little Rex or Fluffy. But I balk at any mindset that says falling in love means total immersion, and that total immersion means the time one spends with oneself is still somehow devalued, considered a perk of a relationship rather than an intrinsic right and a soul-feeding necessity.

So what's all this leading up to? Well, a little more than a year ago, I met Jeffery. I didn't exactly exude a come-and-get-me vibe on our first encounter: I was enjoying my own company at an indie-rock festival when I overheard the cute guy with the Clark Kent specs several seats down from me tell his friend that he was going to go talk to me, but was a little wary because I had been sitting alone all day and "might be sketchy." (Which counted as a strike—let's not even get started on why so many people think it's weird to go solo to restaurants, shows and other public events.) We ended up meeting on our way out of the show, and during the course of a short chat that ended abruptly because I had to catch the last train, I decided that someone who seemed so genuinely nice could— grudgingly—be forgiven the "sketchy" remark. On the long walk to the train station, my stomach aflutter, I kept mentally turning back to find him, wondering if he was feeling the same impulse. And as I stood in line to buy my ticket, I saw a figure come skidding around the corner like Road Runner: It was Jeffery, phone number in hand—and though my heart contracted so hard it felt like it might dislodge from my chest, my face must have registered something totally different. "I took one look at you," he remembers, "and I was sure you were about to pull out a can of mace." Like I said, I've never had a flair for the first impression.

Still, we started dating the next day, and before too long I found myself feeling strangely girlfriendy—and, even more strangely, fully content about it. I relaxed my two-night rule. We took weekend trips, something I'd never wanted to do with anyone before. When we talked in that deliberately abstract, what-if way about the future, I could picture us together easily. (And I didn't feel the need to picture a door through which I could escape.) Once I realized I'd fallen in love, in fact, I spent a lot of time marveling at how easy it had been. Jeffery was smart and sarcastic and talented; he left mash notes on my pillow, photographs and Pez dispensers in my mailbox. He looked at me like I hung the moon, but he also made merciless fun of me when I tripped over my own feet. So one morning when he said he wanted to live with me, I shrugged and smiled and said yeah, I could do that, that seems like a pretty good idea.

Other boyfriends had proposed it, but I'd always refused on the grounds of, yes, needing my privacy. But the thought of painting the bathroom with Jeffery and cooking dinner with him and falling asleep together every single night filled me with a slightly sheepish but undeniable warm fuzziness. I should probably add, though, that the first thing I did after agreeing to shack up was panic. Not a lot, but enough to make me wonder if it could work. Not only had I never lived with a boyfriend, I'd never even felt particularly committed to one. For the past twenty-seven years, my most significant other had been privacy. All of a sudden, the comforts and rituals of solitude that made up my life— the dinners for one, the early weekend mornings sitting in bed, surrounded by books and journals and bowls of cereal, the nights spent out seeing music, or at home drawing and listening to the stereo—seemed threatened. Could I make room for an equally significant other, or did the first one have to go?

My inner critics pshawed this concern. They yawned at my naiveté, informing me that most women resolved that room-of-one's-own crap ages ago. They sniffed that living with a partner wasn't all that different from living with a roommate (as I had for years), except for the extra socks that would start appearing magically in my laundry bag. They told me earnestly that if I wanted to spend my evenings curled up in front of the tube in my undies watching *Sex and the City* reruns with a carton of takeout sushi in one hand and a good book in the other, then I should get on with my bad self and damn the boyfriend. But they didn't do a whole lot to quell my fear that I'd have no choice but to sacrifice a prized part of my life in order to keep the hearts and flowers coming.

I must note here that my mental handwringing over the potential drawbacks of our impending cohabitation wasn't inspired by the significant other himself: Jeffery knew about my long-term affair with solitude since the start, and didn't much care. Which is not to say he doesn't respect it; it just never bothered him. He doesn't think I'm freakish (or even, now that he knows me, sketchy), and he doesn't believe that liking to be on one's own is necessarily a one-way ticket to a town called You'll Be Alone the Rest of Your Miserable Days. The main thing he understands is that it's not all about him. This may sound obvious, but given the protests of my former guys—the Greek chorus of pissy disapproval I still hear when I'm feeling like I should change my ways—it's clearly not. (David, for example, viewed my private-time pinings as part of a larger, more devious conspiracy—a whole secret life whose main function was to exclude him from its excitement and fun. Though far more glamorous than reality, it was a delicious concept for sure, and one that kept me stocked with verbal ammo during the waning months of our relationship—"Oh, did I forget the wine? I must have left it in my *secret life*.") Jeffery not only knows that when I say, "I think I'm just going to hang out by myself tonight," it doesn't translate to, "I'm not sure I like you anymore, at all," but he knows it without my ever needing to explain it.

Also, he knows that my yen for privacy is something that, at times, actually has helped our relationship along. When Jeffery and I met, he was living in a city three hours from me, and consequently I spent a lot of that first summer *not* seeing him. I liked this; it was an organic way to maintain my various private routines. The fact that I saw him for a day or so every two weeks was nice; the distance encouraged me to write letters, make mix tapes and yearn, all of which are very enjoyable activities. But more significantly, the temporary geographic limits forced me to really consider whether I wanted to put my energy into our burgeoning love thing—something I might have been too overwhelmed to think about were we seeing each other every other night from the start. And when the yawning space and miles of telephone line that separated us disappeared at the end of the summer, I knew it was right.

Still, knowing these things didn't quell the interior freakouts that continued as we prepared to set up house. I wondered what would happen when I saw him every day, when a rote domesticity could obscure the clarity I felt when we were apart; I chewed my fingernails as I pictured myself running around the apartment like a wide-eyed junkie, squirmy and snappish, jonesing for a fix of solitude.

For the past few months, I have seen Jeffery almost every day. As I sit here writing, the evidence is unmistakable. There are pictures of us on the desk, flowers he's brought me in a glass mug. His skateboard and cameras sit alongside my books and art supplies; our CDs are heaped together in unalphabetized chaos. After two months of living together, Jeffery's things look familiar to me and feel like they belong in the apartment that, for the past few years, has had just one name on the lease. But when I look at how our possessions have merged, I realize that while I might be used to the stuff itself, getting used to what it represents will take more time.

I think back to the David-Nathan-Hank years of my dating life, when privacy took precedence over relationships in my heart. Though I was reluctant to admit it to myself at the time, I knew exactly why. Privacy served as a subtle, ongoing preemptive strike: As far as I was concerned, those liaisons had a built-in expiration date, and I wasn't willing to push such a substantial part of who I was to the side just to be a better girlfriend to someone I knew I would be leaving—or who would be leaving me—sooner rather than later. In comparison, my relationship with Jeffery has no such foregone conclusion; my decision to live with him means that privacy must now share its previously rock-solid position with compromise, if only so I don't turn the most mundane happenings of our daily life into turf wars.

And entwining the necessary trappings of physical privacy with the minutiae of domesticity has been something of a challenge. The weekend Jeffery moved in, for example, we stood in the graveled lot of a used-furniture store, debating the merits of a large metal desk.

"It only has one file drawer," I pointed out.

"We can share it," he half-smiled, knowing what was coming.

"We can't share it. I have a lot of stuff to file."

"I promise I won't go through your stuff, if that's what you're worried about. We can draw a line down the middle, and I won't cross it." Full smile. He had my number.

In the course of that brief exchange, the desk had become a symbol of my need for uncompromised privacy—or, to put it in uglier terms, my failure to play nice and share. There in the lot, with stacks of desks and chairs towering over our heads, I tried to explain that I'd rather have a desk of my own, but because it was now *our* apartment and *our* office, it was going to have to be our desk too, and I wanted part of it that could just be mine—namely, the file drawer. With no real logic to back up my argument, no practical reason to demand more than my share of our potential desk, I felt selfish and miserable. We did end up buying the desk, though, and the final breakdown went like this: two of the regular drawers for him, two for me, a shared drawer in the middle. And the file drawer? Mine. But every time I open it, its metallic squeaks remind me of the guilt I felt that day.

Then there's the matter of the bed. I've never been much of a team player when it comes to sleeping, and when former flames complained that I denuded them of covers, hogged the pillows and unconsciously kicked them in the shins, I was apologetic but unrepentant: It was my bed, after all, and if they had a problem with my nocturnal style they could take their PJs and go home. Now, of course, my bed has become our bed, and often it's my beloved who's stealing the quilt and throwing elbows, to say nothing of performing a series of nasal bossa novas so loud I've taken to keeping earplugs within a sleepy arm's reach. Are these things small potatoes compared to the rosy warmth of curling up with him night after night? You bet. But there have been times when the urge to fall asleep by myself far outweighs this, when I find myself scooting to the margins of the mattress, certain that even the slightest touch of toenail on my leg will make me jump out of my skin, when I remember fondly the days of sleeping diagonally, limbs splayed with abandon.

But even though living with Jeffery means that physical privacy is often not at my immediate disposal, our daily schedules dovetail nicely, so there's generally an ample amount of time when I'm around and he's not. And I can always supplement these interludes, as I did throughout the roommate years, with time in alternate locations—coffee shops, parks, libraries. But if maintaining my comfort as a loner in the physical realm has been simple enough to resolve—I can leave the apartment, spend an occasional night on the couch or ask him to, buy extra drawers for my stuff—emotional privacy comes to the fore toting a little more baggage. There's a conversation Jeffery and I have had every few days since we started dating, which goes something like this:

HIM: What's on your mind?

ME: Nothing.

HIM [heavy sarcasm]: *Really.*

ME: Yup.

HIM: You are such a liar.

ME: How do you know? There could be nothing.

HIM: There's not nothing.

And so on. By now we have honed the exchange so that it exits our mouths with comedy-routine precision. But every time it happens, I feel, if not exactly like a butterfly on the end of a pin, at least a teeny bit twitchy. I'm aware that, historically, men have been the ones whose thoughts are supposed to be impenetrable to their mates. All the pop culture I've absorbed has dictated that this kind of discussion puts the woman in the role of prying ears and casts the man as the silent stoic, pride rendering him unwilling to give it up. But I'm not flipping the script as a conscious gesture of feminism. I don't hold back information for the sake of holding it back; it's just that I'm more at ease keeping most things to myself, sharing if and when the time is right. In the case of this particular conversation, I'm not interested in taking the treadmill-style loop to the point where it becomes ridiculous, and so I usually do end up telling Jeffery what's on my mind—which has the dual benefit of making him feel good and underscoring that whatever I was holding back was hardly a pungent offering from a bottomless pit of secrets. And even when I don't tell him, it's nice to know that I can.

Privacy is my second nature, my default setting, and though conversations like these have occasionally been a source of frustration for both of us, I can't deny I'm comforted at the thought that they will repeat themselves. Partly it's that I know Jeffery can handle, and even relish, the fact that I'm no open book. When he says he knows I've got something on my mind, he's letting me know he wants to hear about it, not telling me he'll resent me if I don't tell him. And if, someday soon, I have to make like *Happy All the Time*'s Holly and head temporarily for the hills, hopefully we'll both understand that it's a momentary recharging, not a permanent escape.

My relationship with Jeffery, as well as the ill-fated ones that came before, has made clear to me that privacy isn't only a matter of having time to myself, or space for myself, or thoughts that aren't voiced. It's about autonomy and identity, about trusting and loving someone enough to reveal myself on my own terms. Which is why, in deciding to share my apartment and my future, it feels like I've begun a process of fine-tuning the terms of my long-time affair with privacy—adjusting them to fit the me who has fully enjoyed making this person an enduring and consistent part of her life, instead of enjoying him in small doses while waiting for him to go home and leave her alone. I can wish stubbornly that I didn't have to do things like share a desk, but when I'm sitting there and I see on that desk bits and pieces of the life Jeffery and I have started together—the Polaroids and postcards, the mannequin hand I gave him and the little brass elephant he gave me—the compromise seems minimal balanced against the intimacy it's allowed us to create. On another level, I've started to realize that some of the things I never imagined I could or would want to share with another person—from irrational fears to favorite places to even the rare few pages from my journal—are things that I want him to know about, especially now that I know he truly wants to.

I still nod my head in sympathy when Joan Armatrading makes her case. I still imagine the house on the dunes and the nights of savory, bracing solitude. But I believe now that I can have both, in this mixture of companionship and solitude that makes me realize I don't have to be by myself forever to be by myself, forever.

Contributors

Sabrina Margarita Alcantara-Tan is a queer Filipina mestiza and editress of *Bamboo Girl,* a zine confronting issues of racism, sexism and homophobia as they relate to young women of color. Her work is featured in *Dragon Ladies: Asian American Feminists Breathe Fire* and *A Girl's Guide to Taking Over the World: Writings from the Girl Zine Revolution,* as well as in *On the Issues, A. magazine, Asian New Yorker* and *maganda.* Sabrina Margarita is co-founder of Kilawin Kolektibo, a Filipina lesbian-, bi- and transgendered-identified collective based in New York, and a former member of Gabriela network, a Philippine women's solidarity organization. She is also a performance artist, videomaker and graphic designer, and is slowly compiling an anthology of nonfiction essays by young nontraditional women of color. She studies the Filipino martial art of weapon fighting called Pananandata Marinas Style, and her favorite weapon is the balisong.

Diane Anderson-Minshall was the co-founder and editor of *Alice* magazine (in 1999) and *Girlfriends* magazine (in 1994). Her writing has appeared in over thirty publications including *Seventeen, Curve, Teenage, Film Threat, Diva* and *Femme Fatale.* She and her wife of ten years divide their time between Idaho (where the politics suck) and Northern California (where the cost of living is too high).

Erin Aubry-Kaplan is a Los Angeles native and staff writer for the *LA Weekly.* She was previously a staff writer for *New Times Los Angeles* and has written extensively for a variety of publications, including the *Los Angeles Times, Salon, Black Enterprise, London Independent, CODE, Underwire* and *Contemporary Art.* Her essays have been recently anthologized in the books *Body Outlaws: Young Women Write About Body Image and Identity* (Seal Press, 2000), *Mothers Who Think: Tales of Real-Life Parenthood*

(Washington Square Press, 2000) and *Step into a World: A Global Anthology of the New Black Literature* (John Wiley & Sons, 2000). Erin also writes poetry and fiction.

A.E. Berkowitz has written for *Bitch, BUST* and *nebulosi*. She lives with her husband and their cats, Tiny and Peanut, in the San Francisco Bay Area. She is at work on a mystery novel.

Stacy Bierlein is a contributing editor to the literary magazine *Other Voices,* and one of the founding editors of *Fish Stories: A Literary Annual of Fiction and Poetry.* Her current fiction appears in *Clackamas Literary Review, Emergence* and *So to Speak.* She makes her home in Santa Monica, California, where she is finishing a collection of stories titled "Gestures of Strangeness."

Denise Brennan Watson is procurer of poetry critics for the Greater Cincinnati Writers League and is author of *The Undertow of Hunger* (Finishing Line Press, 1999), a collection of culinary poetry. Her poetry and literary nonfiction are included in *Soul Stirrings: Sage Woman Cookbook* (Blessed Bee Press, 1999), and her short story "False Charms & Chitlins" appeared in the anthology *Food and Other Enemies: Stories of Consuming Desire* (Essex Press, 2000). This year, Denise and her husband, Jay Brennan Pattison, will celebrate the fifth anniversary of their handfasting and the tenth anniversary of their uniting.

Kitsey Canaan is a poet and essayist who earns a living as an editor and ghostwriter. She earned her BA at Bennington College and her MFA at Indiana University. She lives in North Bennington, Vermont, with her husband and two young daughters.

Georgette Chen lives, works and writes in San Francisco.

Jennifer M. Collins is a twenty-seven-year-old bisexual dyke who is happily married to a woman. She is a poet and author, a feminist and an activist, tattooed and pierced and transgressive in other ways.

Leigh Cotnoir is a furniture and new media designer living in San Diego, California, with an elfin ceramicist roommate. She looks good in pink shirts.

Jane Eaton Hamilton is the award-winning author of four books: *Jessica's Elevator* (children's), *Body Rain* (poetry), *July Nights* (stories) and *Steam-Cleaning Love* (poetry). Her work has appeared in such places as the *New York Times* and *Seventeen* magazine as well as *Best Canadian Short Stories* and *The Journey Prize Anthology*. It has also been cited in the *Pushcart Prize* and *Best American Short Stories*. She has been the recipient of numerous writing awards including the *Yellow Silk* fiction award and the *Belles Lettres* essay award. She grew up in Ontario, and lived in St. Louis, Phoenix, New York City, Alberta, the Kootenays and on Salt Spring Island before settling in Vancouver.

Karen Eng is a lapsed poet from Los Angeles who's gone prosaic in Berkeley. She contributes to *Publishers Weekly*, *Wired*, *Urban View* and *Bitch* when she's not working on *PekoPeko*, a zine of her own dedicated to food.

Kate Epstein's work has appeared in *Bitch* and online at *feminista!*, *Moxie* and *Moondance*. Her website, http://people.ne.mediaone.net/kateepstein, gives full details. She lives in Whitman, Massachusetts, and works in Cambridge.

Rachel Fudge was born and raised in San Francisco and makes her home there with her special peer, Hugh Hynes. By day she is a freelance grammar queen and fierce defender of the serial comma; by night she unleashes her own mixed metaphors and split infinitives on the world. You can find more of her writing in *Bitch: Feminist Response to Pop Culture* and *Nebulosi,* a zine of cultural criticism edited by Rachel and Hugh (more info: nebulosi@pobox.com). For the record, she is not now, nor has she ever been, as sweet as her name.

Faith Haaz-Landsman and her husband Michael live in the queer mecca of West Hollywood. Faith is the administrator of an HIV vaccine project and is a consultant for various nonprofit organizations. When she isn't baking cookies, making dinner or doing the laundry she makes lists, buys shoes, goes on very strange dates and writes accounts of her queer life.

Noelle Howey is the coeditor of the anthology *Out of the Ordinary: Essays on Growing Up With Gay, Lesbian, and Transgender Parents* (St. Martin's Press, 2000), and author of a forthcoming memoir entitled *Clothes Lines* (Picador USA). She has written for *Ms., Mother Jones,* National Public Radio, *Mademoiselle, Jane, Seventeen* and a whole slew of other magazines. She lives with her husband, Christopher Healy, in Manhattan.

Sonya Huber is a twenty-eight-year-old midwesterner currently studying journalism and trying to figure out what to do next. She has worked in magazines, nonprofits and mental health centers, and in some ways they all felt pretty similar. Her writing has appeared in *In These Times, Sojourner, The Workbook, As We Are, Third Force, Infusion* and other publications, and in anthologies from Queen of Swords Press and Outrider Press. Her work is slated to appear in upcoming anthologies from University of Arizona Press and Prometheus Books.

Katie Hubert teaches and lives somewhere between Seattle and Tacoma. She received her MFA in fiction from the Iowa Writers' Workshop. She and her partner, a veterinarian, live in a 1928 bungalow that needs much love and attention. They share their home with a dog and two cats.

Carrie Jones lives in Austin, Texas, with her partner and their small menagerie. She is a writer, a hedonist, a teacher-in-training, a good cook, a wombat, a proud liberal, a tough femme, a Saturn owner, a pop-culture queen, a wannabe-activist, an obnoxiously enthusiastic cat owner and a loud-mouthed feminist.

Bee Lavender is an editor of *Hip Mama: The Parenting Zine,* and the coeditor of *Breeder: Real-Life Stories from the New Generation of Mothers* (Seal Press, 2001). She is a twenty-nine-year-old mother of two and lives with her family in Portland, Oregon.

Ellen Anne Lindsey is the pseudonym of an author of several lesbian-themed novels.

Jennifer Maher has a PhD in modern studies. She is currently a university lecturer and is working on a book about female desire.

Bhargavi C. Mandava was born in Hyderabad, India, and grew up in New York. Her novel, *Where the Oceans Meet,* was published by Seal Press in 1996 and has been translated into Dutch and Catalan. Her nonfiction appears in the anthologies *Body Outlaws: Young Women Write About Body Image and Identity* (Seal Press, 2000) and *Listen Up: Voices from the Next Feminist Generation* (Seal Press, 2001). Some of her poetry is featured in *Another Way to Dance: Contemporary Asian Poetry from Canada and the United States* (TSAR Publications, 1997). She is currently working on her next novel.

Lilace Mellin Guignard has an MFA from the University of California at Irvine, and is currently studying literature and the environment at the University of Nevada at Reno. Her essays appear in *Whole Terrain: Reflective Environmental Practice* and *English Journal.* Her poetry is published in *Sundog,* the *Asheville Poetry Review, ISLE: Journal of Interdisciplinary Studies in Literature and Environment* and *American Diaspora: Poetry of Exile,* as well as other journals and anthologies. She is currently working on a series of essays about grief and the land, in addition to completing a poetry manuscript, "Lost in the Homeland."

Recent wyfe **Leslie Miller** works as the senior editor at Seal Press, is the editor of *de/scribe* magazine—a journal of modern thought—and is currently editing a book celebrating women and food entitled "Women Who Eat." Her nonfiction has appeared in *Sex and Single Girls: Straight and Queer Women on Sexuality* (Seal Press, 2000) and in *The Unsavvy Traveler,* forthcoming from Seal Press.

Maria Raha is a writer currently living in New York. While acting as advertising services manager for *Vibe* magazine, Maria is working toward her master's degree in liberal studies at the New School University. In her spare time, she does everything she can to write for and empower as many women as she can. Maria would like to dedicate her piece to every kick-ass woman and girl on the planet.

Lauren Smith, with her writing partner Jessie Grearson, is the editor of *Swaying* and the author of *Love in a Global Village* (both books on intercultural families and both from University of Iowa Press). Smith is also a poet and a professor of English and women's studies. She lives with her daughter, Myriama, and her husband, Hassimi, in Champaign, Illinois.

Lori L. Tharps graduated from Smith College with a degree in comparative education and Spanish. After spending two years finding herself in New York City, she enrolled in Columbia University's Graduate School of Journalism, where she developed an unhealthy interest in black hair culture. Her book, *Hair Story: Untangling the Roots of Black Hair in America,* was published by St. Martin's Press in January 2001. She lives in Brooklyn, New York, with her husband and her turtle.

Juhu Thukral is a women's rights attorney in New York City.

Andi Zeisler is a writer, editor, illustrator, textile designer and human Zip disk for all manner of pop-culture trivia. She is the cofounder and coeditor of *Bitch: Feminist Response to Pop Culture,* and the former pop-music columnist for the *SF Weekly* and the *East Bay Express.* Her work has also appeared in *Ms., Bust, HUES, Mother Jones* and the Pottery Barn catalog. She lives in San Francisco, where she spends her private time reading magazines and record shopping, and her nonprivate time playing Nerf basketball with her boyfriend and trying to guess whom their dog loves more.

About The Editors

Jill Corral is an editor, writer and developer of new media content products for Sony Music Entertainment. She lives in San Francisco.

Lisa Miya-Jervis is the editor and publisher of *Bitch: Feminist Response to Pop Culture*. Her work has appeared in numerous magazines and books, including *Ms.*, the *San Francisco Chronicle*, the *Utne Reader*, *Mother Jones*, the *Women's Review of Books*, *Bust*, *HUES*, *Salon*, *Girlfriends*, *Punk Planet*, *Body Outlaws* (Seal Press, 2000), *Sex and Single Girls* (Seal Press, 2000) and *The Bust Guide to the New Girl Order* (Penguin, 1999). A transplanted New Yorker, she lives in Oakland, California, with her husband and their two cats.

Selected Titles

Sex and Single Girls: Straight and Queer Women on Sexuality edited by Lee Damsky. $16.95, 1-58005-038-7. In this potent and entertaining collection of personal essays, women lay bare pleasure, fear, desire, risk—all that comes with exploring their sexuality. Contributors write their own rules and tell their own stories with empowering and often humorous results.

Cunt: A Declaration of Independence by Inga Muscio. $14.95, 1-58005-015-8. An ancient title of respect for women, "cunt" long ago veered off the path of honor and now careens toward the heart of every woman as an expletive. Muscio traces this winding road, giving women both the motivation and the tools to claim "cunt" as a positive and powerful force in the lives of all women.

Body Outlaws: Young Women Write About Body Image and Identity edited by Ophira Edut, foreword by Rebecca Walker. $14.95, 1-58005-043-3. Filled with honesty and humor, this groundbreaking anthology offers stories by women who have chosen to ignore, subvert or redefine the dominant beauty standard in order to feel at home in their bodies.

Wild Child: Girlhoods in the Counterculture edited by Chelsea Cain, foreword by Moon Zappa. $16.00, 1-58005-031-X. Daughters of the hippie generation reflect on the experience of a counterculture childhood, presenting a fresh perspective on our current world as seen through the legacy of sixties ideals.

Dharma Girl: A Road Trip Across the American Generations by Chelsea Cain. $12.00, 1-878067-84-2. Written to the unmistakable beat of the road, this memoir chronicles the twenty-four-year-old author's homecoming to the commune in Iowa where she grew up with her counterculture parents.

She's a Rebel: The History of Women in Rock & Roll by Gillian G. Gaar. $16.95, 1-878067-08-7. *She's a Rebel* tells the fascinating story of the women who have shaped rock and pop music for the last five decades.

From Seal Press

Listen Up: Voices from the Next Feminist Generation edited by Barbara Findlen. $16.95, 1-58005-054-9. In a new expanded edition of the classic collection of young feminist writing, *Listen Up* gathers the women of feminism's "third wave" and allows them to explore and reveal their lives. Contributors address topics such as racism, sexuality, identity, AIDS, revolution, religion, abortion and much more.

Breeder: Real-Life Stories from the New Generation of Mothers edited by Ariel Gore and Bee Lavender, foreword by Dan Savage. $16.00, 1-58005-051-4. From the editors of *Hip Mama,* this hilarious and heartrending compilation creates a space where Gen-X moms can dish, cry, scream and laugh. With its strength, humor and wisdom, *Breeder* will speak to every young mother, and anyone who wants a peek into the mind and spirit behind those bleary eyes.

The Mother Trip: Hip Mama's Guide to Staying Sane in the Chaos of Motherhood by Ariel Gore. $14.95, 1-58005-029-8. In a book that is part self-help, part critique of the mommy myth and part hip-mama handbook, Ariel Gore offers support to mothers who break the mold.

Valencia by Michelle Tea. $13.00, 1-58005-035-2. The fast-paced account of one girl's search for love and high times in the dyke world of San Francisco. By turns poetic and frantic, *Valencia* is an edgy, visceral ride through the queer girl underground of the Mission District.

Lap Dancing for Mommy: Tender Stories of Disgust, Blame and Inspiration by Erika Lopez. $14.00, 1-878067-96-6. Not for the faint of heart, this debut collection of comic narratives is shockingly incisive and offers reams of racy, raunchy and riotous appeal.

⚭

Seal Press publishes many books of fiction and nonfiction by women writers. If you are unable to obtain a Seal Press title from a bookstore, please order from us directly by calling 800-754-0271. Visit our website and online catalog at www.sealpress.com.